Bob Reynolds is a financial journalist. He has served as senior writer on *Business* magazine and was editor of *Business Success*. He has written for a large number of newspapers and magazines in the financial, broadcasting, medical and construction sectors. He is married to Kay Reynolds, who is also a financial journalist, and they live in Beckenham, Kent.

BOB REYNOLDS

The 100 Best Companies
to Work for in the UK

Fontana/Collins

First published in 1989 by Fontana Paperbacks,
8 Grafton Street, London W1X 3LA

Set in Linotron Meridien
Printed and bound in Great Britain by
William Collins Sons & Co. Ltd, Glasgow

CONTENTS

CONTENTS

ACKNOWLEDGEMENTS

The preparation of *The 100 Best Companies to Work for in the UK* has involved the cooperation, advice and assistance of several hundred people. All of those people who made suggestions or offered opinions are too numerous to list individually. However, the research team were the most significant contributors. Their efforts were coordinated by Kay Reynolds, who matched the skills of the researchers to the nature of the companies with accomplished ease. The team included Richard Evans, Stephan Szymanski, Helen Elias, Meiron Jones, Sarah Tree, Esther Kaposi, Charles Whitworth, Richard Leeming, Graham Davies and Gill Charlton.

Thanks are also due to Roger Maitland, of International Survey Research, and to MORI for their help in compiling the final list of one hundred companies. Their insight into how employees and graduates view our 100 was invaluable. Leonard Robinson was a consistent source of good commercial sense and offered a measure of detachment – and occasionally transport! Madge Robinson and Peggy Reynolds were constant sources of administrative help and back-up.

Finally, thanks are due to Lucinda McNeile at Collins for sharpening the text and coping with the pressure of inevitable delays with good grace.

FOREWORD

by John Harvey-Jones

This is one of those simple, straightforward ideas that is so obviously helpful one can only be surprised it has not happened before. Every one of us who has a son or daughter knows the anxieties and problems of trying to find out what sort of outfit it is that our loved one is about to dedicate his or her life to.

Such information tends to arrive from the company itself, who have an obvious self-interest in pushing their own case, or from the occasional friend or acquaintance who has worked for the company – quite often some time ago.

The problem is exacerbated by the fact that potential new recruits are surprisingly tentative about asking hard questions of their future employers. There is an understandable, but incorrect, belief that such questioning will be seen as simply too materialistic or 'pushy', or even that it may possibly lose the candidate the opportunity of the job. At minimum it is often thought the questioner will be marked out as a likely member of the 'awkward squad'.

The difficulties of making any real assessment are added to by the near impossibility of getting any comparative information on which to base a judgement that may turn out to be one of the most important of one's life.

Increasingly individuals are abandoning the idea of joining one firm for life. Not only are 'head-hunters' increasingly on the prowl (again, scarcely a totally disinterested source of information), but many young managers want the chance of looking around and broadening their experience. So I, for one, have no doubt that there will be a large number of people who will wish to refer to this book and will benefit from it.

I am sure that many people will expect the results of the investigation to be self-evident. Everyone 'knows' that oil companies are good employers, and so on. This view, however, misses what I believe to be the greatest virtue of the research. It sets out to compare companies on a very wide range of criteria, some of which do not always combine naturally with the others. We should never forget that each of us is different; each of us has different preferences and places different emphasis on different qualities from an employer. Competitive pay may be more important to some than open communications – or equally some may be particularly concerned about pensions, or promotion opportunities for women. The matching of the ambitions of the individual and the capabilities and values of the employer is a tricky business, but it is very much in the interests of both parties to get it right.

Not everyone knows the strengths or weaknesses of various employers, and the voyages of discovery embarked upon by the author should speedily correct the assumption that the 'good' employees are well known and recognized.

Although it is true that companies who pride themselves on their concern for their people tend to stay that way, it is surprising, and a source of real pleasure, to see how often yesterday's lousy company can be transformed into tomorrow's star.

Not only do companies themselves change continuously, but so too do the expectations of individuals. There seems to me to be a growing distrust of paternalism and a growing appreciation of tolerance. Inevitably, perhaps, with an increasing realization of the impermanence of jobs and the difficulties involved in moving, there is great interest in the prospects for long-term and secure employment.

So it is quite likely that this year's 'top 100' may be viewed in quite different ways in, say, two or five years. This is, of course, why companies have continually to change and adapt their practices and behaviour. What is relatively slow to alter is the value system of the company which is likely to be reflected in the ways it relates to its people.

There is one aspect that I have always valued highly in an employer which is not reflected in the assessment system. I refer to what I describe as 'headroom' – the relative space which is available to you to operate in and the freedom you have to 'do it your way'.

The best companies, and the ones which are most fun to work for, are those who describe exactly their expectations and requirements for achievement, but leave the actual task of how to do it to the individual; where supervision is discreet, and where the boss allows you to go a long way before pulling on the reins. These are the circumstances under which employees can grow, both personally and professionally, and that is almost always the source of greatest excitement and pleasure.

I am confident that this book will also have a good effect on employment practices. While most employers seek to make comparisons on the more readily-accessible employment standards of their competitors, very few can attempt to cover such a large field as is covered by this book.

10

Since the measures and judgements are on a relative basis, I would expect that we will see more attention paid by the better companies to improving those areas where they have been judged relatively weak. In this way, over a period of time, the whole ground shifts upwards, and that can only be good.

The real test of the good employer is the quality of the people he or she can attract, retain and motivate. The future of both the individual and the company are inextricably linked, and the best firms enforce the success of both their businesses and their people. This can only be welcomed by every one of us in the community at large, for it is on the international competitive success of our businesses that all our standards of living depend.

INTRODUCTION

The invitation by Collins to locate the 100 best companies to work for in the UK was an immensely exciting one, and the subsequent project involved vigorous and detailed research into the psyche of British industry. A research group was established to locate the finest employers in the land. This would be a piece of original research since, while the marketplace is full of books on business and business management, none before has concentrated on the merits of companies as employers. None has addressed the question of who specifically are the best for employees.

To begin with we compiled a list of companies which were likely contenders for the top 100. This list was made up from a number of different sources. First, we entered our own observations as journalists working in the financial sector. Our own experience led us to believe that certain companies should be included, but we remained open-minded. Should our later research reveal that these companies were not such strong contenders after all, then we were eager to see them replaced by more impressive candidates.

We then talked to a wide range of professionals who daily come into close contact with industry. Among these were accountants and lawyers who have a unique opportunity to see commercial concerns on an intimate basis. We also spoke to fellow journalists on the national newspapers and in the trade journals, to the editors of the business pages of regional evening newspapers and business journals.

We spoke to careers advisers and head-hunters, and when out in the field we spoke to industrial leaders about their own perceptions: which companies did they most admire as employers? Finally, a questionnaire was posted to *The Times* Top 1000, and this also produced a favourable and helpful response. The result of all this was a list of two thousand companies. We considered each of these in great depth, though it is fair to say that some companies stood head and shoulders above the rest right from the start.

Almost everyone we spoke to mentioned Marks & Spencer. Among the most often recommended were ICI, the oil companies Shell, BP and Esso, the pharmaceutical giant Glaxo, American computer concerns Hewlett-Packard, IBM and Digital, the insurance company Allied Dunbar, and United Biscuits. All of these were obvious candidates for research. Our team produced background on all the companies – first, as business enterprises, and second, as employers. While companies rarely achieve much positive press coverage as employers, there exists considerable material in the personnel press on pay, benefits, conditions of service, pension schemes and employment philosophy, and on companies which are unusual success stories.

Vickers Defence System, for example, is a classic success story, but one which few people outside the sector are familiar with. A recommendation by a Tyneside business journalist led to our discovery that the company had turned an industrial relations nightmare into a profound and lasting partnership with staff. We sent a researcher to visit the company and we were singularly impressed with what we found.

Through this process of research we finally refined our list to a working document of approximately 200 companies that we wanted to see. This proved the toughest task, and it was the persuasive skill of Kay Reynolds which encouraged so many companies to let us visit them. It should be said that American-owned companies could not wait to let us in. Hewlett-Packard, for example, was typical. Communications director Roger Wilson said he would be delighted to let us visit HP. The Japanese on the whole were equally positive – Nissan and Sony invited us to conduct research within a few days of our initial approach. British companies, however, were generally more unsure of our motives, and took some persuading that our objectives were valid and that we were who we said we were. Some took as long as five months to give us an answer – some slightly longer. British companies are wary of journalists by nature. Some have very good cause. Rowntree was hurt by some bad publicity and has since withdrawn into its shell.

Our list of candidates for the book was updated as we went along, and it was also refined somewhat as we discovered more about the employment record of our principal contenders.

Before launching out on company visits, we drew up a list of criteria on which companies were to be assessed. These were: pay, benefits, promotion, training, equal opportunities, environment, ambience and communications. Pay is an obvious criterion. People's motivation for work is usually related to how much they earn. But we wanted to assess companies against how they performed nationally, locally and in their industrial sector. Among the best payers are Mars, Marks & Spencer, 3M and the oil companies. Paying well could not and would not be a sole reason for inclusion. In some cases our top 100 are not the best payers, but they perform well in other areas.

Benefits contribute to the overall rewards package. Some companies prefer to pay well and provide skeletal perks. Others offer a wide range of benefits, including private medical insurance – usually BUPA or PPP

– share option schemes, hairdressing and chiropody, staff discount programmes and sports facilities. Commonplace benefits are holidays in excess of twenty days a year, subsidized canteens (some are free), pension schemes and sick pay benefits beyond the statutory norms. Pension schemes were under particular attention since the government announced changes to the arrangements for pensions which took effect in 1988. We took particular note of companies which offered non-contributory pension schemes. Some companies have unusual benefits, like Kodak, which has an ocean-going yacht for use by staff, Hallmark Cards, which gives every staff member the day off on his or her birthday, and Rank Xerox, which has one of the largest Jacuzzis in Western Europe.

Promotion, and the speed at which individuals can rise, is often linked with the structure of companies. Mars, for example, has few tiers of authority – a very clean and flat structure – while ICI and Shell have a series of levels. Many larger organizations have so-called fast-track programmes. These schemes are designed to promote people with potential to positions of responsibility as rapidly as possible. Shell is clearly interested in the top half a per cent of graduates each year who can provide the maximum talent for senior management in years to come. This is common among very large corporations.

Two grounds of concern emerged in this area. One, which overlaps with equal opportunities, is the rapidity and frequency with which women are promoted. The other is whether companies handle their non-graduate talent with sufficient skill. As graduate talent becomes increasingly difficult to acquire, companies do not, on the whole, seem to be developing their non-graduates with as much foresight and flexibility as they might. Among the best companies for non-graduates are the entrepreneurial businesses like Cala, Black & Decker and The Body Shop, but Littlewoods, Marks & Spencer and Phillips & Drew are also good in this area. Advertising agency Lowe, Howard-Spink & Bell, makes a positive virtue of not recruiting graduates. Many companies are beginning to recognize that promotion from within strengthens and develops the organization.

Training has improved in recent years, and a plethora of training formats has evolved to meet the demand. Some of the American multinationals, such as Digital and 3M, are advocates of training as a means of personal development. Implicit in this is the notion that the company will support an individual's application for training outside the normal spectrum of work-related courses. If a salesman wanted to learn Italian, even though his job is selling software to clients in the West Midlands, the company would listen favourably. The experience

15

would help him develop as a person, and he would be grateful to the organization for spending a small sum of money – in corporate terms – to advance him.

Notably we were impressed by Glaxo's pragmatic approach of mixing internal and external training fashioned to the company's specific needs. United Biscuits, Marks & Spencer and W H Smith all score well here.

The working environment is a fairly obvious criterion. We saw a trend towards open-plan layouts, and cleaner and brighter workplaces. Mars is the only company which is genuinely open-plan. Everyone, including the managing director, is located in the same room. Many companies have pleasant offices, and among them are LWT, BP, Shell, Digital, IBM, HTV and Allied Dunbar. But this list is not meant to be exhaustive.

Ambience is less easy to judge, but we were looking for more than merely a friendly atmosphere in which to work. In some senses it is tied to the culture of the company. If companies have a sense of direction, and people know what that direction is, they often have a better sense of belonging. This is further enhanced if they also feel they are making a positive contribution to the company's wellbeing.

Equal opportunities is an area where great progress still needs to be made. In British industry as a whole it has traditionally been able-bodied white men who have succeeded, but there have been signs in the 1980s that this is beginning to change. Many of our top companies are introducing and extending policies which make the work of women, disabled people and ethnic minorities much more fulfilling. Nevertheless, the path is a long and hard one, and some companies have further to tread than others.

Communications was an area of our research which in many cases proved to be a key factor. Companies which trust their people sufficiently to keep them well informed and solicit their views are by and large those which show the greatest prospect for long-term growth. Communicative companies prosper. It was sad to see in some companies we visited that considerate and generous personnel policies had not always been communicated well enough. The systems for disseminating information vary radically. Some favour briefing meetings, others newspapers and videos.

It would be unfair to look for perfection among any of the top 100 companies. We aimed to find organizations which were moving in the right direction, which displayed a positive approach, and, more importantly, saw their staff as human beings and had a real interest in what they were doing. This was often reflected in their communications policy. It is good to see management who bother to tell people how the company is shaping up financially, and how their competitors are performing. Where they consult their people and ask their advice, this is real progress. The oil companies are generally good here. Esso, for example, went into a long consultative process with its staff before planning its move to Leatherhead. Mars scored highly, but so too did Dana, whose staff could not say enough about how effective communications were. In contrast, Polaroid, which is an excellent company, has yet to bring its communications up to scratch. The result is a work force which feels that it is out of touch with what management are trying to achieve. It seemed good sense to us that if companies expect more and more from their staff in an increasingly competitive environment, then they should be prepared to drop their cloak of secrecy and extend staff involvement.

Nissan and Peugeot Talbot are good examples of motorcar companies, in an industry once beleaguered by strikes and poor industrial relations, which are now thriving. Nissan's employee-relations success even made the national press. Here creative managements have found new solutions to old staffing problems. In some companies unions have been ruled out of the picture altogether; in others, single-union agreements have functioned effectively, and in some cases unions have acted as a dynamic spur to the enterprise. H. P. Bulmer and Petrofina are good examples of companies where this phenomenon has occurred.

Many of the companies we interviewed succeeded in gaining an entry in this book because of the atmosphere they had created. The so-called family atmosphere is one which companies seek to create even if they are not family firms at the outset, and it pays dividends. If people feel themselves to be part of a team, they work harder. When some companies were modernized in the early 1980s, and consequently became more aggressive, some of them lost the family feel of the business while the shrewder companies sought to retain it. The Americans are particularly keen on the family as a concept, and where they have adapted the brash Stateside attitude into a more British approach they have won significant gains.

As a means of providing a quick overview of a company's performance in terms of the eight basic criteria on which all companies were judged, the following key has been used.

1) excellent
2) very good
3) good
4) fair
5) poor

One of the major themes to emerge from the research on this project has been the increasing interest in production quality. Many more companies see quality as an important theme for their activities. The benefits are considerable in terms of sales, but also in employees' attitudes, as the drive towards excellence encourages greater effort by staff.

We have attempted to make the language of the book as accessible as possible for the general reader and we have avoided personnel industry terminology. There are references to salary structures such as the Hay/MSL guidelines which are used by a handful of top companies to compare their pay and conditions. We have also referred to team briefings, usually as defined by the Industrial Society. Information is passed right through the organization within a few hours. It is presented at a series of meetings where staff are invited to make comments which are subsequently fed back.

Some reference has been made to the milk round recruitment process of undergraduates and other students, which general readers may not be familiar with. Each year a wide range of companies participates in the milk round. Visits are made to universities and polytechnics by representatives of the companies. Presentations are made to students, and prospective recruits are interviewed in subsequent sessions. The influence of the milk round has been diluted in recent years by the growth of summer recruitment fairs. These are normally held after examinations have been taken, when students have a clearer idea of their likely results.

Some mention is made of quality circles, currently popular in some sections of industry. They are used as a quality-control device which involves both work force and management. People are brought together regularly to discuss ways of improving the quality of the work carried out.

We have also referred to psychometric testing, which is one of a group of techniques used to assess applicants for jobs. These are designed not to judge specific skills but to analyse psychologically an individual's fitness for the task.

The geographical spread of companies included in the top 100 is reassuringly wide. We have visited – and included in the book – companies as far apart as central Scotland and the West Country. Overseas-owned enterprises have found the northeast, central Scotland and South Wales particularly attractive areas in which to do business. High unemployment in the areas could have tempted them to reduce their standards, but in fact some of our very best enterprises

18

are in these regions. Nissan, Komatsu, Sony, Polaroid, Compaq, and National Panasonic offer good conditions and stimulating work.

In the early 1980s redundancies throughout British industry were heavy and wide-ranging, but the fact that a company needed to reduce staff is emphatically not a reason for debarring them for selection, and some of our companies were among those forced to cut back to survive. We have looked for an intelligent, caring and sensitive approach to redundancy when considering a company for selection.

This is the first time that such a project has been undertaken, the enterprise was in itself a mini-business. The processing of the information flow was a major task alone. We believe that this volume is an indispensable guide to anyone wanting to discover the best employers in industry.

ABBEY NATIONAL

The Abbey National Building Society is the largest building society in the UK. Its 1986 assets amounted to £26 billion, and pre-tax profits were £353 million. The organization employs 12,500 people full time, and 3000 part time. The Abbey National is based in Baker Street, central London, and has 700 branches.

pay	☐	ambience	☐
benefits	☐	environment	☐
promotion	☐	equal opportunities	☐
training	☐	communications	☐

If the Abbey National were a bank its assets would make it one of the 100 largest banks in the world. There are people inside Abbey House who dream of turning that 'if' into a 'when'. Certainly the banks were worried when a mere building society thought up the £100 cheque card before they did. The previously friendly but dozy Abbey National has woken up. It has changed more in the last five years than it had in the last forty.

Seven million people have accounts with the Abbey National. It was created by the merger of the Abbey Road and National societies in 1942. The Abbey has always been known for its unconventional approach to advertising – from paying reporters to write good copy to putting up the world's biggest advertising hoarding in 1935. It was no coincidence that Abbey Road's move to 221b Baker Street took them to one of the most famous addresses in London – fictional home of Sherlock Holmes – nor that they found personalities like Neville Chamberlain and Ramsay MacDonald to open their new premises.

This spirit is prevalent in the modern Abbey National's aggressive approach to marketing – they were the first building society to advertise on television, with slogans like 'I've got the Abbey habit' and the 'thumbs up' symbol.

The National's more radical tradition goes back to the nineteenth-century politicians Cobden and Bright who set up the society to help win the vote for ordinary working people. The idea was to buy up land wholesale and sell it off in small plots so that the buyers would qualify to take part in elections as 40-shilling freeholders. They would then vote in parliamentary reform. This idealistic tradition does not seem to have survived as strongly as the commercial ethos, but the Abbey National still values its employees. After all, 'You don't get profit in this business,' as Terry Murphy, general manager of personnel observes, 'without highly committed staff.' A 40 per cent increase in profits last year bears witness to that commitment.

Apart from the headquarters in central London and computing and finance departments in Milton Keynes, there are 700 branches. Counter clerks have a tough time. They start on less than £5000 and work really hard for their money, although £3000 London weighting does help. Even so, staff turnover is 16 per cent in the capital compared to 1 per cent in the northwest. A cashier might be on £8000 and a supervisor on £9000. Branch managers are on £14,000 plus.

Most counter staff are women, and at assistant manager level too there is an even balance of the sexes, but 95 per cent of managers are men. Women are not applying. 'We could do better,' says Murphy. There are more female management trainees now, but at the top levels of the organization the eight general managers are all men although there are two women on the board. Murphy thinks the Abbey is 'good at getting ethnic minorities to work for us'. He admits that disabled people are not making senior levels of management, although new buildings are being designed for wheelchair access and there are facilities such as talking calculators and Braille typewriters.

Under the chief executive, Peter Birch (on a six-figure salary), and the eight general managers, there are two operations managers on £40,000 and six regional managers on £30,000, with area chiefs earning in the mid-£20,000s. Benefits are good – particularly the 5 per cent interest mortgage which is available to staff after just three months. Employees still complain that this 'only' applies to mortgages of up to £25,000, and that it is not worth much to high earners by the time they take tax relief into account, but it helps most employees buy a house or flat. The profit share was worth a month's salary in 1986 and the Abbey will pay half the cost of BUPA.

The Abbey recruits 'O' or 'CSE' level students from school, and graduates from employment fairs, but it does not participate in the milk round. Mature students are seen as a good bet. It also believes in recruitment tests which look at behavioural, numerical and verbal skills.

Training is a priority as the Abbey expands into areas such as current accounts, portable pensions, insurance and estate agency. Since 1985, the time given to training has gone up from an average of a third of a day per employee to seven days – and that does not include the half hour a week spent in branches. The Abbey uses a mixture of computer-based and off-job training. For their customer-care programme they put 12,000 people through a two-day training course.

The Abbey sponsors promising recruits through degree courses. John Bayliss came in as an office boy and is now general manager of marketing. Graduates enter a management training programme for two years, which gives them experience of head office departments and of the branches. If they choose to stay in the branches after that they could expect to be assistant managers in one or two years, and managers in another two or three years. But the branch network is no longer expanding, so this may slow up in future.

The branches will gradually change in appearance. The Abbey wants to get rid of the screens and go for a more informal, friendly atmosphere. Along with motivation, commitment and energy, communication is one of the new buzz words inside the society. Communications chief Stuart Gowans claims that when he first joined he had to convince old-timers that 'the Abbey habit didn't mean taking a vow of silence'. Since 1984 there has been a move away from the paternalism and authoritarianism of the past, although its effects are still strong. Staff are not unionized and the staff association is dismissed by some members as 'a bit of a joke. They make an offer. We accept it or get nothing. They know that 90 per cent of us would never go on strike on principle.' The Abbey points to a 3 per cent absence rate ('all genuine') as proof of staff commitment. Staff are rewarded for good suggestions – and not just with a certificate or a few kind words from the chief executive. The suggestions scheme has paid out thousands of pounds for employees' ideas.

Statutes are changing and societies like the Abbey may soon take advantage of deregulation to become limited companies, but the outside world has been to slow to realize what is happening. No one knows whether it will still exclusively be a building society in five years' time, and that makes it a more exciting place to work. Training is excellent and with all the new business initiatives there are many more opportunities for promotion than there were in the days of 'dead men's shoes'.

ALLIED COLLOIDS

Allied Colloids is a diversified group, manufacturing chemicals for product sectors in agriculture, mineral processing, oil services, paper, pollution control, textiles and engineering. Its turnover in 1987 was £142 million. It employs 1600 people, of which 1350 are in the Bradford area. The remainder are scattered around the country in small outposts.

pay ☐		ambience ☐	
benefits ☐		environment ☐	
promotion ☐		equal opportunities ☐	
training ☐		communications ☐	

Allied Colloids was fifty years old in 1987. It celebrated with pre-tax profits which were yet again 20 per cent higher than the previous twelve months. *Business* magazine in October 1987 nominated Colloids the sixteenth most profitable company in the UK. This is in spite of heavy dependence on foreign exchange earnings – 80 per cent of the group's revenue comes from outside the UK.

Based on a single-site complex south of Bradford, Colloids research and manufacture chemicals for a large variety of industrial sectors. 'We are certainly quite young among our competitors,' says John Binnie, AC sales director who joined in 1973 after spells with ICI and Esso. Nevertheless, the last decade has shown remarkable growth. Some 250 people nationwide are in sales and 35 per cent of employees are in management.

Managing director Peter Flesher is typical. He joined the company in 1951 as a laboratory assistant. He qualified simultaneously as a chemist at Leeds University in 1961. Employing school-leaver chemists and training them is part of the corporate ideology at Colloids. These apprentices, with seven years' university training and employment experience, are far more valuable to the company than 'any fresh-faced graduate straight from college', says Colin Scargill, a sales manager. 'We are far keener on a policy of promoting from within our own ranks – we have great faith in our own products, both human and manufactured.'

There is a warm Yorkshire pride about the people who work for

Colloids. 'No one is indispensable but it is true that the continuous training we receive at AC does make us more vital than most – my lab would be pretty stuck without me at the helm,' says one research chemist.

What the company is looking for are chemists with a finely tuned commercial sense who can react quickly to market demands and who understand the chemistry and technology of the industries which they serve. 'We're not looking for prima donnas,' says Binnie, 'but ambition which shows itself both personally and corporately is very healthy in a business like this. The personable, reliable and competitive man is who we're looking for in management, especially when this is backed up by the right technical ability.'

After nine years with AC, one research manager says: 'What I like most about working here is the speed with which I see my work being put into production. I waste very little time on work which doesn't eventually have a commercial use. It gives me a great deal of confidence both in the company and my own ability.' He says that the directors will often talk out some chemical problem in the canteen at lunchtime. 'The single-site complex at Low Moor [Bradford] has much to do with the ease of communications,' says Binnie. 'I learn far more in the hour at lunchtime than I do during the rest of the day.'

Colloids has never made anyone redundant – an even greater feat considering the company is sited primarily in West Yorkshire, an industrial location scarred with decay and unemployment. Bradford is not a pretty place in which to work – though Leeds, now a thriving commercial and retail centre, is ten miles down the M62. Scargill points out that it has the lowest cost of living in the country. House prices are notably cheaper than anywhere else.

Ben McDonnell is leader of the workers' council. It meets bi-monthly to discuss issues raised between elected work-force representatives and management. Scargill, one of its recent members, says: 'The atmosphere in there is so far removed from the traditional concept of British management versus British worker – it is genuinely an atmosphere of business colleagues working as a team towards one end. It is one thing about AC that has impressed me more than anything else: the unity of purpose, the awareness of one another.' McDonnell says: 'The only dispute we've ever had while I've been council leader was concerned with weekend rostering. It was quickly resolved at council. The engineers are the most independent division in the company. The problem for them is that they do not see the products performing in real markets like everyone else. So they sometimes feel a little hard done by.'

25

AC does not have a regular recruitment programme. It has done the milk round once or twice in recent years but no particular university is favoured. They take six to seven graduates a year but the preferred route is to take school-leavers and train them at work. Pay is average to good for the sector and promotion occurs roughly every two to three years. Perks are not numerous but the pension scheme is especially good. Share option schemes are available to all employees and currently 75–80 per cent of them take advantage of this. In 1986 a profit-related bonus scheme was introduced which distributes equally among employees a cream of the profit. Above 10 per cent of profits is deemed an acceptable minimum. The first payout brought £200 to everyone. The Christmas bonus is 3.5 per cent of annual income.

The production site is well organized into self-contained units where the research, production and administration for one product is carried out in one area. On a larger scale the power supply, engineering maintenance and packing houses are nearby. The factory floors are a mixture of pipes and convoluted metal structures, that bubble and steam, and high-tech computerized control rooms whose information is updated several times a second. These are noisy and smelly as factories go. Our researchers were issued with stove boots to stop them slipping on the floor. Production is carried out on a continuous continental shift system of four days on, three days off, but safety concerns make flexitime impractical. Overtime is taken up by virtually everyone. A factory foreman might work 55–60 hours a week and take home £15,000 a year. For the area the pay is good, but it is the job security which is the most attractive quality for many workers. There is an atmosphere of willing urgency on the production line, and almost everyone appears to enjoy the work.

There are no unions at Allied Colloids, and pay is not negotiated. 'We are quite paternalistic,' admits Binnie. 'The lack of a pay structure at levels above the shop floor is an incentive to better productivity.' McDonnell said, 'I would probably spend most of the day with my feet up if I knew what salary I was going to be on.'

Allied Colloids has succeeded in making a traditional chemical plant a decent, humane and friendly place to work. The company has established itself in world markets and is going places. Its financial performance is unquestioned. The loyalty and commitment of the staff is remarkable.

Despite management assertions of approachability, some members of the work force are less convinced. When we visited the Low Moor site some employees said they found top management more remote than the impression painted by company spokesmen. When asked what the senior management – or even middle management – could do to improve matters, a consistent reply came back. 'That's what the company council's for, isn't it?' Grievances were nothing more than grumbles about canteen food and the five-minute walk from the car park each morning. But there is a company bus to take people to the front gate.

It is declared policy that the workers must 'communicate and cooperate', and they do, effectively, without the need for a strong arbitration forum. The canteen, the focus for most informal communication, is adequately sized but provides a poor choice of albeit quite good food. Its main drawback is that it closes at night. There is no social centre at AC and organized sports are limited. But the annual Christmas ball is well attended.

The acquisition phase of growth for the company is still seen as some way off, although a plant has recently been acquired in Kent. The rapid growth in the chemicals industry during the last ten years has been mirrored at AC. A whole new breed of young chemists has benefited from this movement. Typical is Ali Ashgar, aged thirty-four, who is fully trained as a sales manager in the oil services division. He says that for young people with ambition AC is a company where they can gain academic and commercial achievement.

David Farrar, the same age, was recently appointed a technical director. He says the work ethic is predominant. 'If you want to get somewhere fast, work hard at Allied Colloids,' he comments. It is a measure of their competence that so little of AC's executive skill is imported. The company is on a high right now, and certainly shows no signs of losing its grip on success.

ALLIED DUNBAR

Allied Dunbar is a wholly-owned subsidiary of BAT Industries. It employs 2500 people in 120 branches nationwide, including 1900 in Swindon. Its actuarial surplus for 1986 was £43.8 million.

pay	☐	ambience	☐
benefits	☐	environment	☐
promotion	☐	equal opportunities	☐
training	☐	communications	☐

International Survey Research company recently conducted an attitude assessment among the work force at Allied Dunbar and it came up with some surprising results. Satisfaction at AD was vastly higher than the national average. On all significant points the staff at the Swindon-based assurance company were markedly happier than in any other comparable survey. Yet senior management argue that the primary reason for their success is the sound business ethic.

'Our attitude towards our staff is not born out of any altruistic motives,' says deputy managing director Sandy Leitch. 'We believe that it makes good business sense to treat your staff well. We are a very positive culture. We are motivated by growth and we aim to achieve more than 10 per cent above the retail price index each year.'

This aggressive approach to its business singles out AD among its competitors. It is dispensing with the traditional image of insurance companies as slow, reticent corporations trapped in their ivory towers. This is an entrepreneurial outfit with a high moral ethic and a determination to double the company's turnover every two years and to take the industry by storm. 'We are not interested in market share or position in the league table,' says Leitch. 'We want growth.'

Formed in 1971 by Sir Mark Weinberg and others, AD was created to find a new way of doing business in the insurance sector. It went public in 1976 and had grown so fast that in 1985 it was acquired by BAT Industries for £660 million. In the early 1980s the company spent a year laying down its basic code of business. This has been summarized in a set of brief value statements called Vision, the most conspicuous of which is 'demanding and caring'. Staff throughout the company reiterate this with a measure of pride and enthusiasm.

'Demanding and caring sums it up,' says Steve Duffy, who has been with AD for the last seven years. He is a complaints controller in the white dome of the Allied Dunbar Centre. 'We work hard but the benefits are very good.'

Maggie Gill celebrated a decade with the company in 1987. She is a deputy manager in the life services division, and has risen quickly through the ranks – as do many others in the organization. 'AD is an equal opportunities employer and I have no reason to criticize the company in terms of its fairness to me or any other woman here.' She has been promoted six times. 'It's down to you,' she adds. 'It's high-pressure work and if you're prepared to work hard then the company will give you every encouragement.'

Sixty per cent of the work force are women. The company notes a reluctance among male school-leavers in the Swindon area to apply for jobs which do not involve getting their hands dirty. While Swindon is a mini Milton Keynes constructed almost entirely of steel and glass, it is surrounded by a vast rural hinterland and country values still apply.

Openness is another compelling feature of AD. Everyone is encouraged to say what they think. This frankness is remarkable in such a tightly controlled, even paternalistic, organization and is being fostered. Early in 1988 AD launched a Speak Out campaign which emphasized the company's desire to know the views of its staff. Employees are allowed to speak freely to the press and the company has few fears that it will be let down. In interviews with 20 members of staff it was difficult to find someone with a seriously bad word to say about AD.

Another important aspect of this culture is honesty. AD will not tolerate underhand dealing or dishonest transactions. Recently a senior manager was discovered to have forged a mortgage reference. He was fired on the spot. 'We recognized that he had been under considerable pressures but we cannot tolerate dishonest behaviour,' said one executive.

'We want to remove barriers to performance and encourage our staff to talk openly about how they might improve their performance,' says Sandy Leitch. The executives seem to be both accessible and approachable. Their willingness to assess what is wrong with the organization and take steps to improve matters is consistently appealing.

AD is also shrewd about its recruitment. Attrition stands at 8–10 per cent per annum. 'Too high,' says Peter Stemp, personnel director. He puts some of it down to the pregnancy factor but admits that other companies are beginning to offer comparable pay packages.

Pay is above average for the sector and benefits are lavish, encompassing 25 days' holiday a year, free insurance, options to buy BAT shares, a generous annual bonus, company cars and BUPA membership. The level of training is high, and Keith Carby, sales director, maintains that it is the best and most comprehensive in the sector. AD is at present building a training centre which will cost the company £15 million. Members of his sales force below manager level are all self-employed and are paid on a commission-only basis. 'Only a certain type of individual is appropriate as an Allied Dunbar associate,' he explains. 'They must have lots of get up and go. They must want to build a long-term relationship with their clients. They come from a variety of sources – some are ex-football players, lawyers or brokers. We have a lot of ex-service people. One is an ex-Jethro Tull guitarist,' says Carby. He underlines AD's commitment to quality, and explains that he devised the sales training course with that in mind. The Fastrak course involves preparation and study before attending. Those who fail the first assessment are sent back to their units. The foundation course lasts for two weeks, followed by four days on investment, two days on loans, a three-day introduction to pensions and a further three days on business insurance. The applicant is then fully licensed.

'The foundation course is very impressive,' says Mark Child, an associate from Birmingham who previously worked for British Telecom. 'The course brings a lot of your character out.' The associates work to industry rates for commission. But AD matches benefits to their performance. At stages of improved performance they add a company car, a secretary and teams of sales people working to them.

For those sales people who work hard according to the AD ethic the rewards are considerable. But its equally large commitment to charities also plays a part in the career objectives of its sales managers. Those who have a good life style and regularly hit high targets also contribute substantially to the sales department's charities schemes. Recently staff contributed £30,000 to a brain scanner at the nearby Princess Margaret Hospital. This sum was matched by the company, which is one of the largest charitable donors in the country.

The informality of approach – everyone is on first-name terms – extends to the communications system. 'We started a communications facility in 1981. We have regular team briefings and we encourage staff to feed back their comments,' says Peter Stemp.

The managing director emphasizes three key value statements: commitment to service, demanding and caring, and positive management. This combination makes Allied Dunbar an exciting place to work. Staff are encouraged to move into different divisions to broaden their experience. It is not the place for an easy life, but for the dedicated it is a stimulating and rewarding environment.

ALLIED-LYONS

Allied-Lyons is a diverse brewing and leisure group, owning hotels, country clubs and restaurants. The group has interests across the UK. It employs 10,000 people and head office is in London. In 1988 pre-tax profits reached £436 million on a turnover of £4.23 billion

pay ☐		ambience ☐	
benefits ☐		environment ☐	
promotion ☐		equal opportunities ☐	
training ☐		communications ☐	

If you go out to certain pub restaurants for Sunday lunch, enjoy a pint of Tetley's beer, take a six-pack out from the Victoria Wine chain of off-licences, or spend some time at the Gloucester Country Club, you will be a guest of Allied-Lyons. This sprawling group includes breweries, hotels, wine bars, restaurants and clubs. But the Allied-Lyons name would probably be unfamiliar to most customers – they would recognize only the brand names.

Rather like Unilever or United Biscuits, Allied-Lyons as a group prefers to operate invisibly and may not be apparent even to many employees. Chairman Sir Derrick Holden-Brown says that the company learned from its mistake in the late 1960s when a group of advisers suggested that all of the group's small brewing interests should be submerged under the one company name of ABUK – Allied Breweries United Kingdom.

Holden-Brown, who was then boss of the Showerings, Vine Products and Whiteways division of the group, disagreed with this policy and refused to be bulldozed into adopting it. He later said that it would have meant losing such brand names as Britvic, Harveys Bristol Cream and Coates Gaymers. Employees would no longer be able to associate with a brand that was instantly recognizable to the consumer. He says that it was a telling adventure: the companies in the same brewing division, having each lost their identities, became rudderless for almost ten years.

A decision was finally made in the late 1970s to re-establish the personality of the brand labels. It took a full five years for those companies to get back on course. The story reveals something of the leadership style of the chairman and the attitude of the company, and it also shows why Allied-Lyons is now such a good place to work. Staff can again feel affinity with specific products. It should also be said that the group is highly secretive about its work practices and does not like members of the press snooping around its premises.

Like many concerns in the brewing industry, Allied-Lyons is a mixture of the traditional and the modern. It is one of the liveliest-minded of the brewers in terms of marketing – it is most definitely brand led – and some of its outlets reflect the leading edge of pub and restaurant design. Many of the group's restaurant chains have a distinctly US design. Calendars, an American-style café, restaurant and bar in Watford, is typical. It seats nearly 250 people and the menu caters for the young and old with a blend of traditional and more unusual fare. Such is the success of Calendars that the chairman of Allied Breweries says he plans to open another twenty-five early in the next decade. The company also owns a selection of steak bars under the names Cavalier and Chester, and has christened a selection of pubs 'Gamebirds'. A young designer has been taken on to fashion these pubs for the youth market.

The company has also been innovative at the richer end of the market. The Soho Brasserie is a famous haunt of artists and PR people, and is one of the vogue restaurants of the district.

In the same way that TNT and Federal Express expect their drivers to bring in sales by watching out for possible leads, Allied-Lyons is also keen to involve its staff. Tetley-Walker, for example, has increased its market share in the free trade section of the business by involving staff from sectors other than the sales departments.

Sales people visit clubs and halls to try to win new business. They often take with them some draymen, office staff and even some of the brewers themselves. The aim is to get people involved in other business in addition to their own jobs, to motivate them to believe in the company. The entire staff of the Tetley office act like a team of management consultants. They explain how they achieve sales or exploit premises to their fullest potential.

The logical extension is for the Allied-Lyons staff to advise customers on how they can better run their business. There is no charge for this consultation, but it is strong encouragement to buy the product. The campaign has been very effective within Tetley and it has made people aware of how the business operates and of what the commercial pressures are. It is typical of the group's innovative thinking.

Allied-Lyons shares the same reputation as all brewers for being far from progressive in their employment of women. Brewing, it is said, is a business which has been male-dominated for years and it will take some time to shift attitudes. On the hotels and restaurants side the company is moving forward, and, like Bass, is able to push its women through faster here than in the brewing area.

The group has a good share option scheme which has a savings plan and an option. As many as 4000 workers have taken up the facility to buy shares in the group. Many of these are at the top end of the management structure of the group, but there is nonetheless a wide selection of people who are shareholders.

The group is seen as being average to good in pay and conditions, although conditions vary from operating company to operating company. There is, however, strong loyalty for the individual companies, something which the current group management has encouraged.

Allied-Lyons is a diverse group within the brewing and leisure sectors. Its outlets and products enjoy considerable esteem in the public domain. Allied restaurants and bistros win awards for their design and general appeal. It is fortunate to own a large reservoir of pubs with which to try out new ideas and move people around. The organization has a good sense of experimentation, and is one in which people who like that type of environment will prosper.

AMERSHAM INTERNATIONAL

Amersham International is based in the Buckinghamshire town of Amersham. It specializes in products related to radioactivity and molecular biology. It employs 3000 people worldwide, the majority of whom are based in Amersham and Cardiff. Turnover in 1987 was £148 million and pre-tax profits were £22 million.

pay □		ambience □	
benefits □		environment □	
promotion □		equal opportunities □	
training □		communications □	

Amersham International is located in the most unlikely setting. Its ultra-modern-tech plant nestles in the Chiltern Hills in the traditional Buckinghamshire town of Amersham. But the sleepy rural backdrop should not mislead. The company is at the forefront of its sector. Amersham has bases worldwide but the largest part of its work force is sited in the town. It also has a large R&D centre in Cardiff.

Founded in 1940, as a government research laboratory manufacturing products based on radium, Amersham has developed a considerable reputation for its radioactive materials which are used mainly in health care. Despite privatization in 1982, there is still a strong emphasis on research and development, for which the company is justly internationally famous. The main body of its team concentrates on new products.

Output is produced exclusively in the UK, but some 88 per cent of sales are overseas, mainly in Europe and North America. Around 40 per cent of sales are health-care linked, and another 40 per cent is derived from the biological, genetic and biochemical markets. The final 20 per cent comes from industrial requirements.

Until privatization, Amersham grew at a steady pace as an adjunct of the UK Atomic Energy Authority, with a strong Civil Service culture. There was a cosy relationship between management and staff and a sense of dedication, but a rather lax approach towards commercial values. A veil of secrecy clothed the operation since the organization worked with radioactive materials, and everyone had had to sign the Official Secrets Act.

After 1982 the family feeling stayed but management tried to engender a greater awareness of the marketplace. Sixteen years later turnover and staff numbers have doubled. The old guard remain suspicious but newcomers comment on the friendly attitude of the company. Paul Woodward, a project scientist recruited in 1986, says, 'The managers are a lot different from the way I imagined them to be. I thought they would be aloof but it is more like a family.' Adrianne Hutchins, PA to the manager of one of the operating groups, joined in 1977. She says that the management are open-minded and approachable. 'There's always someone to go to for help, if you need it. Someone will always listen.'

Part of this intimate culture is generated by the arrangement of operational groups within Amersham. Most people work on specific projects in teams of four or five. There are some larger groups, but never more than twenty in a team. Each one has a team leader, usually a science graduate with three or four years of working experience post qualification. Team leaders are normally appointed internally, but increasingly they are being drawn in from outside. Each team has a set of objectives which are based on the company's business plan. Commercial deadlines are very tightly set.

Cathy Sturrock, a technician working in molecular biology, started at Amersham in 1986. 'Each member of the group has an area for which they are responsible and you have some freedom to make up your own experiments, but you also get a great deal of support,' she says.

The company concentrates on products which can be put on the market within two years. The new emphasis on speed has, to a certain extent, been brought about by the stock market quote. It also means that product lines are planned with an eye to marketing. Moving away from the purely scientific tendency has caused some resentment among the science professionals. Some of them feel there is a little too much management and that there have been too many reorganizations with too little effect. But as Gareth Griffiths, director of personnel, comments: 'Prior to 1982 the business was something of a cottage industry, with a feeling that everyone could have a go at what they liked. Now we're trying to bring some order into the business.'

The pay and benefits package is nothing special. It lies precariously between the low pay of the National Health Service in pure research and the comparatively huge salaries of the pharmaceutical industry. A graduate could expect to start on £10,000 and a laboratory worker with 'A' levels on £7000. Increments are unremarkable. Pay is increased according to length of service rather than achievement – an obvious reminder of the Civil Service days – but things are on the move. Performance-related pay will become increasingly important, especially in middle management.

Fringe benefits are few and far between. There are cars for middle and senior managers and a Save As You Earn share option scheme. One senior project leader says that he could get more money elsewhere but that the atmosphere and teamwork keeps him at Amersham. One of the company's most pressing problems is its proximity to London and the soaring prices of houses. Most of the younger staff live at least ten miles away, and in that part of the countryside public transport is at best inadequate.

Set against this is the spectacular setting – one of the buildings is a converted manor house in fifty acres of woodland – the highly informal structure, the positive environment, the single-status canteen and the quality of teamwork.

The company still has the Civil Service type of union negotiating structure, but it has few real problems in this area. Training is still somewhat informal with great emphasis on on-the-job training. The academic staff keep pace with the latest developments in their fields and spend some time communicating these to their staff. Lab technicians are encouraged to take a sponsored higher national certificate on day release and it is even possible to take a part-time degree. Many staff attend conferences – some overseas.

The management are aware of the deficiencies in formal training and have established several programmes to remedy the situation. Managers and staff enjoy an easy, informal communication, and the grapevine is still the most efficient means of passing round information. Peter Brand, a group personnel manager, says, 'You'll never get rid of the grapevine but we'd like to be sure that everything you heard on the grapevine would be confirmed by managers within twenty-four hours.' Team briefing now operates as a main conduit of information.

Amersham enjoys a special reputation for quality. William Ellaby, finance director, comments that the company aims to double in size every four to five years and to increase staff by 5 to 7 per cent per annum. This points to opportunities for promotion, especially in the newer fields.

Griffiths talks about the management's desire to create an atmosphere of stability and controlled change. They are lucky to benefit from a powerful loyalty which binds Amersham staff to the company and to one another. It is indicative that staff turnover is remarkably low. Hutchins says, 'I have a lot to thank the company for in terms of my career development. They've given me a lot of confidence.' Susan Matthews, an operations manager, says, 'Amersham generates a lot of loyalty in me and I'm not usually especially loyal to a company.'

While Amersham may not yet have completed the transition from public sector to privatized concern, it is becoming a commercial business. It is responsive and sympathetic to its staff, and, notably, it has skilfully managed to retain its friendly, family atmosphere while it makes some radical changes.

APPLE COMPUTER

Apple Computer UK is a subsidiary of the California Apple Computer Inc. UK domestic figures are unavailable but worldwide the company reports a turnover of $2.67 billion. In its current home of Hemel Hempstead the company employs less than one hundred staff, but when the business moves shortly to Stockley Park, a site close to Heathrow Airport, its intake will grow to between 200 and 250 employees by mid-year 1989.

pay	☐	ambience	☐
benefits	☐	environment	☐
promotion	☐	equal opportunities	☐
training	☐	communications	☐

The legend on Apple's 1986 annual report makes a simple statement. In a few words it encapsulates the style, some of the history and the reason for the company's spectacular success: 'Sometimes you have to go against conventional wisdom to succeed.' Conventional wisdom held that Apple was washed up. IBM's strategy had left the company with little more than liabilities, but with the same entrepreneurial energy with which Apple was launched in 1976, it fought back. In 1987 Apple worldwide reported a 40 per cent increase in turnover and a 32 per cent rise in pre-tax profits. This is powerful testimony to the will, commitment and single-minded determination of both Apple management and employees.

The same youthful but indomitable drive which characterizes Apple in the States is present in its smaller offspring in the UK. Despite protests to the contrary, it is very much the British son of the American father. Around the world the same high-pressure, high-innovation management style recurs in Apple outposts. Allowing for regional and cultural variations, Apple Values hold true wherever in the company's global network you might be. Its lively, friendly and open approach is typically Californian and parallels can easily be drawn with other West Coast computer businesses in the UK.

What sets Apple apart from many UK companies, apart from some obvious differences in style, is the excellent level of pay and benefits. Salesmen on 100 per cent achievement of their individual targets take away £70,000 a year. Secretaries are on a bare minimum of £10,000; a supervisor would earn £16,000, and managers earn between £22,000 and £35,000 depending on status. These salaries do not take into account the benefits structure. Salaries are reviewed, along with other aspects of career and performances, at intervals of six months.

Status is not a big deal at Apple. More emphasis is placed on a combination of personal initiative and teamwork. An essential enthusiasm hovers on the edge of fervent dedication. Apple employees have a passionate belief in their product and it takes understanding spouses and partners to tolerate such vibrant commitment. Harold Beirne, director of finance, has no illusions, 'We pay 'em a lot and we work 'em to death.'

His analysis is borne out by his people. Peter Davies, market development manager, says, 'Apple's goal is to be in the top 5 per cent in terms of salary paid. They prefer to pay a bit more money and take fewer people on board to encourage the individual.' Davies has been with Apple for three and a half years. He started as a field sales manager and now earns £35,000 basic. But with a management bonus, other benefits and a company car, his real income measures between £55,000 and £60,000.

Tony Perks, who joined three years ago from Apple Holland, is an information systems manager. His starting salary of £20,000 has risen to £29,000 and he reckons his bonuses bring him in another £12,000. He also runs a company car. He sums up his appreciation of the company's salary and benefits package: 'Everybody benefits from everything there is to be benefited from.'

Two-thirds of all staff up to the level of supervisors are given company cars. A creditable share option scheme is available to everyone after a year and is based on an allocation of shares according to salary. Everyone is covered by life insurance, a voluntary pension fund is open to all staff after three months and BUPA membership is granted to all Apple people based in the London area. Holidays, which are well earned, are fixed at 26 days, rising to 28 days after five years. An additional four weeks' sabbatical is awarded after five years, and is repeated every five years thereafter.

Single status applies to profit-sharing – everyone gets the same amount. When company profits hit 30 per cent above target in 1986 everyone received £1000. Hero awards are made for work done which is over and above the call of duty, and a gold and diamond tie pin or brooch carrying the Apple logo is given after five years of service.

Some 48 per cent of staffers are women, and maternity leave is one area where Apple excels. Apple women receive all their state benefits plus 50 per cent of their salaries. Rita Boughen, a customer service supervisor who joined Apple as a temp eight years ago, has left the company twice to have a baby. She is full of praise for the maternity package and says that the company was extremely generous. What impressed Clarissa Hunt, an event liaison officer, about Apple is the commitment to personal growth. 'You progress as an individual in every way. You expand the job to do what you want to do. You are in control of your own destiny. It doesn't matter how you come into the company – you will get to where you want to go.' It is really all a matter of attitude at Apple.

A high accent on initiative is pointing the company in one direction – creativity in product design and sales. Apple UK won the parent's Country of the Year aware in 1986 as a recognition of its innovation and achievement. These are the qualities with which the original Apple I personal computer, the Macintosh and its desktop publishing equipment were developed.

It is remarkable that a company with such a high profile in the marketplace is so small in the UK. But the move to Stockley Park should change this: Apple looks forward to increasing its staff and sales. On an international scale, Apple is reputed to be teaming up with another major-league computer manufacturer for joint ventures. With such ingredients, the Apple recipe for success can only get better.

BASS

Bass are brewers with interests in catering, soft drinks, hotels, travel and bookmaking. In 1987 the company turned over £3.2 billion with pre-tax profits of £365 million. The company employs 80,914 people in the UK. Head office is in central London.

pay ☐		ambience ☐	
benefits ☐		environment ☐	
promotion ☐		equal opportunities ☐	
training ☐		communications ☐	

The mock machismo of the drinkers of Carling Black Label is familiar to television viewers across the country. The superhuman individual, always a man, is accompanied in his record-breaking deeds by a can of the frothy lager. The ads appeal to the traditional buyers of beer and pokes a little gentle humour at them.

But in some senses the hero of the Carling ads is none other than its parent company Bass. Even the name can conjure up images of northern redbrick breweries or Black Country pubs dispensing Brew XI, favourite beer in the West Midlands. However, while these impressions are accurate, the company has moved into new areas.

It was a surprise to the researchers on this project that Bass owned Horizon Travel, Britain's third largest package tour operator, and Coral Racing, the chain of betting offices, but it proves to be entirely logical when the path of the group's development is traced.

Brewing remains the Bass core business, but the expansion into other related areas makes good sense. The brewing side is based on a selection of key products; among them Allbright, the most popular beer in Wales, Brew XI, Worthington Bitter, which is number one in the East Midlands, Stones Best Bitter, strong in the north and the takeaway market, Toby Bitter and Worthington Best. Its lagers include Tennent's and Lamot.

The range of beers and lagers means that Bass covers the UK with its product. It is the largest brewer in the UK. The company runs thirteen breweries and three maltings which distribute their product through five operating companies to more than 7000 pubs, more than 800 off-licences and a variety of free trade outlets.

The main operating companies are Charrington, Bass Wales & West, Bass Mitchells & Butlers, Bass North and Tennent Caledonian Breweries. Bass is also active in the soft drinks world, owning Britvic Corona. This company runs all the Britvic lines, the Pepsi licences in the UK, Canada Dry, Corona, Quosh, Tango and Barbican.

One of the key developments in 1987 on the leisure side was the acquisition of eight Holiday Inn hotels – four in the UK and the remainder in Europe. This was added to the existing strength that the company has in the hotel market with 170 Holiday Inns and the Crest chain. Bass owns 50 hotels in the UK and 37 in Europe.

In May 1987 Bass bought Horizon. This runs its own airline – Orion Airways – and owns hotels in resorts abroad. Additionally, Bass Leisure supplies gaming and amusement machines and juke boxes to a wide range of companies. The organization also operates 73 bingo clubs. Finally, Coral Racing runs 822 betting shops, which puts them among the big four bookmakers.

Hedges & Butler is engaged in the wine trade and the list of its products is too long to enumerate, but among them are familiar names such as Hirondelle, Veuve du Vernay, Charbonnier, Moussec, Wincarnis and Colman's of Norwich.

The company has evolved a code called the Bass Philosophy. Referring to its people policy, the code says, 'We aim to provide our employees with the security of working for a successful company, with job satisfaction, good remuneration and good working conditions, acknowledging their right to be informed and consulted on matters which affect their work.'

The statement shows a degree of awareness by Bass which is not normally associated with brewers. In some senses it is an ancient industry with exceptionally traditional views. The fact that Bass has put this policy down on paper and is attempting to live up to it is a step in the right direction.

The company straddles many differing areas of operation. The holidays sector is more free and easy than brewing. Catering is notoriously underpaid and the hotels industry demands long hours and hard work for scant return. However, Bass is making steps to provide good basic minimum standards of pay and conditions.

The company has introduced an employee profit share scheme which is designed to encourage greater staff participation in the company and its activities. Up to 1987 Bass people were allocated £48.4 million worth of shares.

The group is keen that everyone should play a part in pushing the business forward, and it has established a communications policy which allows every employee some say in the future direction of the company and the group.

Bass is still behind the times in some ways, and women must display greater abilities than men to get just as far. Nevertheless, in its industry Bass stands out as a positive and fair-minded company moving into new sectors every year with enthusiasm and drive.

BAXTER HEALTHCARE

Baxter Healthcare is based in Thetford in Norfolk. In the UK, this American-owned company has 1400 staff. Sales in 1986 were £74.4 million.

pay	☐	ambience	☐
benefits	☐	environment	☐
promotion	☐	equal opportunities	☐
training	☐	communications	☐

Baxter Healthcare may be more immediately recognized, especially to those working within the health-care sector, by the company's original name of Travenol. The name-change took place early in 1988 in a move to illustrate the wider range of products now manufactured by the organization. Travenol linked the company closely with the vital intravenous solutions manufactured, but did not help to describe the whole, vast range of 120,000 health-care products now included in the Baxter portfolio worldwide.

Baxter Healthcare has provided health-care products since the company first began trading in America in 1931. Worldwide, the company employs a work force of around 60,000 with 600 facilities in 33 countries. In the UK, the payroll currently totals a staff of 1400, based at manufacturing sites in Thetford, Norfolk, and Nelson, Lancashire; with corporate offices in Egham, and distribution centres based in Basingstoke, Compton and Warrington in England, and Cumbernauld in Scotland.

In December 1988 the company commissioned a new centralized UK distribution centre in Northampton, which will mean the closure of the other English distribution sites. The Scottish operation will remain to serve health-care clients north of the border.

Baxter's UK work force includes over 600 direct production operatives, and around 100 clerical and administrative staff supporting the management, research and sales teams for the company's many products. With such a high proportion of on-line staff, the actual turnover of employees is relatively stable: about ten new staff join, usually in a replacement recruitment situation, across the UK in any one week, according to personnel manager Geoff Hull.

The main Baxter manufacturing centre is in Thetford, which Hull describes as a 'honey pot town', because the community happily experiences an almost non-existent rate of unemployment. Currently, policy is to employ a high number of temporary workers to meet fluctuating manufacturing volumes. Hull points out that the taking on of temporary staff naturally affects the overall staff turnover figures. The average length of service of full-time staff is high, and there are more than 340 members of a staff 'ten-year club'.

'We want creative people, able to be creative and challenging within an environment that dictates a way of doing things. Because of the nature of our products, there are some serious rules and regulations here,' says Hull. 'You need to challenge, but in the right way. People need to be pro-active, rather than re-active. Because of the way our company operates, you have got to be able to handle, on occasions, quite high levels of ambiguity. I believe that no one can guarantee a career path for large numbers of people. Where we do have responsibility for career success, it is a blind date between opportunity and the individual being prepared. Our responsibility lies in making sure our people are prepared to take the opportunity when it occurs.'

As an equal-opportunity employer, Baxter encourages suitably qualified women to apply for all jobs, including disabled workers and members of ethnic groups. Women workers who have a child are given statutory maternity leave arrangements, and jobs are always held open for them. 'Maternity leave is regarded as just a temporary absence from work,' says Hull.

The company operates a standard voluntary pension scheme, based upon a 1 per cent contribution from members. A share option scheme is available to all workers, with a 15 per cent discount. Purchasing of shares is limited to up to 15 per cent of an employee's salary in any one year. The scheme has been very successful, with many employees buying in. Although there is no management bonus scheme, sales staff do work on an incentive programme. Plant graded staff enjoy a loyalty service bonus, with £30 being paid to them on the anniversary of their joining for every year that they have spent with the company, up to ten years. The figure is paid at the ten years' service level on a continuous basis after that. Staff also enjoy a subsidized canteen, and membership of a social club which has its own bar and gym.

Management salaries are paid within professional scales reached through the Hay job evaluation scheme. 'We aim to be in the upper third of the marketplace that we compare ourselves with,' says Hull. On the shop floor, salaries are arrived at in a formal annual agreement with the Employee Consultative Committee (ECC).

Baxter is one of the largest employers within Thetford, yet the company chooses to avoid dominating the local community, preferring instead to build up strong ties with local affairs and events on a low-key but supportive basis. Funding of groups or charitable donations will often go unrecognized in the local press, as these are not seen as a PR exercise.

Management style is open, and managers are not necessarily solely responsible for decisions made. Issues are agreed by working closely with the ECC, which represents production operatives in the UK. 'We try to delegate down as much as possible the basic decision-making,' says Viaflex filling product manager, Charles Hawkins. 'We are putting a lot of responsibility on to people and they are thriving. People appreciate the chance to have an input with ideas and suggestions. We've even closed down the whole plant or stopped individual production lines in order to give people a chance to get a better appreciation of ourselves and the products. I would say that for people who have got a level of ambition and are prepared to give a high level of commitment there is more opportunity in this company. Teamwork is critical in this industry as so many people are interdependent.'

The ECC was established in 1974, and the current chair is held by technician Sean West, who is elected along with the rest of the seventeen committee members by line operatives, taking on the extra responsibility on a voluntary basis. Ninety-nine per cent of the staff at Baxters would not want a union, according to West, even though the subject is discussed at intervals. 'The major role of the ECC is to act as an information-giving process between senior management and the work force,' says West. 'Monthly departmental meetings are supported by a bi-monthly meeting of the full committee and senior management. Staff are asked about issues before the meetings, and briefed after them. Information from this company is good, and everyone has an input on things that need to be changed. Everyone on the shop floor and management are on first-name terms.'

'This is an environment that people can flourish in,' says manufacturing accounts manager Trevor Webster. 'People do not work long hours. It is a matter of quality, not quantity. If I see a lot of people doing overtime, it means that there is a problem in the system that needs addressing. In a company this size, there is every opportunity to be innovative.' Every Friday a random selection of line operators are asked to have a boardroom lunch with the management team to discuss ideas, and to get to know people, reflecting the open-management strategy which encourages people to be constructive rather than destructive. If an employee has an idea which generates a cost saving, for example, the employee will be given 10 per cent of the savings made.

'We are a very quality-oriented company,' says Gerry Jenkins, quality control manager, 'but then this is probably one of the most sensitive areas of the health-care industry, and we manufacture about 100,000 units a day of intravenous product. Our induction process particularly emphasizes good manufacturing practice. We try to cultivate a sense of trust and honesty, as well as identification with the product. In October 1987 we had a quality commitment day, when we closed the plant for half a day and took everyone through a programme of quality education, with exhibitions, displays, talks and videos, all trying to push home how fundamental the issue of quality is to the company. It was very successful. The setting-up of quality working teams across the plant involves people at all levels, underlining the company belief that everyone is an expert.'

Communications officer Linda Van Driel, who has been with Baxters for over six years, says, 'This is an up-beat, fast-moving company where you are given enough space to exercise your talents. The atmosphere is committed, and helped by visits of patients to the plant. We know that some jobs are repetitive, but it is important that the people making the products are aware that they are not making baked beans. The product is for sick people, and has to be perfect, to help make them better.' Sending groups of workers to visit local hospitals has helped communicate the responsibility for quality in production.

Health-care products have to be produced with accuracy, within controlled environments. So training at all levels is paramount in order to ensure standards are maintained. Ultimate end-users of many of the company's products are sick people, so it is vital that no mistakes are made in production. 'We try to make sure that all staff receive training on an on-going basis,' says Hull. 'There is an in-house training department and three training managers within the UK.' A graduate entry management trainee scheme to the company was introduced in 1987.

Baxter Healthcare combines a friendly and positive atmosphere with a highly professional approach to its products and markets. Pharmaceutical companies can, so often, be austere places, but Baxter stands out as one that is precisely the opposite.

BLACK & DECKER

B&D is an American-owned company which makes power tools. Turnover in 1987 was £120 million. It employs 1700 at its plant at Spennymoor, County Durham.

pay	☐	ambience	☐
benefits	☐	environment	☐
promotion	☐	equal opportunities	☐
training	☐	communications	☐

When David Fanthorpe and his colleagues visited Japan they were surprised by what they found. 'We went out there with the view that the Japanese won on technology. What you actually see is some very ordinary technology. The difference you spot straightaway is the immense contribution that Japanese companies get from every single employee – the obsession with success from every single employee. And one of our key strategies became to build on what was already an extremely good base in employee relations. We were looking for the same commitment and contribution from our employees. We wanted to free our people to make their biggest contribution,' he says.

Black & Decker is based in the commercially uninviting territory of the northeast. The region's industrial relations history is one peppered with closure, discontent and strife. Despite this, B&D's own history is largely positive – albeit with some redundancies along the way. The company is non-unionized, and it has operated in the UK for sixty years. Initially it was a marketing enterprise, but in 1965 it opened its plant at Spennymoor.

'I suppose the really formative years, apart from all the work that was done in establishing our culture before that, were the early 1960s when we set out to establish a consumer marketplace,' says Fanthorpe, who is the MD. 'We would claim total credit for the DIY electric power tool market in the UK. We have very high market shares. We have also backed up an enormous product range with thirty-six service centres across the country,' he comments. The company also dominates the light lawnmower market.

But the recession in the 1970s bit hard at B&D, not least because exchange rates were so unfavourable. 'For an exporting company –

and we exported about one half of what we made – this was disastrous. We also felt that things were going on in manufacturing which were beyond the horizon. Things that we needed to get a grip of,' says Fanthorpe. In 1979 his predecessor went to Japan. He was impressed by many things, especially quality circles, in which groups of workers and management attempt to find ways of improving production techniques. Eddy Jones, personnel director, takes up the story. 'We ended up with thirty-five active circles, which meant we had over two hundred people on the shop floor actively engaged in problem-solving.

'People found their jobs were more enriched. They started stretching themselves, using their brains on a lot of things that they'd not done before. The problem was that it was involving only a minority of the work force.'

As David Fanthorpe says, 'People had immense skills and a lot more to contribute to the business than we were actually allowing them, given the old rules of the game.' The management fashioned TCS – total customer service. Again, it was based on Japanese experience. 'The aim is that everybody gets involved in TCS,' says Jones. 'At B&D that means that everyone has a customer. The next person to you is a customer. So is the receptionist dealing with an outsider. It's somebody in the machine shop who is supplying a part for someone in assembly.

'So we wanted to develop a TCS attitude with everybody in the plant. The programme we embarked on in 1985 to get the whole plant geared towards quality, excellence in everything we do is a five-year plan. The main rewards you get from allowing people to show their potential is that you get far more commitment, more loyalty to the company and you get people who are satisfied with their work,' says Jones.

TCS works so well that staff who spot flaws in material supplied by competitors get in touch with the source factory and discuss improvements. On one occasion staff were complaining about some faulty goods and visited the supplier's plant. Once they had discussed what was wrong, the other side had a few words to say about some black bags which B&D supplied in dirty condition. Through similar meetings and connections the quality of work on both sides improves immeasurably.

The company is looking for the sort of people who are capable of holding their own in a discussion. 'In the marketplace we are seen as dynamic and positive,' says Jones. Fanthorpe reinforces the message. 'Ambitious people succeed, enjoy the freedom of decision-taking and achievement. We look for people who would also enjoy the accountability which goes along with that, and people who aren't hidebound by hierarchical views.'

If you enjoy that sort of environment B&D is a first-rate employer. Pay is among the highest in the area. Benefits are among the best in the industry. The company is also a great communicator. 'As we are non-union we have to be an excellent communicator. In most unionized companies the communication is done by the unions. We have to have very strong communications. One supervisor we recently recruited from another company had only one reservation about joining us. Here he will need to address his team of people which could be twenty or thirty people. At his present company he deals with a shop steward on line issues,' says Jones.

'A lot of companies are strong on briefing groups. We've been through briefing groups. We have found that the supervisors are not comfortable with that. We have a weekly newsletter, a quarterly product brief and we have a joint consultative committee which meets every six weeks,' he adds.

B&D is moving positively towards being one of the very best employers in the land. Its human face is particularly kind. There are children's parties, dances and outings. Typical of the generosity of the company was when B&D was offered four tickets for a Buckingham Palace garden party. The MD took one set and the other pair were won by a member of staff and her husband. So she was presented to the Queen as a representative of the company.

BLACKWOOD HODGE

Blackwood Hodge is an independent UK company engaged in the worldwide distribution of construction, mining and earth-moving equipment. Turnover in 1986 was £204.4 million with pre-tax profits of £8.8 million. The company employs 2800 people at sites in the UK and overseas. Head office is in Northampton.

pay	☐	ambience	☐
benefits	☐	environment	☐
promotion	☐	equal opportunities	☐
training	☐	communications	☐

Blackwood Hodge is one of those companies which rarely achieves national prominence. Its figures are reported soberly in the financial press. Comment is sometimes made on its acquisitions, yet quietly and steadily the company is achieving a major position in its sector.

In 1983 the story was quite a different one. The company was at the bottom of a recession when its shares collapsed to 11p. The team of Arthur Richards and Ken Scobie, now chairman and managing director, was brought in to rescue the position. Jointly they planned a revival strategy which pulled the company back from the brink.

So much so, in fact, that a broker report from Capel Cure Myers described the company in the summer of 1987 as the world's foremost distributor of construction, earth-moving and mining equipment. 'By 1985 the group had been restructured. From a pre-tax loss in 1983 of £20.6 million, a pre-tax profit of £7.1 million was achieved,' says the report.

Scobie recalls what happened: 'When I walked in there was a large question as to whether the company would survive.' The company sold off its loss-making businesses and concentrated on those which could earn worthy profits. While attending to the profit-and-loss account, Scobie discovered that the group was seriously overstocked. Once this was remedied a much deeper flaw was addressed. The company had always 'followed the flag', which is to say that it operated in Commonwealth countries. In doing so it was ignoring the biggest market in the world. A rights issue in 1987 allowed Hodge to buy Roland Machinery in Illinois, Midway Equipment in Illinois and Missouri, and Mitchell Distributing in Virginia.

Scobie spent time and effort winning over Japanese manufacturer Komatsu to the idea of a strong Blackwood Hodge involvement in the United States. Mitchell was Komatsu's distributor in North Carolina. The *Sunday Telegraph* recorded how successful Scobie had been. 'The rapidity – just forty-eight hours – with which Komatsu gave its blessing to the Blackwood acquisition of Mitchell indicates that the message is getting home to the Japanese.' Scobie told the paper that it was his aim to build the company into a major third force after Caterpillar and Komatsu.

The financial turnaround and the excursion into the States has created a bubble of excitement within the group. The company believes that its success depends on the quality of its work, and the new impetus will encourage extra performance. Morale has been given an extra fillip by the huge improvement in internal efficiency which management have achieved.

The company's apprenticeship scheme has a good name locally for being both long and well structured. The decision to maintain the scheme during the toughest points of the recession is a key indicator of the company's commitment to its people, and its understanding that it would always need skilled people no matter how long it took to turn the company around.

The programme, based on a City and Guilds qualification, is traditional. It lasts four years and at the end of the apprenticeship period participants can choose the shop in which they would like to operate and specialize in particular areas of work.

Alan Smith, now a service engineer, was a product of the apprentice programme. He says, 'When we went to college everyone was a little bit envious of anyone who got a Blackwood Hodge apprenticeship because it was recognized in the town.' Smith's rise in the company illustrates the possibilities for promotion. As a multinational, Blackwood Hodge offers opportunities for travel within the group. Apart from the States, the group has interests in Australia, Africa and Canada.

Jim Smith, another worker in the Northampton headquarters, was selected to represent the UK in the World Veteran Games in Australia in 1986. He approached the management for sponsorship and they gave him a free flight. While he stayed in Australia, the group's subsidiary took care of him.

Alan Smith confirms that the company normally takes good care of its people abroad. In the late 1970s he was working on secondment in Romania. The Romanians liked his work so much that they did not want him to leave. 'It got sticky at one point. My boss had to come out and almost physically drag me away.'

Steve Cauthen is a local councillor and says that he has never had any trouble getting time off to attend council meetings. With the change in management came a significant change in communications. 'Now everyone talks to each other,' says Cauthen. 'Five years ago the place used to run on rumours.'

The company has changed radically in attitude in the last half decade. Alan Smith says that empire building was very much in evidence, whereas today 'there is an increased flexibility and communication which leads to teamwork'.

Cauthen says that despite this valuable teamwork people are encouraged to work on their own initiative. They are particularly keen on staff taking responsibility for the quality of work.

Nick Baker, director of personnel, says that after the financial turnaround the management sat down to a highly self-critical meeting on employee relations. The result has been fresh strategies to improve training, communications, personnel work and recruitment. Pay and conditions are average for the locality and the company is also addressing how best to renumerate their people.

The positive surge in Blackwood Hodge since the turnaround has created a vital and vibrant company where people are given the opportunity to contribute. The management is bright and responsive and its people can be enthusiastic about the future.

BLUE ARROW

Blue Arrow is the world's largest recruitment agency. Its turnover in 1987 was £406 million, showing pre-tax profits of £29 million. Based in central London, the group employs 8000 people.

pay	▭	ambience	▭
benefits	☐	environment	▭
promotion	▭	equal opportunities	▭
training	▭	communications	▭

Not so long ago Brook Street Bureau was successful but staid, competent but complacent. Now it has removed the talking feet posters on the Underground and its twin-set-and-pearls image. The new Brook Street screams out from the TV in eye-popping ads.

In 1986 Brook Street was taken over by Blue Arrow, the same group which absorbed many of the other familiar High Street employment agencies. In 1984 Blue Arrow was a small recruitment and contract cleaning company, turning over less than £17 million. Under the guidance of chief executive Tony Berry, it acquired the Reliance and Brook Street agencies to become the biggest source of temporary staff in Britain. Late in 1987 Blue Arrow swallowed the American giant Manpower to become the biggest employment agency in the world, with nearly 2000 branches in 33 countries.

Around one in fifteen of all the temps in the world are working for Blue Arrow at any one time – 250,000 on a typical day. With just seven weeks of Manpower figures included, the 1987 Blue Arrow turnover was over £400 million and analysts confidently expect the 1988 figures to be measured in billions. 'Temp' still means typist to most people, but Blue Arrow can supply oil rig drivers, accountants and social workers by the week. On the permanent recruitment front, Blue Arrow's head-hunting operations like Hoggett Bowers can supply six-figure salaries.

Company secretary Bruce Gray admits that the group 'has grown by acquisition', but the individual performance of each part of the group has also improved massively. Blue Arrow believes in putting incentives 'on the desk' for its full-time agency staff. Bruce Gray wants to encourage an atmosphere in which bureau staff 'make a few extra phone calls – stay till six to crack it'. Without incentives, 'It is hats and coats on at five-thirty – and why not?'

Incentives are brought in on top of basic wages. Companies that fall under the Blue Arrow banner find their head offices diminished in importance. 'We encourage businesses to run from the bottom up.' Gray does not see Blue Arrow as a dozen big groups but as 2000 separate enterprises. Blue Arrow itself has small but prestigious corporate headquarters in the City, and an ambiguous attitude to the stock exchange, institutions and the trappings of financial success.

Group human resources director Hugh Teasdale is looking for 'entrepreneurial self-starters who enjoy pressure' but not loners. 'Our successful people can also work as part of a team. They must also be consistent – they can't have a bad day, morning or afternoon because clients tell more people if something is bad than if it is good.' He sees money as 'a powerful motivator' but would rather keep the perks down. 'We prefer to pay money.' Gray agrees, and believes that even now they are too liberal with cars. 'They're not minis,' he says ruefully.

Blue Arrow does not tolerate unions but claims that there is no demand for them. 'It's not a sweated industry. A union has to be able to offer something.' Since employment is Blue Arrow's business, they believe they can only succeed by being good employers. 'If we can't get it right for our own people, how can we get it right for other people?'

Benefits for temps are improving because demand is increasing quicker than supply: 'The big problem is applicants not clients.' Top secretaries can earn £6–£7 an hour in central London, and regular temps are increasingly demanding – and getting – the same benefits as full-time workers, such as holiday pay and sickness benefit.

Brook Street was the creation of Marjery Hurst just after the Second World War. Originally she was finding temporary work just for herself, then a few others – 'my girls' – before it evolved into the first real temp agency in the UK. It soon became big in the London area, specializing in the supply of secretaries. Blue Arrow had bigger plans, and the introduction of incentives was popular with interviewers – even if it did mean working 50-hour weeks or even 60 hours in City branches to meet targets. 'If you work hard we'll look after you – we're looking for a little bit extra someone who can give 150 per cent rather than 100 per cent.' The effects were dramatic, with 1987 turnover up by a half over the previous year and profits more than doubled.

Brook Street is still very much a woman's company even if recruitment has been widened. Most managers are women, and the group was sensitive to this when bringing in Di Cornish from Blue Arrow

Personnel Services to head up the operation. Women who leave to have a baby are encouraged to come back and work two or three days a week, but only 'when it's people we want to have back'. Di started as a branch manager. Blue Arrow, and particularly Brook Street, is proud of its reputation for developing talent within the firm. They are also aware of the 'secretary trap' and can point to an ex-PA who is now a head office manager.

In anything from one to three years a good Brook Street interviewer could hope to become a branch manager with four or five full-time staff, placing about sixty temps a week. Brook Street believes that 'a branch manager has to have done the job', but it now recruits ten trainee managers a year in addition. Branch managers earn between £11,000–£15,000, and with bonus in a high-performing location that could be as much as £20,000. Incentives are important and every branch has a target. Holiday competitions are another incentive. A quarter of Brook Street's 500 permanent staff win free trips each year – weekends in New York, cruising in the Greek islands, seeing the pyramids or going on safari.

People find out pretty quickly whether the Brook Street life style suits them, and the grouses of the staff that stay are confined to grumbles about the lack of perks – no Luncheon Vouchers or season ticket loans, and a reluctance to part with company cars. Staff get 40 per cent off private health insurance and senior managers at area and regional level, who are paid between £12,000–£20,000, get a car and full private health cover.

The story is similar in the other companies which have been 'Arrowed'. Manpower is still such a recent acquisition that the full effect has not yet been felt, but incentives and extra emphasis on the branches are the key. 'We provide the basics, but branches are one-man businesses,' explains Teasdale.

Blue Arrow does not see a need to 'rationalize' its branch network. For the moment at least we will continue to see Brook Street, Manpower and Blue Arrow Personnel Services offices lined up next to each other on the High Street. In theory they are all in competition, but managers admit, 'We don't undercut each other.'

Blue Arrow oozes Thatcherite values. 'Historically,' says Teasdale, 'we haven't had such an entrepreneurial spirit growing in the country.' Norman Tebbit is on the board and Blue Arrow pays its subs to the Conservative Party. It may be a billion-pound giant with monopolistic tendencies, but it still prefers to be seen as 2000 small businesses. As a career, working full time for Blue Arrow offers quick rewards for those prepared to put in the effort, and more responsibility at branch level. As Gray puts it, 'Blue Arrow is run by 1800 people.'

THE BODY SHOP

The Body Shop is a cosmetics company based in Little-hampton, West Sussex. In 1987 turnover reached £28.5 million, with pre-tax profits of £6 million. In head office and the eleven principal shops which Body Shop owns, the company employs 351 people.

pay	☐	ambience	☐
benefits	☐	environment	☐
promotion	☐	equal opportunities	☐
training	☐	communications	☐

The evolution of The Body Shop is one of the famous business stories in recent years. Managing director Anita Roddick has made a name for herself pioneering a chain of herbal-based franchises. The company is well known for its social commitment – its identification with Friends of the Earth and numerous charity projects. Its values of care for the community, the environment and wildlife have set it apart from other retail ventures.

It was a brilliant commercial idea – one of the more eccentric adaptations of the 1960s which has made money. While the business is little more than a decade old, it has a depth of tradition which would put an ICI or Shell to shame. Every year at Body Shop is like ten anywhere else.

Body Shop used to be a family business, and for those people who work at head office and in the principal Body Shop stores it still is to some extent. Charlotte Treeburn, who originally approached Roddick with the idea of running a dance studio above the Brighton shop, is clear about the relationship between Body Shop people. 'It's like a big family. We did some research about people's attitude to the company and they said it was a family. When we meet up at franchise meetings there's lots of hugs and kisses and people catch up with the news.'

Roddick herself says that there has been a change in culture. 'In the old days we all used to muck in to build the shops. People mortgaged their houses to pay for them. Now we pick prime High Street sites and it is a problem knowing what's at the heart of someone who applies for a franchise.'

Today the franchises are some of the most expensive – and sought after – on the market – rivalling Wimpy and MacDonalds. Roddick says that they take £40,000 a week in prime locations. That's understandable. Body Shop has a name, a high-profile image, and a product that almost sells itself – with no direct competitors.

The eleven stores owned by Body Shop International are the flagships of the company. New products are tested out here and the company can control their development. Their market potential can be assessed before releasing them on to the franchisees.

The business is composed of two sectors: head office and production at Littlehampton and the eleven principal shops which the company owns; and the 268 franchise operations in the UK. The company carries out a rigorous analysis of franchisee moral credentials. Since Body Shop franchises are keenly desired, this is something which the company can enforce. It makes no stipulations on the pay and conditions of the staff in the shops.

What Body Shop is good at is its communications within the business. Meetings are regularly held to let people know about changes in the business, its products, its social activities and its market. People are told to speak up and make their views heard. Ideas for improving the business are eagerly sought.

People who have the energy and commitment can go far in the company. Qualifications – or the lack of them – makes no difference. If you are intelligent and dedicated you can go a long way. Take Pat Jarvis. 'I was working for a franchisee in the northeast. I wanted to move to London. So my boss said, "Shall I ring Anita?" An hour and a half later I had a job in London.' Jarvis transferred from franchisee to franchisor – Body Shop International. She nows works in the training centre in Great Portland Street in west London. Margaret Hendon, who runs the centre, has seven trainers who service the shops and, more recently, head office and overseas franchises. 'We are different from most other retailers. We are not looking for 100 per cent education standards. We are looking for commitment, for enthusiasm, for a loyalty and for an empathy for our beliefs and the way we do things.'

Much of the training is sales-driven. Staff in the franchises are fully briefed on new product lines, the preparation of gift baskets, how to handle customers and putting their own views forward. Staff in head office complained to us that they did not get much training unless they pushed hard, but that this is now being rectified. In 1988 training was extended to them.

A video is circulated once a month to all the stores, briefing management and staff on new developments within Body Shop. The training centre also runs specialist programmes. In 1987 people were invited in to talk about ageing, and how the skin changes. Since many of the assistants in Body Shop are quite young, and older women are now patronizing the stores in greater numbers, this was especially valuable.

With the international expansion of the company, Roddick is keen to promote Swap A Job. People can change jobs with personnel in the Bondi Beach or New York branches. It is one of the few exciting perks of the job, but people mainly work for Body Shop because they enjoy the product, the atmosphere or have an affiliation with the social objectives of the company. Pay is not bad for the retail sector, and head office people rate it highly.

There is a limited share option scheme, private health insurance for directors only, and a staff discount scheme. In many senses Body Shop has not looked after its people extraordinarily well. There is no pension scheme, for example. The improved shoe cleaning and ironing facilities in the stores could be seen as only another way of improving the corporate image.

There is little doubt that Body Shop is a company committed to its principles. Many of its positive attributes reflect its culture – the right to speak out, good education and training, staff discounts, mobility between the stores. Yet it comes across as a very commercial enterprise, and one that is particularly adept at exploiting the opportunities of its market. It has a vocal and opinionated managing director, a strong market profile, a wide range of products and a cogent business strategy.

CHRISTIAN BRANN

Reporting a turnover of £14.3 million in 1987, Christian Brann is a wholly-owned subsidiary of Business Intelligence Services. BIS itself is part of the American-owned NYNEX Corporation. Christian Brann employs 320 people at its headquarters in Cirencester, Gloucestershire.

pay	▭	ambience	▭
benefits	▭	environment	▭
promotion	▭	equal opportunities	▭
training	▭	communications	▭

'We have a total belief in ourselves and our place among the top three direct-marketing companies in the UK,' says Juliet Williams, the energetic managing director of Christian Brann. A former teacher, Williams is forthright about her company and its role in the industry. She is equally positive about her staff. 'The growth of the company depends on the growth of its people. We want to satisfy aspirations. In short – people matter.' This ideology underpins every activity at Brann. In everything it does its people are paramount.

This policy is the touchstone of the Christian Brann success story. Brann is a small company. It has grown in the last few years from being an unremarkable venture, resting in a rural idyll in the Cotswolds, into a force to be reckoned with in direct marketing. Founded in 1967 in Cirencester, Christian Brann has been transformed into a quality concern boasting a client list of major enterprises: British Gas, Butlin's, Barclays, General Accident, House of Fraser, ICI, Mothercare and Do It All are among its customers.

The humble beginnings of the business founded by Christian Brann and his wife Mary Rose have been superseded in the mid-1980s by rapid growth, a high intake of staff, and introduction of a new tier of senior management when BIS took full control in 1983. Alan Bigg, group marketing director, says: 'Direct marketing has come a long way recently. It's become the most fashionable and fastest-growing branch of marketing. Some 71 per cent of top companies are now using it.' Bigg maintains that CB's achievement has been the marriage of creativity and technology: 'When you put a direct-marketing agency on the same site as a production facility an unusual chemistry develops.' This 'chemistry', combined with the recognition that a highly motivated, determined and well-trained staff are essential to the success of a service sector company, has boosted sales from £4.3 million in 1983 to £14.3 million in 1987.

CB is split into six divisions. The agency handles customer accounts; the creative department houses copywriters and art directors; the production area covers studio, darkroom, printing and mailing; the computer sector includes program and systems operations; corporate group looks after marketing, accounts and finance; and the technical planning group projects the future pattern of business. Each division is kept at approximately 10 per cent below full strength to obviate the need for redundancy.

Bryan Johnson, a darkroom supervisor, who has worked for the company for eighteen years, is father of the chapel for the National Graphical Association. He believes that the level of expansion proposed by the company will add to job security and improvement in salary. 'It is a modern, forward-thinking company. For the person who recognizes that he can go somewhere if he tries, there are no closed doors.' He attributes the success of the concern to the non-corporatist philosophy of its founder. Inevitably, though, the management are beginning to lose touch with the shop-floor staff as the company expands, and in an attempt to redress the balance, management are keen to have an attitudes survey. At the time of our visit the company was preparing to present a new pay package. Pay is a sticking point. The unions, the NGA and SOGAT '82, argue that the area, once relatively cheap, has prospered. The cost of living has gathered pace and salaries are more out of kilter with demands on their pockets. A survey by independent consultants shows that Christian Brann pays the going rate – or more – for the job. Individual assessment plays a major role in determining what each member of the work force will be paid. On average, trainees start at about £8000, and can expect a 15–18 per cent increase after the first six months. Gary Smith, an account manager in the agency, started on £6500, and two years later (at the end of 1987) was earning £13,000.

After three years in the creative department, staff could expect to be earning around £19,000. Salaries are less good in the agency but a senior account manager could expect to get £15,000 and a car. In printing the scales are 30 per cent above the union minimum rate for the area. Secretaries average £8500. The benefits package is quite generous. Everyone gets 25 days' holiday a year. The company grants average maternity leave, operates a fair pension scheme and staff eat in a subsidized canteen. Additionally, the firm sponsors in-house football and cricket teams.

Communication is rapid and effective. Gary Smith says that the degree of openness in staff relations is an especially attractive quality. 'We hold meetings every three weeks with the director of the group. We hold regular team briefings and we receive detailed information on the company's performance. Being in one location does help. It creates a friendly and enthusiastic atmosphere. We get support from above and below. As individuals we are judged on our work which encourages a sense of pride.'

Ron Fulton, a senior shift supervisor who has been at CB for thirteen years, points to the informality of relationships. 'The growth rate is quite substantial and the loss of contact is inevitable. But everyone is on first-name terms and there's no Mr This and Mr That. The office door is always open.' Fulton says that the friendly approach and the cooperation between all departments contribute to the general enthusiasm.

Forty per cent of the work force are women. Managing director Juliet Williams explained that there was no set policy to encourage the employment of women or ethnic minorities. 'If they are the right people for the company, we employ them,' and there are other women besides herself who have reached senior positions in Christian Brann.

The company has a powerful commitment to training. It recruits on average ten new graduates a year, and the training scheme lasts six months. Candidates spend time in each department, and attend lectures and seminars in-house and externally. Williams has introduced the policy of sending trainees on secondment to a variety of other companies.

For such a small company, the dedication to training is extensive. CB people are encouraged to continue developing their skills to add to their proficiency – and to increase their value to the company. Its 1986 mission statement set the target of leading the direct-marketing industry in the planning, management and development of skills. In 1986 82 people received induction training, 75 people went on special courses to upgrade their skills and 12 new training courses were opened. These varied from telemarketing training, interview techniques and effective computing, to Dale Carnegie courses on effective communication and human relations.

The training programme is evolving and some gaps still exist. Gary Hammond, who has been a programmer group leader with CB for nine months, says: 'I was sent on a management course that was good, but from the systems department viewpoint the training was too immediate. It did not take account of the long-term aspects of the accelerating pace of technology. But with the expansion of the company, I am sure the management will become more aware of this.' Nevertheless Christian Brann has a package of training courses which outshines many companies and much larger businesses, and demonstrates its exemplary commitment to staff development.

Nick Richardson, creative group head, says that he has been given opportunities for training, and subsequent promotion, which are not offered to people in similar positions elsewhere. 'This company challenges rather than ties you. People are encouraged to put forward detailed ideas and they will be considered, although encouragement of your imaginative ideas is tempered with sound business sense.'

In 1986 the company set out its mission. One of the principal aims was to provide the most exciting and rewarding working environment in the industry, and there is every sign that this aim is being fulfilled.

BRITISH AEROSPACE

BAe is Europe's largest aircraft company, and is made up of five separate entities in the form of British Aircraft Corporation, Hawker Siddeley's aviation and dynamics sections, Scottish Aviation and Sperry Gyroscope. In 1986 its sales amounted to £3.14 billion with pre-tax profits at £182 million. Its 75,000 people are based in several locations around the southeast.

pay	☐	ambience	☐
benefits	☐	environment	☐
promotion	☐	equal opportunities	☐
training	☐	communications	☐

At the beginning of 1988 the City was taken by storm. The government, in its thirst for privatization, prepared to sell off its holding in the troubled motor manufacturer the Rover Group. While the timing of the move was surprising – it was far earlier than had been forecast – the decision to find a potential buyer in advance of the sale was unprecedented. Analysts could see no logic in the plan to sell Rover to the aircraft company and defence contractor British Aerospace. Where did the synergy lie between the ailing car company and the increasingly competitive aerospace group? asked financial journalists and brokers' analysts alike. BAe was itself a product of privatization and had grown to become Europe's largest aircraft manufacturer.

Observers did note that other leading defence contractors had motor interests, but still the link was puzzling. BAe, described by *Financial Weekly* as Britain's flagship aerospace company, faced its own problems, and to bring Rover into the arena would only seem to add to them. Nevertheless, BAe chairman Professor Roland Smith was positive when introducing the possibility of the merger. One powerful caveat remained. Rover must come over free of debt and with some greater government investment in the company.

This kind of tough negotiating style is typical of British Aerospace. Since full privatization in 1985 the company has emerged as Britain's largest exporter of manufactured goods, Europe's biggest aircraft company and its largest producer of defence goods. *Financial Weekly* quoted Smith as saying that the company faced tough battles on three fronts: the need to consolidate its international position; to increase productivity by as much as 75 per cent; and to win a battle with the government to increase development. The government holds a so-called 'golden share' which allows it to veto major issues. The company wants to lift its 15 per cent limit on foreign holding but the government will not give way. National concern for protecting British expertise is valid but over-egged, according to Smith.

The 1980s have not been auspicious for BAe, but at long last profits are improving. Turnover in 1985 stood at £2.65 billion. In 1986 this had risen to £3.14 billion. The improvement was reflected in pre-tax profit figures which rose by 20 per cent to £182 million in 1986.

This improvement is also expressed in orders which rose by a staggering 67 per cent in 1987. The defence and aviation sector is volatile and continued success is exceptional. The better performance is mirrored by the renewed confidence of the staff. 'There is a new breed of engineer at British Aerospace who is acquainted only with the company as it exists now, who is competitive on the company's behalf and filled with optimism for the future,' says Peter Sparkes, recently recruited personnel officer for BAe. 'In years to come these engineers will reach senior levels of management, and in the meantime BAe will reach levels of international cooperation unknown in its earlier years. It will really take off.'

A clear sense of corporate identity, which was lacking before, has now emerged. This has bonded the organization and created a feeling of community. It would be unfair to place too much emphasis on the high ratio of profits to employees, as this is not unusual in the industrial sector in which BAe works. It spends £450 million on R&D and vast amounts of cash on projects intended for a bright future which do not always materialize. But a competitive pressure is instilled in the company by the flood of able graduates who have pushed their way upward in the company since privatization. Alan Startin, of BAe's public relations department, is quick to point out that six out of every seven engineering students applying for work in their final year at university opt for British Aerospace.

Smith and his team do not have everything right by any means yet. When we visited the Weybridge site some 300 staff in the military aircraft division had been laid off. The buildings which stand on the old Brooklands racetrack are antiquated and do not match up to BAe's high-tech image. Equally, at the Hatfield site in Hertfordshire you could be excused for thinking that you had wandered on to the set of the old *Dambusters* film. The civil aircraft division, with more than

5000 employees, operates from Nissen huts, but this does not seem to worry the graduates who work there. 'The first thing that impressed me when I arrived here was the warmth of the welcome I received,' says John Coverdale. Sparkes made the same comment. 'By comparison with my first day at Marconi, it made a pleasant surprise.'

At Hatfield there is a marked shortage of accommodation, and associations have been established to overcome the problem. They also offer sporting and social facilities. One graduate entrant says, 'It is very like college to begin with – the graduate associations are much like college unions. The sporting facilities are excellent. The England football team used to practise at Stevenage and the cricket ground at Weybridge was used regularly on Sundays in the John Player League days.'

The recruits are asked in what specialist fields they would like to work. 'The requests are usually met. For instance, if you are a specialist in radar you will probably spend six months working on one project as a fully-fledged member of a research or production team,' says Coverdale. 'But equally, if you are looking for more general experience, the matrix structure means that you will not be working solely on one project and you will easily find your feet.'

During the first year the recruit is under the watchful eye of a line manager who will report progress at a quarterly meeting and will ensure that the individual's prearranged requirements are being met.

'A friend has just gone to the States to give a series of lectures on recent work that he was doing here. It was his own idea but one which was picked up and encouraged by BAe,' says one worker. The company likes its engineers to move between departments, developing a cross-fertilization of skills and personnel. Coverdale admits that this has yet to find full fruition.

The perks at BAe are probably less visible than in any other employer of its size. Bonuses and pensions are standard, company cars are for senior managers only, and pay is certainly not as attractive as elsewhere, although it is competitive for the sector. BAe's training, however, is so good that it creates engineers who are attractive to competitors. 'We have suffered a great deal from the temptation of higher salaries elsewhere,' says Coverdale. Sparkes states a company truth: 'British Aerospace is very much what you make of it. If you are ambitious and you are good then there are no limits to the possibilities available to you. The pay is not particularly good – graduate starting salaries are around the £9000 mark – and neither is promotion very quick.'

John Nicholas says that the lack of early promotion can be deceptive.

'Nominally I have stayed in the same position for the last two and a half years, but in that time I have gained more experience than I could have done anywhere else. There are temptations to move elsewhere – I can't say that I haven't considered them – but working for the foremost aerospace research company in the world means that you are constantly making a globally significant contribution to the aerospace market.'

BRITISH AIRWAYS

One of the world's largest airlines, British Airways employs 48,000 people. Its pre-tax profits in 1988 were £228 million from a turnover of £3.7 billion. Headquarters are at Heathrow Airport.

pay		ambience	
benefits		environment	
promotion		equal opportunities	
training		communications	

Package tours, near-misses and Luton Airport have taken some of the glamour out of flying, but British Airways has more to offer than good pay and excellent training. Most people join an airline because they want to see the world. You do not have to be a pilot or a member of the cabin crew. Even if you are a BA accountant, cook or cleaner, you can fly anywhere in the world – as long as there is a vacant seat – for around 10 per cent of the normal cost. So, if a return flight to Tokyo for £90, or Sydney for £115, sounds attractive, read on.

British Airways is the biggest international carrier. What is often forgotten is that it is also one of the largest engineering operations in Britain, one of the biggest software houses, a massive caterer, and a major force in a dozen other industries. In short, it can offer not one but a hundred different careers. 'We employ everyone from consultant psychologists to sewage workers,' says human resources director Nick Georgiades.

BA and its forerunners BOAC and BEA had a reputation for relying on its monopoly of the airways and failing to adapt to the needs of the traveller. 'It was managed by people who won the war,' says Georgiades, and the officers, gentlemen and other-ranks attitude persisted with information given out on a strictly 'need to know' basis. 'You would be having a meeting and somebody would come in and cut the table in half with no consultation,' says one old hand. Biggles only really retired in the 1970s.

Some say that 'it used to be good because you couldn't get the sack', but since then there has been a change of culture. In the early 1980s BA shed 20,000 staff and it had to find new ways to sustain the loyalty of those who remained. Training was developed, and more mobility within the company was created. Communications were improved: 'Staff need to be told the truth,' says Georgiades. A new attitude to staff was combined with a new approach to customers. 'The British have a bad time with the concept of service,' says Georgiades. 'They confuse it with subservience.'

BA tried to give front-line staff more confidence in the product and more responsibility. They hope that staff will stay with them for more than ten years. 'You don't get good customer service unless you care for service providers.' All British Airways staff go through the Putting People First customer care programme.

Staff turnover is now very low and BA carries out termination interviews to find out why people have left. British Caledonian staff suffered heavy redundancies when the two airlines merged, but BA does not expect any more sudden reductions of its work force. During the slump in summer 1986, when Chernobyl and the bombing of Libya combined to scare off American tourists, BA encouraged staff to take unpaid leave or extra days off and so avoided lay-offs.

BA is making slow progress towards single status. Badges of rank have been deleted from uniforms, except on the flight deck, but it is still a common complaint that the top brass 'are preaching it but not carrying it out'. However, with the main office complex at Heathrow built around the hangars, head office is not as cut off as in many big organizations.

BA has 48,000 staff, but even after the British Caledonian merger, less than 200 planes. About one-third of the employees are involved in marketing – anything from selling tickets to planning advertising – and the other two-thirds keep the operations going.

There are 3000 pilots earning anything between £15,000 – for a raw recruit – and £45,000. It is hard to get on to BA's pilot training scheme. All potential recruits have to go through psychometric testing, and for cockpit crew the airline is looking for people who will fit a very definite psychological profile. For most jobs the parameters are wider, although BA is not keen to take risks and would-be senior managers have to go through a heavy session of tests and interviews with psychologists who produce ten-page reports on them.

There are 400 engineering officers – 'They're the ones who play with the engines' – and 8000 stewards and stewardesses. Back on the ground there are about as many working in engineering as there are in the cabin crews, with similar numbers in ground support, administration, and overseas. A driver might earn between £7000 and £9000, a supervisor £12,000, a trained steward or stewardess £10,000 or £11,000 and middle managers £15,000–£22,000. BA recruits locally and nationally. There are graduate recruitment programmes in investment, purchasing, finance and engineering. Graduates come in on around £10,000.

The real growth area is in information management – the harnessing and distribution of increasing volumes of data on flights, cargo, ticket sales, accounts, personnel and locations. This is swallowing 300 recruits a year – 200 of them graduates – as it builds towards a target of 3000 staff by 1990. Both the information management department and the top 400 managers are paid on performance, with results assessed every six months.

Most staff say that pay is still good, but on the decline compared to the outside world. A mixture of loyalty and benefits keeps them with the company, and some admit that the airline business gets into their blood. Concorde still gets an admiring glance as it taxies past the window. Familiarity has not bred contempt.

BA has a fast track for high flyers, but it is not a good option if you are looking for the quiet life. 'In the fast lane you've got to keep going or get out – you can't slow down.' BA is looking for personal skills, entrepreneurial flair and a general aptitude for business in their senior managers of the 1990s. Fast-track employees spend four weeks in jobs where they have to deal directly with customer problems, then go on to three projects in different departments. Travel is an important part of their training, 'if only to learn how to cope with jetlag'. Most of the dozen fast-track recruits each year are graduates, but not all, and significantly there are now as many women as men on the fast track.

BA is the right kind of company for young people with ambition. Its style and influence as a world-class carrier make it an inviting prospect for many potential recruits.

BRITISH PETROLEUM

BP is one of the world's largest oil companies. It employs more than 128,000 people in 70 countries around the world. In 1986 the company reported profits of £1.8 billion. The company is currently based in Moorgate, London, but is moving to Hemel Hempstead, Hertfordshire.

pay	☐	ambience	☐
benefits	☐	environment	☐
promotion	☐	equal opportunities	☐
training	☐	communications	☐

In the last half of 1987 and the first few months of 1988, barely a day went by without fresh mention in the press of BP. While the oil major has a high profile, it probably attracted more publicity than it wanted. First there was the share issue. The government put up for sale its holding in BP as part of its sequence of privatization. But the issue failed and chancellor Nigel Lawson was forced to put up a compromise package. BP's share price was badly hit by the stock market's Black Monday in October 1987 when stocks collapsed.

Attention was focused on the purchase of a sizeable holding in the company by the Kuwaiti government, which was rumoured to be mounting a takeover bid. Finally BP successfully bid for Britoil. Speculation continued on the implications for the oil industry of all these developments. But BP, the company at the centre of all the coverage, was remarkably unaffected.

The company remains highly profitable and one of the largest industrial concerns in the world. Its history began with the discovery of oil in Persia in 1908 and the formation of Anglo-Persian the following year. It was a classic British adventure, but one that developed with sure enough foundations to evolve into one of the greatest oil companies in the world. That uniquely British brand of paternalism, reinforced by nineteenth-century liberalism which characterized some of the best late Victorian and Edwardian concerns, lingers on as part of the present-day culture but is really only an echo of a past age.

The present-day culture of BP is not static. It has the characteristics of a company in evolution. The old paternalistic veil is being dropped to reveal a multi-faceted, highly skilled and forward-looking enterprise. There is a powerful streak of internationalism running through the business, and for individuals to succeed they must be prepared to serve in BP locations across the world.

Flexibility – the ability to adapt to changing circumstances – is one of the strengths that a new BP recruit must show. Yet lingering still in the corridors is a certain stiff upper-lippedness which, with the lively commercial zeal, is a strange blend. While its core values will still exist ten or fifteen years hence, the character of BP will have moved further away from being very British and formalized and increasingly become extrovert.

Despite some major difficulties in recent years, BP has quashed unfavourable comparisons with Shell and other oil majors and has sharpened its management team. One facet of the fresh management style introduced by chairman Sir Peter Walters is non-interference in the operating style and objectives of the ten companies which make up the BP group. This extends, more or less, to personal achievement within BP. Individuals are encouraged to take up ideas and run with them.

The company has also improved its pay performance. Until September 1987, pay had lagged behind other dominant forces in the sector. Andy Leonard, a sedimentologist with BP Exploration, says that a pay and benefits increase has now more than made up for the relative deficiency before. 'We used to talk about rewarding people on merit before. Now it is actually happening.'

Leonard, who came to the company six years ago after qualifying from Exeter University, points to a change in attitude among BP staff. Previously the company had taken their leads on developments from Shell. 'They did something and we would follow it some while later with our reaction. Now we believe we are at least as good as our competitors and we take our own initiatives.'

BP people become quite edgy when talking about the supremely confident men at Shell. Until the end of the 1960s Shell and BP shared a joint marketing operation. 'At the break-up some of us were sent to Shell and some to BP,' says David Garaway, management development manager. 'People used to say he's a Shell man or he's one of us. Now that has all gone.' BP's style is a vibrant and innovative one. Analysts are quick to credit the company with a lively and quality approach to their markets and a resourceful position of diversification.

BP Nutrition is one of the companies which is mentioned regularly by employees as the proving ground for new management talent. Both

Garaway and Ian Conn, who spent three years with this company, are especially positive about their futures.

The relationship between the group and the operating companies is clearly defined. The policy guidelines are laid down centrally and it is up to the operating companies to interpret them. For example, there is an excellent pension scheme administered centrally. Financial assistance is provided with relocation, whether domestic or overseas. Annual increments are now divided between cost of living and merit. Like many large enterprises, BP provides a share option scheme allowing purchase of up to £1250 worth of shares annually. This has been greeted with such enthusiasm that as many as 60 per cent of the UK employees have shares in BP.

There is a superb canteen where meals are provided at the outrageously cheap rate of 5p for a three-course meal. The quality reputedly extends to the oil rigs which the company operates off Aberdeen. One former rig denizen says that facilities are comparable to a top-class hotel.

There is a panoply of clubs and societies based at head office, and sports functions proliferate around the country. This is a socially minded organization which does not expect its initiates to eat, sleep and breathe BP. Communication is a high priority and various mechanisms exist for the dissemination of information. These take the form of formal or informal briefings, and house magazines in the operating companies. Staff comment that the company keeps them well informed about new policy decisions and approaches to the market.

Equal opportunities are a major concern at BP. Vicky Wisman, equal opportunities manager at head office, explains that since 1984 the company has taken active steps to encourage ethnic minorities and women. Part of the problem has been the predominantly male culture which often exists in technical concerns. However, the movement towards change has begun: recruiters are now told why it is desirable to improve the quota of excellent women graduates, and to date policy targets have been achieved. In 1987 some 29 per cent of all graduates inducted were women, which is the highest level of female graduate intake at the company. Five years ago the figure was 15 per cent. In addition the company encourages the Women In BP group which meets to discuss and advance the role of women in the company. Recently the group produced a maternity help-pack for working mothers and prospective mothers. There has been a more demonstrable success with women's rights – some women have managed to get jobs reasonably high up in BP and staffers expect a woman on the

74

board of one of the operating companies within five years – than with ethnic minorities, but the two projects have strong priority.

BP retains its historical association with quality work, sound judgement and understated management. It enjoys the standing of being one of the nation's flagship companies, and in recent years this has been matched by a commercialism which has encouraged it to flourish still further.

H. P. BULMER

H. P. Bulmer are cider-makers based in Hereford. In 1987 the group produced a turnover of £183.4 million, with pre-tax profits of £18.1 million. The company employs 1400 people.

pay	☐	ambience	☐	
benefits	☐	environment	☐	
promotion	☐	equal opportunities	☐	
training	☐	communications	☐	

At first glance H. P. Bulmer might best be viewed through a sepia photograph of an age long since past, with rural draymen carrying flagons of cider to pubs in the depths of the Welsh border country. It is a romantic notion, but one which is divorced from the reality. Bulmer is an important business. It is the UK's largest cider-maker, it acts as agent for Perrier and Orangina, sells Red Stripe lager and markets Domecq sherries, Pol Roger champagne and Glenmorangie Scotch.

There is definitely more to the company than originally meets the eye. Eddie McMenamin, deputy chairman of the employee council and Transport and General Workers Union senior shop steward, says, 'I reckon they are the best in the area. Look at the long-service record. The quantity of long-servers is probably greater than any other company for miles. I think the track record proves that they are the best. Terms, conditions, attitudes – a multitude of reasons for it.'

It is rare for a union man to be so forthright in his praise for his company. Bulmer does have something special, and it goes back a long way. In 1887 Percy Bulmer started making cider. 'He was the uneducated son of the local vicar. In his first year he made four thousand gallons. Today we serve half the cider drinkers in the country and turn out thirty-five million gallons,' says George Thomas, public relations manager.

The Bulmer family embraced the enterprise with enthusiasm and skill. They became even more active in the local community and were ultimately the dominant employers in the county. In the 1960s the Bulmer family recognized that, while they were aiming to retain the atmosphere of a family firm, they wanted to bring in outside management expertise to meet modern commercial challenges.

76

Peter Prior was brought in as managing director and he introduced many innovative ideas. Outward Bound-style leadership training was created and the manager who ran the courses left the company to launch the Leadership Trust. The aim was to put managers and staff into situations where they would all have to work together to find a solution to a problem. For example, a group might be put at the side of a river and given the task of getting a beer barrel across with limited implements. 'If you can work together over a weekend solving problems you should be able to cooperate on Monday at work,' says personnel director Mike Pearce.

In the 1970s the group initiated several industrial relations moves which were five to ten years ahead of the majority of industry. 'There is a major commitment to communication. We have the employee council which was set up in 1977. It has been hard work. But the company is committed to the whole spectrum of industrial relations. We are innovative in a lot of areas. The employee council was just one of these. Not that we were the first ever. We looked at the best and the worst and we picked the best,' comments McMenamin.

'It is part of an overall employee package. You cannot take it in isolation. It is so intermixed with everything else. Wage negotiation, permanent health insurance, sickness benefit are all part of the picture. Contrary to trade union dogma that you will not participate in BUPA, if we get the chance to participate in BUPA we will actively encourage it,' he adds.

The 27-member council meets up to eight times a year to thrash out a wide range of issues. One of the most painful was in 1984 when the company announced that it was going to have to make people redundant.

'It wasn't just the management who made the decision, it was the employee council. We spent six months working out what the redundancy policy was going to be. The Inland Revenue hit us with a major tax bill. The management said let us sit down and talk about it. Everyone was involved from the lowest of low to the highest of high. Whatever level of the company you were at you were told. We sought the attitudes of the people we represented.

'The management said that the Christmas bonus which was paid at the end of November would have to go. We said no, you must pay it. But over the next twelve months we negotiated it away. Last year we got some extra money up front. We constructed a package. People were treated as human beings,' says McMenamin.

Pearce adds that only a few who did not want to go were made redundant. Some people took early retirement, others were beyond retirement age anyway. The company brought in consultants who helped some people to set up their own businesses. 'One fitter was particularly interested in bee-keeping. He now ensures that our orchards are correctly pollinated,' recalls Pearce. 'The package for those people who were made redundant was vastly more generous than anything which the government lays down as a minimum.'

The enlightened attitude towards redundancy is commonplace in Bulmers. It is a generous and understanding company. Training is heavily accented on its relevance to the company and to the individual's job. People can move from department to department with ease.

A major concern about Bulmer must centre on its long-term survival as an independent producer. 'Eventually we may get taken over,' says one senior manager at Hereford. 'It is the way the market is going.' There is no doubt that if Bulmer were taken over the future might not be so rosy. At present it is a highly conscientious enterprise as far as its staff is concerned. Problems are discussed openly and serious attempts are made to resolve difficulties. Pay is very good for the area. Benefits are extraordinary for the county and match any American multinational. It would be a great shame if Bulmer were not to remain independent.

CADBURY SCHWEPPES

Cadbury Schweppes is the largest confectioner in Britain. In 1987 its turnover was £2 billion and its pre-tax profits were £176 million. The company employs 27,500 people. Head office is in London.

pay ☐	ambience ☐
benefits ☐	environment ☐
promotion ☐	equal opportunities ☐
training ☐	communications ☐

At the beginning of 1988 Cadbury's emerged ahead of the pack in the UK chocolate market. While it did not run the largest selling brand – that was down to Mars – Cadbury could claim 30 per cent of the UK chocolate confectionery market. Previously, the three dominant forces in British chocolate – Cadbury, Mars and Rowntree – had all stood equal.

The British have the sweetest tooth in Europe, according to an article published in *The Times* in March 1988. We spend more on chocolate than on milk, bread, beverages, snacks or breakfast cereals.

Cadbury has been in the business for years. In the early nineteenth century John Cadbury opened a small factory and began producing cocoas and drinking chocolates. In 1879 the expanding business moved to Bournville, the south Birmingham suburb, which was to achieve its own fame; first, as the name of a bar of chocolate which continues to this day, and second as a social experiment.

The Cadbury family were deeply interested in the welfare of their workers and constructed their business in ways which would make the work as pleasant as possible for the staff. The family built houses nearby for the workers and they were considered exemplary for their day. The tradition was extended down through the generations. While the Cadbury family does not own the business today, it continues to run the enterprise. Sir Adrian Cadbury is the chairman and Dominic Cadbury is chief executive.

The company bought J. S. Fry in 1919, which was the spur to a greater international identity, and in 1969 it merged with Schweppes to form Cadbury Schweppes. Over the next decade the new company went on a strident acquisitions tour, picking up confectionery and drinks companies in Europe and America. It even diversified into health and hygiene products.

Then came the hammer blow. While the chocolate brands were strong, the market started to decline – both here and in the United States. Cadbury never really captured a significant toehold in America and suffered heavy losses. At the same time the drinks market was not faring too well. In 1984 the company sold off its beverages concerns to a management buy-out team called Premier Brands.

Profits in 1985 collapsed from £40 million to £34 million. The poor currency exchange rate did not help. The company was being written off by the financial press as being run with 'gentlemanly incompetence'. But in 1988 the company was on top again. Cadbury had secured a bigger proportion of its market, the Schweppes side had picked up through a joint venture with Coca-Cola and threatened to wipe the floor with the opposition, and the international picture had improved.

This represents a graphic illustration of the tenacity of the Cadbury management. The company, which is fitter than at any time for years, is taking on more people after painful redundancies. The Coca-Cola Schweppes bottling plant will add 470 jobs in Wakefield.

The company would not allow us official access to their work force, so all our research has been done externally, but both employees and ex-employees were enthusiastic about the company. The company remained true to its people during the difficult period, and the loyalty of the Cadbury work force was not breached even though morale did sag.

'They are a superb employer. They are highly ethical, care deeply about their work force and offer excellent opportunities,' says one former Cadbury man who moved to United Biscuits. 'They are very similar to UB. They both want the same high standards for their customers and their staff.'

This view was confirmed. 'The Cadbury family have the capacity to inspire tremendous loyalty from their people. This remained throughout the difficult period of the mid-1980s and it has been justified.'

Jobs lost at Bournville and Somerdale, near Bristol, have largely been taken up by natural wastage and early retirement. The cuts will lead to extensive modernization of both sites to allow the company to compete more effectively.

Sir Adrian has gone on record as saying that he believes that Cadbury Schweppes should stick to its core businesses which are chocolate and drinks. His strategy seems to be paying off. Cadbury is number one in the chocolate market and Coca-Cola Schweppes will command the top spot in the drinks market.

With healthier companies and a motivated work force, the group is vigorously pursuing personnel policies. Pay is good but not great, and staff enjoy a range of benefits which are comparable with other companies in the market. Cadbury must always suffer unfortunate comparisons, however, because its principal competitor Mars is probably the best payer in the country, and has a range of benefits which would put any American multinational to shame. Nevertheless, Cadbury does have a case to make. It was in the business of treating its workers well long before Mars was born and has continued a policy of equity and decency throughout its history.

It enjoys a high degree of respect as an employer among other major companies, particularly for its training, and Mars and Rowntree accord it due respect as a major competitor. The company recruits a handful of graduates each year for its management training scheme and others for inclusion in specific areas of the company.

Sir Adrian Cadbury and his team have achieved something which did not appear possible four years ago. Cadbury and Schweppes are the top of the tree in their respective markets, and even the international market has swung back in its favour. The company is well regarded both by its people and industry. It is a caring and decent employer, whose future looks secure.

CALA

Cala is a company which develops high-quality housing. Its headquarters are in Edinburgh. In 1987 the company reported turnover of £42,388,000 with pre-tax profits of £4,385,000. The company employs 209 staff.

pay	☐	ambience	☐
benefits	☐	environment	☐
promotion	☐	equal opportunities	☐
training	☐	communications	☐

Cala may be an unfamiliar organization to most people. Formerly the City of Aberdeen Land Association, it is an innovative housing development which grew out of the Aberdeen association created in 1875.

After almost a hundred years of successful history, Cala was taken over in 1972 by Greencoat Properties, whose managing director was a lively-minded and commercially astute accountant called Geoffrey Ball. He aimed to use Cala as the vehicle for the development of the business. He saw that there was a demand for high-quality housing development with advanced concepts on design and layout.

Such was the success of Ball's vision that he was named Young Businessman of the Year in 1983. He has presided over more than a decade of unprecedented growth in the company. At first he concentrated at the top end of the market in Scotland and made it very much the company's own.

Part of the secret of Cala's success was its open-minded attitude. 'They have their own ideas but they are not rigid in their slavery to them, preferring to note that circumstances alter cases,' noted the *Glasgow Herald* on the launch of a new classic range of house and bungalow styles in 1987.

The prices of the Cala developments in Scotland in 1987 fell between £60,000 and £110,000. They were described by *Business Scotland* as 'an easy combination of the traditional with the modern to give a pleasing sense of solidity rarely found in today's hastily-constructed artefacts'.

Developments in Aberdeen were complemented by growth in the Lothian region around Edinburgh, and as oil wealth started to peter out the company began to look south of the border. After the management buy-out in 1978, which formed the basis of the present company, Cala acquired Anns Homes for £1.2 million in 1982. Anns was converted into Cala Homes (Southern). Southern was the base for the Cala attack on the lucrative market in the south of England.

In 1986 Tern Residential, acquired for £1.4 million, became Cala Homes (Wessex), and Dominion Homes, added to the group for £7.2 million, spread its work in progress among Wessex, Southern and Cala Homes (Midlands). In 1987 the progress continued unabated with regional companies in Strathclyde and the west of England. In all the company has nine subsidiaries.

'The company has grown in several ways,' says Ball. 'Organically, by start-ups and by acquisition. We have done well in Scotland and the south of England. We are now looking at the Midlands and the area between Manchester and Edinburgh.' He says the reason for their success is their insistence on quality and originality in their work. 'The marketing and presentation of the product has always been at a consistently high level,' he adds.

In an industry which has concentrated on volume Cala has preferred to appeal to the upper end of the market. It has spent time and effort ensuring that the product is right. Its decentralized structure has also helped. 'There are ten people trying to increase the profits each year,' says Ball.

A great deal of leeway is given to the operating company managing directors. They decide their objectives with Geoff Ball, but they are given the freedom to make their own decisions. In fact they are positively encouraged to stand or fall on their own ability to make sales, plan developments and negotiate with suppliers.

The company has a high emphasis on enterprise. In some senses it is a Thatcherite dream company: effectively started from scratch, built on the hard work of its people and progressively expanded by the vision of its directors. But another reason for its glowing path of undiluted advance is its consideration for and development of its employees.

From the start Ball wanted his people to enjoy the best working conditions he was able to offer. He has been helped by the small contingent of retained staff – only 209 full-timers. But he has aimed to pay well and provide good training facilities for everyone. 'We are very keen on training,' says Ball. 'It strengthens our people's talents.' Nearly the entire company went on a negotiation skills course in 1987 and all the technical staff have been sent on a financial course to improve their understanding of budgets.

The company is setting up a performance appraisal scheme to

83

monitor people's progress and their development needs. 'Wherever possible the people for our new companies should come from within Cala, because the company demands a high quality of work and an energetic approach which it knows it can get from its own staff, and internal promotions create incentives for others to aspire to greater things,' adds Ball.

When Cala people in the south heard that we were visiting, they wanted to put their thoughts down on paper, with no prompting from the management, as to why they think Cala is such a great place to work. 'Within all Cala subsidiaries there is a tremendous feeling of team spirit at all levels and all locations. Much of this team spirit stems from a real feeling that any individual can contribute and therefore affect the end product,' they commented.

Cala is the sort of company where people do feel that they can progress. Steve Rosier, for example, has risen from the ranks of quantity surveyor through various operating companies to managing director of Cala Homes. It is a quality enterprise, run by committed people but it has a visibly human side. Ball and his team are a focus for high standards within their industry, and champions of good, practical, industrial relations.

JAMES CAPEL

James Capel is a leading stockbroking firm in the City of
London. It employs 1500 people in London and another
700 worldwide. It is owned by the Hong Kong and
Shanghai Bank.

pay	▭	ambience	▭
benefits	▭	environment	▭
promotion	▭	equal opportunities	▭
training	▭	communications	▭

For a number of years the annual poll among professional investors to
find the best stockbroking firm has been about as dull as the English
Football League first division championship. Just as you always suspect
that Liverpool will win the league, James Capel is always favourite to
be the most popular broker. Like a football team, the broking house
depends on the quality of its players – analysts and market-makers in
this case. And you are only as good as your last result.

The stars of stockbroking change hands for telephone-number
transfer fees, and a couple of bad seasons can leave you playing in the
fourth division. Capel, like Liverpool, has shown itself consistently
superior.

There is a happy combination of home-grown talent and judiciously-
purchased stars. This is reinforced by the fact that people do not
choose to leave Capels, and most successful brokers want to work for
them. Rosemary Banyard was recruited to James Capel as a graduate
in 1980, and after three years was asked to start up a research facility
in textile companies, an area in which the firm had no previous
experience. Four (male) analysts dominated this field, but by 1987
Banyard had climbed to second place and was determined to become
the number-one analyst in the field. Bob Barber, the motor analyst,
who was number one in 1987, had just moved to the company.

Stockbroking was traditionally a business centred on buying and
selling securities (shares like British Telecom or British Gas) or gilts –
bonds issued by governments for individual investors or institutions.
The market used to be operated by jobbers, but since the Big Bang in
1986, firms can do both broking and jobbing. This function is now
called market-making. Some organizations have attempted to become

financial supermarkets, while others have stuck to what they are good at.

James Capel adopted this latter course. They have relied on their expertise in research to do agency broking – essentially what the company has always done – and make markets in gilts. It has expanded its international coverage, and has acquired a Dutch firm, a share in a Parisian broker, and has set up an agency in Frankfurt. The company has traditional strengths in the Far East and has gained a presence in the US. 'But,' says Graham Wallace, public relations manager, 'the aim is to become the dominant player in Europe.'

This objective concentrates minds at James Capel on its people policies – since the only way to achieve this objective will be to poach talent from competitors and grow some at home. Ian Collier, in gilts at Capel since 1979, commented that 'Research is expensive and success is based on your history – it is building up a tradition. You know that if you leave James Capel you are going "down-name".'

The company does not pursue a formula approach. Danny Schulter, personnel director, who has been there for ten years, says, 'There is no James Capel type. There are 1500 types who work here, with backgrounds ranging from Eton to the East End. All we look for is enthusiasm – controlled extroverts and self-starters.'

It has always had a loose organizational structure, partly because the business depends on instant decisions and partly as a matter of preference. There is little formal hierarchy, but there is a coherence in the firm created by the fact that most of the personnel people have worked there for ten years or more.

Much more important is the recognition of individual success conveyed by promotion to associate or senior executive status – which are more like courtesy titles than job descriptions. There are a hundred each of these in James Capel now, and senior executives are viewed as equivalent to partners.

After the Big Bang James Capel did not have enough capital to compete effectively, and the only way to proceed was to sell the firm to a commercial bank with financial muscle. The result was a deal with the Hong Kong and Shanghai Bank, but on terms which meant that the parent would not interfere.

The investment made by the bank has enabled James Capel to expand rapidly in the past two years – from 700 to 2200 staff. Some of the older hands regret the passing of the intimacy of the smaller organization, but everyone we spoke to thought themselves lucky to be working for James Capel. Objective assessments would probably fail to find a reason for this. The decentralized structure means that

86

communications are, at best, a little creaky. The company has no particular emphasis on training – most of which you learn on the job. By the standards of the megabuck wonderland of the City, pay and benefits are not outstanding. An annual bonus of 50 per cent of salary is not generous by City standards.

One major selling point is that James Capel is not a hire-and-fire agency, which many City organizations have become. The chairman has said that no redundancies would be made in 1988. That must be unique in the Square Mile. People spoke to us about the caring attitude of the company, the camaraderie and the informality. The company also sponsors *ad hoc* sports teams.

The only black spot – as so often is the case – is their attitude to women. 'There are a lot of old-fashioned attitudes here. You have to be able to take a lot of stick and to give as good as you get. You probably have to be twice as good as the men,' was one fairly typical comment. In fairness, some women are doing well, and the company is probably no worse than much of the rest of the City, but it is something to which James Capel should address itself.

People want to stay at James Capel because they believe it to be the best stockbroker in the City. An aura of success hangs around the dealing room and individual market-makers, which is why Capels remains at the top of the pile. As Peter Marsh, senior international equities dealer, says, 'People outside fall over themselves to work here.'

CHARTERHOUSE

Charterhouse is the merchant-banking arm of the Royal Bank of Scotland. It is based in London and employs 1000 people. In 1987 the company reported pre-tax profits of £32.8 million.

pay ☐		ambience ☐
benefits ☐		environment ☐
promotion ☐		equal opportunities ☐
training ☐		communications ☐

In June 1986 Charterhouse began a new life. After an unhappy association with Jacob Rothschild, Charterhouse moved into bed with the Royal Bank of Scotland. The metamorphosis effectively created a new company, with a distinctly different approach. Three divisions spread out from the central holding company. Charterhouse Bank, well on its way to becoming a first-division merchant bank, Charterhouse Development Capital – the venture capital arm – and Charterhouse Tilney, the stockbroker.

A new style of dynamic leadership, epitomized by chief executive Victor Blank, emerged. Blank symbolized the resurgence in Charterhouse and the fresh vitality that it presented in the marketplace. First, it was a young company full of zeal to create business; second, it was an open, flexible, relaxed but lively culture; and third, people were given the support and training to make the business come alive.

These factors combined to life the organization away from its sluggish past. 'Success has bred success during the last few years,' says Roy Bowley, an assistant director at Charterhouse Bank. Against the background of a volatile environment in the City, Charterhouse has displayed a clarity of purpose and a sense of direction which has escaped other operators.

A belief in the possible exists at Charterhouse. People talk animatedly about how, in this burgeoning atmosphere, the business has grown. At the start of the RBS link-up Charterhouse employed 750 people – by early 1988 this had risen to 1000 people.

'To date we have had support without interference,' says Mike Osborn, a director in Charterhouse Tilney. 'It is a cooperative relationship not a hindrance. Communications are very good and there is not much red tape.'

Communication is a key facet of the business. Meeting are held every fortnight among senior managers. 'We devise our own business strategy and communicate to our staff,' says personnel director John Smythe. Every year Victor Blank addresses meetings in the important locations – London, Liverpool and Edinburgh.

'But we are keen to move within the communications area. The briefing process will probably be extended throughout the three divisions. When the Royal Bank commissioned an attitude survey among its staff we came out very well in terms of communications.'

The divisions hold team briefings once a month on the Industrial Society model. Two-way messages are encouraged, and in such a communicative environment people are not afraid to say what is on their minds. There is an effective grapevine within Charterhouse which is often a good deal quicker than any other means of communication.

Charterhouse is flexible in every aspect of the work that it does. 'The company is good on job descriptions,' says Nicola Nicholls, a manager in development capital. 'They let you try, and they give you an opportunity to succeed.' Pay is regarded as excellent. The City commands high wages and extensive benefits. Charterhouse responds with a housing purchase scheme, personal loans, insurance, a generous profit-sharing scheme, free lunches, season ticket loans, an excellent non-contributory pension scheme and free private medical insurance.

Blank was determined when he took charge that training at Charterhouse would be of the first order. The package Training For Growth is one of the best in the financial world. 'We depend for our success on the quality and skills of our people,' says Blank. The package includes planning for growth, leadership skills, presentations, sales management and time management.

A true meritocracy, people – both men and women – get on according to their ability and nothing else. It is a refreshing company where staff spontaneously congratulate management on the achievement since 1986. 'Charterhouse is better placed to seize opportunities than a lot of organizations,' says Paul Bryons, a manager. 'This is an organization of opportunities and self-starters. A lot of ideas here come from the lower levels.'

His view is supported by Stephen Clarke, director in development capital. 'There's a very positive atmosphere here at Charterhouse. There are no politics – it's all very healthy. People are given a lot of freedom of manoeuvre provided they come up with the goods. If they do perform the rewards are there.'

Clarke is right that the company is generous to those people who bring in the business. It is unmistakably a hard-working company. The staff in each of the divisions are under considerable pressure, the stress levels are high. But a light-hearted and sometimes jovial atmosphere is also apparent. 'This place is fun,' says one manager in CDC. What gives Charterhouse an added fillip is the fact that it is young, inspired by a mission and determined to succeed.

C. & J. CLARK

Based in Street, Somerset, C. & J. Clark is a major shoe manufacturer and through its subsidiary Clarks Shoes employs 10,750 people at its headquarters and various retail outlets around the country. Its turnover in 1988 was £602 million, showing a pre-tax profit of £29 million.

pay	☐	ambience	☐
benefits	☐	environment	☐
promotion	☐	equal opportunities	☐
training	☐	communications	☐

A panoply of influences makes up the unique personality of C. & J. Clark. Among the most important is the tradition perpetuated by its Quaker founders, which blends in with the classical and conservative values of the West Country where the company has been based since its inception in the early nineteenth century. The Clark philosophy and the rural viewpoint meant that change came long and hard: it is only in the last half decade that the company has faced up to tougher and more ruthless times.

The Clarks have been making shoes in Somerset since 1825, and the company has been the dominant employer in Street for as long as anyone can remember. The family were almost as much a part of the landscape as nearby Glastonbury Tor, until they stepped down from active involvement in company affairs in 1987. But their influence is still felt in the newly aggressive and harder-hitting business.

Quaker conviction shaped the company into one which fuses dedication to quality and craftsmanship with the welfare of its staff. Its privileged status in the town could have allowed it to exploit its work force, but this has acted only as an incentive to offer its people a better deal. The family were eager to be seen as benevolent employers, and they have always paid above-average wages. In addition, they introduced standards which were exemplary for the time.

Their shoes are legendary, especially among school children, most of whom at some time in their lives have gone to one of the company's retail outlets for fitting. But times move on. And the family realized, reluctantly, that the paternalistic style of management had had its day.

A tough reappraisal of business goals pointed the company in new directions. An outside managing director was introduced in 1985, and turnover and profits have rocketed.

There are now six constituent companies which act as independent profit centres. The most important of these is Clarks Shoes which operates from the headquarters in Street. In 1988 a new Clarks Shoes plant will open at Radstock near Bath, providing jobs for another 120 employees.

Its reputation for an unswerving devotion to quality is well known. None of that has been lost in the new regime. Melvin Coate, who has served in the Street plant for thirty-one years and is now a foreman in the making room, says: 'From the outside I see it as a forward-going company with a good name for quality and deliveries. Internally it has changed in style from a family company to a hard-headed business.'

Company culture, like many UK concerns, is still evolving. The locale and tradition of the industry mean that change has moved at a slower pace than competitors in the footwear industry. Some employees still look back longingly to the days of the family, but in the main they recognize the need for change. Bill Waldron has been at Clarks for twenty-four years and is a manufacturing manager. 'The company realized some time ago that it had to move forward. But possibly it has not moved at the rate that it should have done. Every day brings a greater realization that there is more to do.'

But this gentle transformation is symptomatic of Clarks' desire to keep its people content and eager to contribute. Waldron's view is that 'Clarks is a fair taskmaster. As a company the strategy is that we are seen to be human beings and to treat people in that same vein. A caring philosophy works in the long run and I believe that we care as a company.'

For the past three years C. & J. Clark has been simplifying the organization structures within its companies. The remodelling of the top executive levels led to the creation of Clarks Shoes in May 1985. A stringent reappraisal of costs was made in 1986 and some redundancies followed. But the company handled these with sensitivity and with little loss of support from the body of the staff.

Although there is little record of establishing sports grounds or social clubs, the Clark family has built houses within the town for its workers and provided the town with a swimming pool and a theatre. It even gave the land on which a modern shopping centre has been built.

While the company is certainly no longer run on Quaker ethics, a Quaker influence still shows through in some of the corporate regulations and practice. No smoking is permitted anywhere on company premises – and this has been the case for more than forty years. All meetings take place around tables – not across desks. All staff are encouraged to listen to and have respect for what others in the company – at whatever level – have to say.

Progress of the individual within the company is based on merit and ability, which can seem at variance with the somewhat patrician outlook of the founders. All recruits must demonstrate commitment to the ideals of Clarks and reflect the sure but modest nature of the enterprise. To succeed in this environment it is necessary to have a good grasp of basic management technique matched by a humanity often lacking in similar companies. Andrew Pierce, who is a product manager in the girls' shoes division, sums it up: 'Clarks is becoming more market-orientated but with the residue of being a family company.'

Each of the 3500 shop assistants follows an on-site induction programme, which is monitored at every stage. The company is also in the process of introducing a pre-retirement programme.

Every year Clarks takes on about fifteen graduates, including a few which the company has sponsored through university. It has a part-stake in the MBA chair at Bath University, and runs a course on design at the London Business School for some of its employees. Clarks management have seen how the right type of individual with proven degree-level education can complement the bulk of the senior grades who rise up from the shop floor.

The most senior female member of staff, the project planning manager, is just below board level. Five of the sections within the organization are headed by women and of the 500 branch managers, 230 are female. In 1972, only one-seventh of the candidates for management training were female, compared to two-thirds today. On this basis, senior management posts will be occupied by women within the next ten years.

The pay is on a par with, or better than, most other companies in the industry. In a Hay salary comparison programme, Clarks emerged level with those in the top group. Since more than 700 companies were surveyed, this has given Clarks people good reason to feel pleased with their pay. Clive Wyatt, a shop-floor worker, comments, 'People tend to join the company because the pay is so good. Jobs here are sought after. Not many leave.'

COATS VIYELLA

Coats Viyella is one of the largest textile businesses in the UK. It is a diversified group with more than 200 individual profit centres. Turnover stands at £1.8 billion. The company employs 45,000 in the United Kingdom, and a further 45,000 abroad.

pay ☐		ambience ☐	
benefits ☐		environment ☐	
promotion ☐		equal opportunities ☐	
training ☐		communications ☐	

Coats Viyella is a weird and wonderful collection of businesses based around the textile and clothing industries. Among the businesses which are not commonly associated with the CV stamp are Jaeger, Dynacast, Van Heusen, Donaghadee carpets, and Pasolds leisure wear. It owes its present state to a charismatic Iranian. David Alliance merged Coats Patons with Vantona Viyella to fashion one of the largest textile and clothing enterprises which Britain has seen.

Growth has been principally by acquisition. Each acquisition has been larger than the previous one. Formative for the Coats Viyella group were Carrington Viyella, producing mainly cotton fabrics; Nottingham Manufacturing primarily supplying knitwear to Marks & Spencer; and Coats Patons, an international conglomerate pre-eminent in threads and yarns.

Alliance's story is rags to riches and deserves a book in its own right. He was apprenticed to the textile industry after growing up in Kashan, a world-famous Persian carpet centre. He came to Britain in 1951 believing Manchester to be the centre for excellence in world textiles. Two years later – and without a work permit – he borrowed £8000 from a money-lender to rescue a supplier who had fallen into receivership.

In 1958 he was joined by his brother and they started buying businesses by the yard. The 1960s earned him a reputation as an asset-stripper, but he argues that he had to close some businesses in order to keep some going, while the textile industry was in a state of wholesale collapse. With this background Alliance bought Spirella, the bra maker, and eventually merged it into the newly acquired Vantona.

Vantona was among the largest textile outfits in the UK. Among the others were Nottingham Manufacturing and Coats Patons. Nine years later came Carrington Viyella, a company with a distinguished history and, more importantly, brand names with character. But its recent performance had been a record of horrors. With the cash mountain at Vantona, Alliance paid off the Carrington debts and merged the two to form Vantona Viyella. Within a couple of years, Nottingham Manufacturing was added to the roster. In March 1986 he took his biggest gamble – raising £700 million to fund the purchase of Coats Patons.

What Alliance has done in a remarkably short time is to beat the international importer by producing quality goods cheaply and efficiently in the UK. He has also taken his people with him. Trade unions confirm that industrial relations at Coats Viyella plants are good. He has committed himself to improving conditions to a level that he would be prepared to work in himself.

David Miller, group personnel director, says that while the business philosophy is to keep profit centres small, 'We needed a group philosophy. People needed to see that there is an overriding benefit of being in the group.' Miller recognizes that it is not an easy task.

The way people like Alliance and Christopher Hogg of Courtaulds survived the textile crash was by making goods that people wanted to buy. John Raybold, CV's director in charge of management development, reinforces the corporate message. 'We want people to have their eyes on the customers not on head office.'

Miller has laid down some basic operating principles about terms of employment. Salaries and benefits are entirely in the hands of the operating companies, but headquarters outlines minimum and maximum levels. These cover health and safety, training, industrial relations and remuneration.

On company cars, for example, the group prefers to offer subsidies rather than vehicles. On the other hand, they want, as Miller says, 'to avoid being seen as a low-paying industry'. CV is keen to boost salaries as long as they do not impede production budgets.

In 1987 the group launched its pension scheme. Prior to this operating companies could offer as much or as little as they liked. One of the group's less well-known subsidiaries sells educational and rehabilitation equipment in Nottingham. Geoff Slater, a sales office manager, says: 'Day to day I see no involvement with the group. As far as I am concerned the main benefit of the merger with Coats Viyella was the pension scheme and the share option scheme.' The

95

share option scheme was also introduced in 1987 and is tied to a savings account with the Leeds Permanent Building Society.

The group personnel department is trying to pave the way in terms of training. It has announced that 3 per cent of all sales should be spent in development courses. Again, the operating companies are left to introduce their own courses. But if central personnel hear about good schemes they will try to get places for people in other CV subsidiaries. While some of these initiatives need to be approved at board level, CV is having some success in melding the best of the old with some new ideas. The new organization has only been in existence since 1986, so progress may appear slow. In practice, new concepts are being introduced at a fair pace and in concert with improvements to the companies as a whole.

Coats Patons, for example, had a good reputation as an employer. Personnel policies are not therefore being tampered with, and they are being supplemented only where necessary. Lyndsey Welch, now in charge of the young managers' development programme, was personnel officer at Coats Patons' Alloa factory at the time of the merger. 'There was quite a lot of concern among the work force – everyone waiting for dramatic change – but after a while everyone realized that nothing terrible was going to happen,' she says.

At Nottingham Manufacturing, a highly centralized base was quickly broken up into semi-autonomous profit centres more in line with the challenge of the 1980s.

In the Nottingham group of Coats Viyella, Stephen Plummer, group sales and marketing director, is adamant that the merger has made little difference. 'We are successful and the Coats Viyella management understood this. The main difference has been the introduction of a performance-related bonus for all members of staff – this can make up to 40–50 per cent of salary – and is very much encouraged by Coats Viyella.'

Jamie Heather, who deals with complaints from customers, has worked there for eleven years. 'You're pretty well looked after here and as long as you get the work done no one's screaming.' But the work is extremely hard and one employee says that the company will not employ one and a half people if it can get away with one.

An unfolding appreciation of the attitude of the group, hard work, incentives and better rewards seem to be the future pattern of Coats Viyella.

CV is still developing a strategy concerning the transferral of people within the group. At the moment the top 300 managers in the company are looked after by head office and there is a lot of movement between the operating companies at this level. Lower down CV is still feeling its way. If group personnel hears of a vacancy and someone in another subsidiary seems appropriate then a recommendation will be made. But nothing more formal exists. Internal vacancies are not yet advertised across the group. One graduate was critical. 'It's a waste. If I wanted to move away then Coats Viyella is going to lose out. They should make us aware of career opportunities within the group.'

Yet the diversity of the group is one of its strengths. You could be managing a textile mill in Penn or answering the telephone in Nottingham.

The personnel managers are working towards a uniform policy for the whole group in an effort to even out disparities. As the organization becomes more efficient it will improve pay and benefits – and promotion opportunities – all the way round.

Any job in textiles is going to be tough. It is a hugely competitive arena. Alliance and his team are moulding a well-run business which cares for its people. Step by step Coats Viyella is becoming an exciting – and rewarding – place to be.

COMPAQ

With world sales of $1.2 billion, Compaq is one of the fastest-growing computer companies in the world. Its UK operations are based near Glasgow in Scotland. It currently employs 200 people but this figure is expected to rise to nearer 350 in the future.

pay	☐	ambience	☐
benefits	☐	environment	☐
promotion	☐	equal opportunities	☐
training	☐	communications	☐

On 13 March 1987 Murray François stood on a muddy Glaswegian building site and announced that within nine months Compaq would be producing portable computers in a brand-new factory. By Christmas Eve not only was the plant up and running, but the first batch of micros were already on the way to Australia.

Compaq itself was set up in 1982. By 1985 it was in the Fortune 500 and its 1987 turnover made it the fastest company ever to break the billion-dollar sales barrier. It was also in 1987 that the company spread out of America and into Singapore and Scotland.

Compaq has convinced big corporate customers who might normally rely on IBM to depend on them. Boeing uses Compaqs to process flight-test data on new versions of the 747, and to demonstrate an electronic maintenance manual which will be introduced on the Boeing 7J7 in the 1990s.

Compaq has not had time to get arrogant. It is still relaxed and informal. Rod Canion, the overall boss, will turn up to work in his Houston HQ wearing denims, unless there is a good reason not to. As François, boss of the Scottish plant, puts it, 'Rod has never contracted that dreaded disease known among start-ups as "Founderitis".' At the same time Compaq is not a free-thinking West-Coast style of computer company.

This is the first plant François has managed outside the USA so you might expect him to have difficulty adjusting to local attitudes. But he finds that the culture and work ethic are much the same: 'The only difference between Texans and Scots is six inches in height, and there's a common language – almost.'

In Scotland Compaq is enjoying a honeymoon with its staff. There is no union agreement at the moment, and little call for one, but that may change if the good times stop rolling. As a new start-up it offers tremendous opportunities for anyone who is prepared to work hard and to take responsibility. Nothing is certain in the world of computing, but Compaq's plans for Scotland are certainly ambitious. While the US plants aim to cater for the Americas, and Singapore will specialize in producing circuit boards, Scotland will produce finished computers for the rest of the world.

Compaq was the first company to produce micros based on the Intel 80386 chip, and these are expected to be the dominant processors in business microcomputers of the early 1990s. Its machines can run the OS/2 operating system which should become the industry standard following on from MS/DOS. The future therefore looks bright – and so does the factory. The work floor is separated from the offices by the cafeteria – a long thin mall scattered with seats and tables intermingled with exotic plants under a Crystal Palace-style roof.

François is proud that he has managed to attract some of IBM's fiercely loyal staff from down the road at Greenock. Compaq's plant at Erskine Bridge on the outskirts of Glasgow is in the middle of what Murray calls 'the best electronics infrastructure in Europe'. There are 350 electronics companies employing 40,000 people in Silicon Glen, so there was a large potential work force, and local sources of components, which attracted Compaq to the area.

What attracts the locals to Compaq is not the pay – which is good but not the best – but the prospects. 'Pay does not motivate – although low pay can de-motivate – it's the work itself.' School-leavers with few qualifications come in on £5000–£6000, and first-level managers – none of whom have more than fifteen people under them – earn £15,000–£18,000. There is 100 per cent BUPA cover for employees and their families.

Some 9000 people applied for the first 200 jobs. By 1989 the second phase of the plant will be in gear, and there will be 350 working on site. François believes that 'the most important thing you can do is hire people'. Everyone who is interviewed makes two or three visits to the plant and is seen by around six to ten different people in the company to make sure that they are suitable. There is no clocking-in and everyone is on first-name terms.

'We haven't hired mice,' says François. 'We're looking for the same things in everybody – 51 per cent drive and 49 per cent skills.' Aggression, flexibility, humour and informality are the qualities Compaq wants. They are looking for a good education, but ultimately

99

track record is more important than paper qualifications. They do not want people with airs and graces, or status-seekers. They want risk-takers who are individually competitive, but not so much so that they cannot work in a team.

Compaq is also keen on job security. 'It's hard to do a good job when you've got fear. I have confidence,' says François, 'that the last thing Compaq would do is lay people off.' He contrasts this with the much-vaunted Japanese principles of no redundancy, which only apply to male employees in top companies. A third of the workers at Compaq are women and they are seen as 'disposable', as are all those working for subcontractors.

Training schemes are still being set up but Compaq will encourage day release, further education, and other personnel development schemes. The company philosophy states that this is an 'essential for individual satisfaction and the growth of the company'. Most of the staff are locally recruited, but Compaq sees the location in a greenfields site near Glasgow as a plus even when they need to bring in expertise from outside. The company is planting limes and beeches around the plant, reverting to an eighteenth-century landscaping plan. The mountains and the coast are close by, and all the attractions of Britain's second largest city are down the road, from music and museums to two of the best football teams in Europe.

News of the company's latest successes worldwide is communicated straight to the work floor because 'success is important for morale'. Compaq encourages its staff to speak up about problems. Each team has a half-hour meeting in the morning before starting: 'There's no fear about messengers getting shot here,' says François, who also believes in management by walking and talking around.

Research and development will stay in the States for the moment, but Glasgow will develop local modifications for different telephone systems and country-kitting to make machines suitable for particular markets. Compaq also has a UK marketing and sales operation based in Richmond, Surrey.

Compaq Computer Corporation turned over $1.2 billion last year, and they expect to turn that dollar sign into a pound by 1989. The Glasgow plant will eventually be responsible for a quarter of Compaq's worldwide production, so despite the relatively small staff numbers it is a major operation. On 11 December 1987 Compaq's staff moved out of a tent and into the new factory, which represents a £20 million investment.

Compaq offers a good balance between security and opportunity. Start-ups are exciting, if exhausting, places, but some of the recruits have worked with other new companies in the area only to find 'that they got worse over the years'. Compaq has started very well but no one can predict what it will be like once the adrenalin ceases to flow.

CONTINENTAL CAN

Continental Can dominates the US packaging industry. In the UK its staff complement is very small – only 276. Most of these are based at its plant at Wrexham in Clwyd, with ten in the head office in Windsor. UK turnover is £70 million.

pay ☐		ambience ☐	
benefits ☐		environment ☐	
promotion ☐		equal opportunities ☐	
training ☐		communications ☐	

The Japanese car manufacturer Nissan is one of the few companies to achieve national press coverage for its personnel policies. Much justified applause has been received by director Peter Wickens for the fresh insights which the company has brought to the human relations area. But much of the groundwork for Nissan was done at a small Welsh canning operation.

Continental Can, a wholly-owned subsidiary of the world's second largest packager, was set up in 1979. The first non-American to work there was Wickens. 'The plant was built in 1979 and officially opened in 1981,' says personnel manager Keith Gibson. 'The credit for creating and pushing the philosophy of the place goes to Wickens. He was an ex-industrial relations manager at Fords.

'We capitalized in three areas. We set ourselves the mission that we were going to be a low-cost producer, we would build a reputation for quality, and we would have a flexible work force based on a single union agreement. The agreement was absolutely key.

'We considered five unions. We needed a union that represented the different workers equally. We believed that the Transport and General Workers would be the most appropriate union – it is very forward-thinking – and it's been a very successful partnership with them,' says Gibson.

'The beauty of the system is that you can go for anything you like. We have a job-evaluation scheme that tells people exactly the criteria we use. There is a clause that says everybody will do whatever they are capable of doing. There are no barriers to that. You can be asked to do a job in the next grade up and you will be paid at the appropriate salary,' he comments.

After about two and a half years the company realized that it needed the job evaluation which Gibson speaks about. 'We needed a scheme which would evaluate everyone from a toilet cleaner to a production manager. We are also conscious that we must not discriminate between men and women. Some guys came down from ACAS and said, "You can't do it. You have to have two schemes – one for your manual workers and one for your staff." I said absolutely not. I am not prepared to draw a line through this company which says you are manual and you are staff.

'We came across this guy from ACAS in South Wales and he thought he could do it. So we sat down with a blank sheet of paper – myself, the guy from ACAS, two other managers, the full-time union official, and three shop stewards. It took us ten months to come up with the scheme which is quite revolutionary in its simplicity. In fact ACAS published it in their guide to job evaluation,' Gibson recalls with a rueful grin.

'We did it by listing all the factors which we thought you should measure in a person's job. We listed about twenty-two or -three things. We short-listed them and knocked them into shape and came up with ten factors. We got everybody to write a job description and we evaluated their descriptions against our criteria. We came up with a nine-grade structure. We implemented it in January 1983 and it has remained the basis of our job evaluation ever since.'

On pay the company plans its awards on three criteria: local conditions, rate of inflation and how well the company has performed. Generally Continental is regarded as a high payer. One worker in charge of quality of production was on £15,000 when we visited, which compares well both with the sector and the area.

The benefits are also generous. Everyone gets PPP at the most expensive rate. The excellent pension scheme is 4 per cent contributory. Everyone is issued with work clothes, and the canteen, which is subsidized, is open twenty-four hours a day, seven days a week. Two courses costs around 65p.

The company closes between Christmas Eve and 2 January, during which time there is a children's Christmas party and a disco. There are also visits to some of the suppliers.

Communication is a high priority. Alan Sims, the manufacturing director – the highest official on site – talks to the workers five times a year. He discusses the business, the state of trade, profitability, customers, new equipment changes, people coming and going, and so on. They know when Continental is bidding for a new contract, who the company is and where it is. In between each of these five sessions, shift managers talk to their own group about their performance, quality, absenteeism, production records and all the things that are happening in their group.

Carole Oldknow, a systems coordinator, has been with the company since the early days. 'It is a very hard-working company. They like you to give 110 per cent. But at the same time it is very well paid and it is a pleasant company to work for. I think the fact that the senior managers are young and that we are all treated as equals means that they don't hold you back. If you can get on with the work you can progress as far as you are capable.'

She adds: 'It doesn't really matter if you are male or female. I came in after working in a bank. I really had no qualifications for the job. They haven't got any of that Old Schoolboy atmosphere. In the bank you didn't get promoted unless someone died.'

The close cooperation between Continental and its work force has paid tremendous dividends. One worker started taking photographs of cans with defects in them – this pointed up a fault in the production. So much impact did this discovery make that America wanted to use it. Gibson recalled when they wanted a training manual and asked members of the shop-floor staff to write it for them. The result far exceeded their wildest expectations, and became a standard text.

Continental Can has a loyal and dedicated work force, and a sense of direction that many companies would envy. In March 1988 they announced that they had secured a contract with Britvic-Corona, which will mean the opening of a joint facility in Rugby. The new site will mean an increase in sales of more than 40 per cent.

DANA

Dana is a distribution and manufacturing company in the motor industry. The UK organization is owned by an American parent. Dana UK employs 3000 people across the country, and produces sales of around £185 million. Headquarters are in Swindon, Wiltshire.

pay	☐	ambience	☐
benefits	☐	environment	☐
promotion	☐	equal opportunities	☐
training	☐	communications	☐

On the second floor of the Dana headquarters lies the control room. This is not some marvel of high-tech engineering, but a centre of numerical communication. Staff come here to be briefed on the latest position of the company, its divisions and its profit centres. In many senses it is an unremarkable room. It could easily be a reception area, save for the panels of figures on each side. But it has greater symbolic significance. The mere existence of this room demonstrates how far Dana has moved in the last ten years. The control room bears testimony to Dana's enthusiasm for communicating its message to its people. It is part of a network of mechanisms which make Dana staff some of the best informed about their company of any employees in the country.

In 1986 Dana introduced team briefings, on the Industrial Society model, which are conducted every third Monday. Dana is typically informal about when groups hold their meetings. Some prefer the end of the working day. The advertising department, never missing a chance for a free sausage roll, have their meeting over lunch. All company offices, plants and depots are obliged to hold the briefing, and to supplement nationally originated material with local news. Detailed notes come down from the centre, and branch managers are expected to extemporize on local financial information.

Staff are extremely positive about the communication flow. 'If anything they tell us too much, but that's much better than nothing at all – which is how it used to be,' says one secretary at head office. Dana staff talk about the external courses they attend, and how they come back glowing with the perception that Dana communications are much better than in most other companies. 'When we meet we usually sit in groups of ten to twelve, and we are invited to offer our opinions and observations. There is a real sense that the management listen to our ideas and act on them,' says a credit controller.

Dana people display a quiet pride. It is a company where individuals can make their mark by working hard and with some degree of creativity. Background is irrelevant. While the company does draw in 40 graduate trainees a year, Dana prides itself on the extent of promotion from within. At branch manager level all appointments are made internally.

Dana is a company which has been completely reconstructed. A little more than ten years ago, a visitor would have found a somewhat sleepy, unstratified organization with numerous interests in the motor trade. In 1975, the American corporation Dana took over the interests of Brown Brothers, the distribution company in Swindon, and Turners, the manufacturing concern in Wolverhampton. These two businesses, plus a specialist engineering company in Colne on the Yorkshire–Lancashire border, formed the basis of the Dana companies in the United Kingdom. But despite the US takeover things remained much as they had been before. However, in the late 1970s a recession hit the motor trade which dented everyone's profits and caused some companies to go out of business. It was a shock for Dana. But in 1981 Brian Ferguson, now vice-president of Dana Europe, was appointed to kick the company into shape.

Ferguson is an impressive figure. He opened all the doors in more senses than one, and a blast of fresh air blew through the company. The present divisional structure was created. Each unit became an independent profit centre with the line manager accountable for reaching targets.

Information on company performance was made freely available to staff, and opinions were sought on improved functioning. The formal methods of address were dropped and everyone, including the boss, was on first-name terms. Few people at head office refer to the company as Dana. For them, it is and will always be Brown Brothers. 'We have many long-servers here,' says one accountant. 'People tend to stay. If they don't like it here – or we don't like them – they tend to go very quickly.'

The company today is composed of three operating divisions: distribution, manufacturing and special engineering. Distribution accounts for around 70 per cent of sales and 2000 staff. Many of these are located in depots around the country, selling a wide range of Dana products and other market leaders to motor retailers. Distribution is the leader in automotive paints, and it also makes a strong showing in component parts, accessories and tools.

Peter Sonley, personnel director, says that the company's attitude towards staff is outlined in the parent company's policies and philosophies document. It states: 'We are dedicated to our belief that our people are our most important asset.' Sonley explains that its operating subsidiaries translate the code according to local demands, conditions and legal frameworks.

The qualities which resulted in Dana's inclusion in the top 100 began to unfold with Ferguson's appointment as leader of the UK enterprise. He has encouraged a sense of confidence within the company which has enabled the business to emerge from its unhappy years. The staff display optimism and loyalty which have been reinforced by success.

There is some concern about high attrition rates among certain sectors within the company. Drivers in the distribution business leave at the rate of 35 per cent a year. 'Too high,' says Sonley. They are often tempted away by an extra fiver a week and the use of a company van for the weekends. Dana's main competitors are a string of 2000-plus independent operators. They have the flexibility to fix rates by the person rather than according to a set policy.

Sales-force people, too, can be lured away, especially in the southeast. Pay at Dana is not the best. An optimistic observer would suggest that it is between average and above average. The same could be said of benefits. Everyone is on 22 days' annual holiday, there is a 5 per cent contributory pension scheme and subsidized canteens. Staff also get company products such as spanners, dusters and antifreeze at 5 per cent less than cost price.

People do not work at Dana for the pay and benefits package. They like the friendly atmosphere, the sense of corporate direction, the good communications and training, and the opportunities – not only for the graduate management trainees – to climb to the highest levels within the company.

DELTA

Delta is a major industrial group comprising businesses in the electrical equipment, engineering and industrial services sectors. The company has businesses all over the country. Turnover in 1986 was £533.6 million, with pre-tax profits of £57.8 million. Head office is in London.

pay ☐		ambience ☐	
benefits ☐		environment ☐	
promotion ☐		equal opportunities ☐	
training ☐		communications ☐	

At the end of a meeting with one of the senior figures in the retail industry, we were discussing potential candidates for inclusion in this book. 'You must have Delta,' he said. 'They were at the forefront of good human relations decades ago.' Delta is a combination of businesses which may lack glamour but do produce vital parts for industry to function. Many of the group's companies are based in the industrial heartland of the Black Country and south Birmingham.

In recent years Delta's reputation as an imaginative and caring employer had slipped. Not through any failing on the part of the company, but because other companies began to make more noise about their personnel policies. In any case, Delta is not the sort of company which attracts much public attention outside industry and the geographical areas in which it operates. It is highly regarded by suppliers and customers alike as an efficient and personable network of businesses.

Its core businesses are electrical equipment, engineering and industrial services. Electrical engineering covers cables for mining, marine and offshore work, for housing and commercial property, and for signalling and communications. It also makes products for use in the control of electricity. Engineering has two divisions – fluid controls and metal products. Fluid controls includes building products, gas controls and precision engineering. Metal products covers four areas: extruded and drawn products, components, special alloys and distribution. Industrial services is an international business focused on extending the life of plant and equipment by repair and providing maintenance.

108

Electrical engineering is based mainly in north London and Birmingham, engineering in West Bromwich, and industrial services worldwide. While there is a small head office in London, it is arguable that the heart of Delta lies among the canals, motorways and Wulfrun ways of the Black Country. Here there is a selection of companies which all retain their independent identities, but which remain part of the Delta family.

A typical company is Conex Sanbra – based in Tipton, West Midlands. It is decentralized and its staff think of themselves as Conex rather than Delta people. No company in the group employs more than 700 people, which means that they can be easily managed and employees encouraged to feel that they are important. A strong sense of belonging exists at Conex. One staff member says, 'If you cut my leg off you would see the company's name running through it like a stick of rock.'

Such commitment is not inspired by superb pay and excellent benefits, although there are central guidelines laid down by Delta to ensure that pay and benefits are kept to an acceptable level, but by the family atmosphere. People are listened to and their ideas are discussed.

Senior management throughout the group have worked their way up through the ranks. To add a spur to internal promotion and personal growth, the group has opened a large new training centre in Birmingham. It has an engineering centre with a large workshop, but there are also computer courses and management schemes. The group takes 40 Youth Training Scheme people who, after sessions at the centre, will go into companies around the West Midlands.

The sector is not generally great for women, but Delta is making an effort. Women are rising slowly through the group's companies and, unlike some other organizations whose roots are in metal bashing, Delta managers are aware of the need to promote female staff. The intake of YTS and graduate people also reflects a willingness to find women and push them through the training schemes. There are 15 graduate vacancies in the group each year.

Treatment of staff varies from site to site depending on the nature of the management, but on the whole Delta has grasped a basic fundamental – that treating staff well pays dividends. As most of the component companies are small, interpersonal skills are considered important and much of the contact is informal and very direct.

Customers from around the world are encouraged to wander around the site. They talk to staff and discover how the place works. This has a twofold benefit. The client feels a greater affinity with the company and staff experience increasing involvement in the affairs of their business. 'We are not an inhibited firm. We get some hassle, a little bit of cheek and a serious ability to criticize the company, but it is very democratic and very healthy – a healthy core to the firm,' says one staff manager on site at Conex.

To reinforce the identity of the group a monthly staff newspaper, *Delta News*, was launched in 1973. Each year there is a special edition to summarize the company's performance and to present the comparative states of the different divisions. In April 1987 the group share option scheme was launched. It is open to all full-timers with three years' experience. Ten per cent is deducted from the share price which is fixed at the time they join the company. There is free dental treatment for all staff, and middle managers get BUPA.

Delta manages to combine an enlightened approach with good commercial sense. Their people are dedicated and enjoy the work. The company's figures have proved that the group with its three core divisions is moving ahead.

DIGITAL

The Digital Equipment Corporation in the UK is the wholly-owned subsidiary of its US parent. Head office is in Reading but the company has sites throughout the country. In 1987 turnover was £671 million. The company employs 7245 people.

pay	☐	ambience	☐
benefits	☐	environment	☐
promotion	☐	equal opportunities	☐
training	☐	communications	☐

The vision which created Digital belonged to one man – Ken Olsen. He left the Massachusetts Institute of Technology in 1957 to form a new company with ideas which were derided at MIT. Today Olsen presides over a business earning $1.16 billion, the second largest computer business in the world.

Olsen's persona is omnipresent. Even people who have never met him quote the founder. 'Ken wouldn't like that,' someone might suggest about a practice which does not fit in with the Digital philosophy. The structure is a loose one – people are flexible and need to be. There is a matrix grid. This means that managers are responsible to a functional director and to subsidiary management.

Digital enjoys a freedom which is unlike that of many other companies. The personnel department talks about people being free to make their own careers: 'You own your career not us. We will give you all the facilities to make a success but it is up to you,' says Steve Preece from personnel services.

That is the way Olsen wanted it. Digital established a reputation in the 1960s and 1970s as key instigators of change in the industry. But in the early 1980s the recession in the sector hit the company hard. 'We didn't stop growing but the rate of growth slowed from 12 per cent to 4 per cent,' says Ray Whitfield, who was personnel programmes manager until 1988.

'We were spending money like water and the sales weren't there to justify it. Ken Olsen cut back on some programmes but he said that no one was going to be made redundant,' adds Whitfield. True to his word, no one was. It is company policy that there should never be any redundancies.

A salary increase programme was deferred, which meant that increases due in January were paid six months later. 'It was the employee's way of making his contribution to the belt-tightening,' says one Digital software engineer, and nobody minded.

Growth now is better than ever, and the company opened four new sales offices between mid-year 1987 and spring 1988. It announced an £82 million silicon chip factory at South Queensferry, Edinburgh, creating 300 jobs, and a new headquarters for the company at Thames Valley Park on the east side of Reading is to open in 1991.

'We have a very open approach to communications,' says one manager. He's right, too. It is one of the few companies which has a genuine open-door policy. People are expected to voice their opinions, especially if they feel that some aspect of their work is somehow jeopardized.

Digital holds team briefings every quarter, with material agreed centrally. Each member of the management board visits one of the twelve locations of the company every three months to discuss developments in the company's business. A wealth of high-quality literature is produced every year which would keep a small library groaning at the seams. Booklets with high-definition colour photography and detailed accounts of Digital performance, products, policies and benefits shower out of the company.

Communication is a vital part of the way the enterprise does business. It is an entirely ethical company, believing in fair treatment, and it demands that its people are open and honest in return. 'We have a process called the job plan and review process where we can discuss anything. And the individual can gain the support of the manager or supervisor to develop them in the way they want to go,' says an administrator at DEC Park.

The group's commitment to training and the range of courses available to the staff is awe-inspiring. The purpose of the training at Digital is not only to prepare individuals for the job or train them up for some future direction, but also to add to their personal development.

In 1987 Digital set up DEC College, which is aimed at giving outsiders a taste for and an understanding of the computer industry. 'We rarely get computer graduates on the milk round these days,' says Lorna Hirst who is a personnel consultant. 'They generally know where they want to go and concentrate on getting their degrees before applying for jobs.' The college is one way of creating an awareness of Digital in its community, especially among school students and school-leavers.

In principle the company could not be anything other than strictly egalitarian in its attitude towards women, though some women are not convinced. 'The opportunities are there but it is tougher for us than for men. In some departments, like sales and administration, there has been a dramatic increase in the number of women rising up through the company. But in some departments it is the attitude of some managers which needs changing,' says one woman manager.

Rewards are competitive. Digital prides itself on being one of the top companies in the land as far as pay is concerned. On average, pay is assessed every six months and the marketplace will be judged. Incentives are offered in many departments. In 1987 the top ten performers in the company went to Hawaii.

The sales force is wholly salary-based, and the team experiences a turnover rate of only 6 to 7 per cent. For the southeast, and particularly the Thames Valley, this is tiny. Many of the people who go can transfer within Digital, and so the loss to the company is even smaller.

The benefits package includes free private health insurance, contributory pension scheme, life insurance, a subsidized canteen and a range of sports and social activities is given financial backing by the company.

Paul Biddle, finance and administration manager, recruited from the more steely Rank Xerox, says that Digital's subsidiary companies in the UK, Germany and France are enjoying much greater autonomy. 'Historically the role of the subsidiary was one of a distributor. Now we are seeing a transition to a much broader solutions-provider, from which a much wider business strategy is envisaged.'

Digitial is an open, creative and lively company. It is distinguished by an excellent philosophy of management which encourages originality of thought and creation among its people.

DU PONT

Du Pont is a major international chemical company. This US-owned enterprise employs 2000 people in the UK, from a worldwide work force of 140,000. Global turnover is $30.5 billion.

pay ☐		ambience ☐	
benefits ☐		environment ☐	
promotion ☐		equal opportunities ☐	
training ☐		communications ☐	

Lavoisier discovered oxygen and was one of the founders of modern chemistry two hundred years ago. Unfortunately, the French Revolution was uncertain what to do with him and sent him to the guillotine. One of his ex-students fled to America in 1800 and set up one of the biggest commercial explosives factories there.

The company he set up still bears his name — Eleuthère Irenée du Pont de Nemours, or Du Pont for short. It claims to have invented the modern chemical industry. Teflon for non-stick frying pans, Lycra which makes swimming costumes stretch, Kevlar fibres used in high-performance tyres, bullet-proof vests and the body shells of Formula One racing cars are some of the 50,000 products patented by Du Pont.

Throughout this century the old power mill company on the banks of the Delaware has been diversifying and spreading its geographical area of operations into 135 different countries. Fifty years ago, in the main headquarters labs in Wilmington, Delaware, a Du Pont chemist called Carothers invented nylon, and with it the whole artificial textile industry. This strange experimenter came to a sticky end too — committing suicide just as his invention became a household name.

Du Pont is still as powerful and innovative as it ever was, spending a billion dollars a year on research. After nearly two centuries Du Pont finally pulled out of the explosives business in 1987. Most of today's products use petroleum as a feedstock, but the oil crises of the 1970s showed how vulnerable the chemical industry could be without any control of its raw materials. One of its suppliers was Conoco, and Du Pont was so impressed by the oil that it merged with the company in 1981. It was the biggest ever corporate marriage at the time, as Conoco and Du Pont were the fourteenth and fifteenth largest companies in America.

Conoco has 3500 staff in Britain working on oil and gas fields in the North Sea, at the Humber Refinery, in London offices, and driving 250 tankers supplying the 1200 Jet petrol stations in the UK. Conoco even operates its own 'mineral motorway', a 520-mile pipeline loop which allows different products to be pumped in batches from the Humber Refinery to Yorkshire, Manchester, the West Country and Berkshire. Conoco still operates completely separately from Du Pont in the UK. It has been recruiting graduates in Britain for fifteen years. Conoco looks for geology and geophysics postgrads for the Exploration department, engineering graduates for the upstream operations, chemists for the Humber Refinery, business and accounting students for the Administration departments, and various degrees for the computing jobs in the Data Centre in London. Training is a mixture of on-the-job projects, in-house courses and tuition from outside specialists. Pay, as you would expect in the oil industry, is good, and there is plenty of opportunity to travel. Unlike Du Pont, Conoco also operates a stock acquisition scheme for employees.

Du Pont itself came to Britain in 1960, setting up the Maydown plant in Northern Ireland. Initially it produced synthetic rubber – neoprene (also invented by Carothers) – but as technology and demand has changed, so has the product to Hylene and Orlon and now Lycra and Kevlar. Employment peaked at round 1800 and is now 'stable' at around 1100. There are also 500 at Du Pont's Stevenage headquarters and 150 at the Hemel Hempstead polymer division, and smaller numbers in distribution and at the Hilcote plant, which makes polypropylene gas pipes, the Leicester fibre plant and the Bristol factory, which makes small connectors for the electronics industry. Although Du Pont employs over 140,000 people worldwide, it deliberately tries to keep units small enough for everyone to know each other.

Maydown is unionized although the other locations are not, and, according to Craig Cameron, the director of employee relations, 'We respect the wishes of the employees.' There are 800 on the wage roll with craft workers on around £10,000 and shift workers on £13,000. There are 500 technical and administrative staff on around £10,000–£12,000, and 700 professional and managerial grades earning between £12,000–£30,000. Pay is theoretically performance-related, with any individual getting between 80 per cent and 120 per cent of a guidepoint, but in practice most people seem to get around 107 per cent of the guide wage. The 200 most senior managers also get bonuses, and the top 120 get cars. Another 200 Du Ponters have cars because they need them for their work.

115

Some of the subsidized cafeterias have video screens which put out up-to-date company news. New products, trading information, statements by Du Pont bigwigs, award-winners and safety statistics are the staples. There is also a quarterly Du Pont UK magazine called the *Courier* as well as European and worldwide publications.

Until recently legal restrictions prevented women from working in many of the jobs which require shiftwork, and this is one of the reasons why most of the work force are male. There are now more women than men in some of the newer growth areas, such as medical products. Du Pont has amibitions to become a major drugs company. Most of the technical and administrative staff are female, but fewer than 6 per cent of the professional and managerial grades are women. Management attribute this partly to the knock-on effects of shiftwork requirements. Women with young children can opt to work a 7 p.m.–10 p.m. evening shift.

Du Pont gives training a high priority and has a good record of promoting its managers from within. The average employee gets between six and ten days' training a year, and the company has an educational assistance programme giving time off and paying exam fees. Many of the Maydown managers started on the shop floor.

Du Pont looks for 'technical excellence in specialized fields, not generalists,' according to Cameron. It does not like the high-flyer programmes which some big companies favour to develop head office managers for the future. 'We don't have the film star view,' says Cameron. Senior employees characterize it as 'a traditional big company – you cannot be a vice-president at thirty-one'. Everything it does, it does with quality, but it is usually slow.

Du Pont is keen on corporate philosophy. 'Safety is the single highest value,' says Cameron, and the official handbook spells out the economic justifications for these principles. 'A company such as Du Pont can thrive over the years only if there is a generally favourable view towards the company on the part of the public and the government, and if the interests of the corporation are balanced with those of society.'

Du Pont does not believe that environmentalism is a threat to the future of the chemical industry. Du Pont talks of opportunities rather than problems. For instance, in response to the fears that chlorofluorocarbons – the substances which are found in aerosols and fast-food packaging – are damaging the ozone layer, Du Pont has developed alternatives.

One issue of Du Pont's European magazine has articles on a new water pump for the Third World, a 100-foot-long escape chute from oil rigs, the detection of AIDS, a new corkscrew, designer climbing gear for yeti-hunters, and undersea optical fibre cables – all of which involve Du Pont products. This gives you some idea of the range of activities of this $30 billion turnover giant. Joining the company is a 'safe' option, and there are no short cuts to the top, but the pay and training is good, work can be exciting and there are plenty of options. The chemical industry may not be as heroic as it was in the days of Lavoisier, or even Carothers – but who wants to come to a sticky end?

ESSO

Esso is an oil company. It is owned by Exxon, one of the largest corporations in the world. In 1987 Esso UK produced a turnover of £5.8 billion with pre-tax profits of £527 million. The company employs 4500 people.

pay ☐	ambience ☐
benefits ☐	environment ☐
promotion ☐	equal opportunities ☐
training ☐	communications ☐

When analysts or journalists write about Exxon, which has claims to the title of the world's largest company, they use words like hard, tough, ruthless, aggressive, go-getting and dynamic. It is an archetypical model of a corporation. It is on a par with IBM in its capacity to get the ear of presidents and prime ministers alike. It demands a lot from its staff. It pays well, offers extraordinary career opportunities and inspires commitment.

With this somewhat awesome impression of the parent, we visited the UK subsidiary Esso. Yet we were greeted by pleasant, warm, enthusiastic people. The receptionist was friendly and attentive without being overwhelming. It was a combination of qualities that we experienced throughout the London headquarters of the company in Victoria Street.

Emotionally, Esso UK is fairly distant from its parent. It is largely autonomous. Head office in New York certainly wants to know what the British are up to, and their figures are keenly scrutinized. Capital spending is noted, but since the European headquarters was closed there is no longer a sense of the corporation peeking over its shoulder. That is just as well, since Esso appears to be noticeably different in approach.

Not that the Esso UK people are any less professional in what they do. Esso has a technical expertise which would be difficult to equal. They have also responded well to the upheaval in the oil industry by retraining rapidly, and finding new solutions to problems which affect the company and the industry.

The name Esso comes from SO or Standard Oil, the first of the American oil companies. When the company was launched in the UK in 1888, the founders preferred the Anglo-American Oil company, but later opted to spell out the initials for the name of the business. Standard Oil of New Jersey itself was launched in Cleveland by John D. Rockefeller in 1863.

Esso has always been populated by locals who have carved out a special name in the corporate history of Exxon; a name for innovation, teamwork, collective vision and individuality. It is a more relaxed organization in style than Shell. It is less distant than BP. The men at Shell regard Esso as their number-one competitor. They recognize its shrewd understanding of downstream marketing and intelligent exploitation of resources in upstream production. These two qualities combine exceptionally well in the harnessing of new technology in the industry.

On its own account Esso has a strong research and development capacity which is focused at the Esso Research Centre near Abingdon in Oxfordshire. The centre does work for the company in all areas, but concentrates on marine lubricants, automotive and aviation fuels and lubricants for Exxon worldwide.

The centre is an important facet of the company, which is composed of Esso UK and two operating subsidiaries. These are Esso Exploration and Production, responsible for the exploration and production of crude oil and natural gas, and Esso Petroleum, responsible for refining, distribution and marketing petroleum products. Esso accounts for 15 per cent of all oil and gas drilled in and around the UK.

The company's refinery at Fawley, near Southampton, has capacity to produce 15.6 million tonnes a year and is the largest in the UK. It serves a network of ten terminals, eight airport installations, various bulk plants and a number of distributors.

Most people are familiar with Esso marketing – the tiger is the hallmark of the company. An attempt in the 1960s – perhaps bogus – to do away with it only reaffirmed its position. Modern marketing requires more than symbols, though, and the company, like its competitors, has been modernizing its image at the pumps. Garages are taking on a mini-supermarket feel, with tea bags as well as maps and cans of oil on sale.

Like Shell and BP, Esso has been engaged in novel ways to persuade the motorist to spend more money at their petrol stations. Price-cutting is not regarded as appropriate, but vouchers for videocassettes, sundae dishes and beakers certainly are.

The company recruits about 50 to 60 graduates a year from a variety of disciplines, most of them technical. 'We are looking for engineers primarily,' says Jim Platt-Higgins, recruitment manager at Esso head-

119

quarters. The company rarely has a problem inducting people of sufficient calibre. It has a reputation as an excellent payer, backed by good training and significant experience on site.

Graduates can expect diverse experience in their early years, moving through the UK and overseas – although experience outside Europe is less likely than with either BP or Shell.

Communication and consultation are keystones of the Esso approach. Typical is the move to Leatherhead, which is planned to happen in 1990. The reaction to a possible transfer of the company out of London, and the suitability of Leatherhead, has been discussed long and hard at all levels.

'Management are very good at keeping us informed about the company and where we stand in the market,' says one engineer. There is a positive and open environment, and one – like BP – which has gone through a transformation. Esso people find it hard to specify the culture of the company which they work for. They talk about an environment which is conducive to team spirit. They say that ideas are welcomed but prima donnas are not. Women are now encountering less barriers. Ten years ago the company was more old-fashioned, but its entrepreneurial energy has always kept it from being too stuffy.

Esso is by far the most informal of the Big Three oil companies in Britain. It has a sharp commercial cutting edge, but it remains decidedly human in its approach to its employees.

FEDERAL EXPRESS

Federal Express is a delivery company. It operates depots nationwide with clearing centres at Nuneaton in Warwickshire and Higham Ferrers in Northamptonshire. The company is American-owned. Turnover in 1987 was £90 million, showing a pre-tax profit of £6 million.

pay	☐	ambience	☐
benefits	☐	environment	☐
promotion	☐	equal opportunities	☐
training	☐	communications	☐

Wilf Carr drives a lorry for a living. He also chats with managing directors and has brought in thousands of pounds worth of business for his bosses at Federal Express. He is a typical envoy for Federal Express, a company which realized at an early stage that if you look after your staff they will take care of your customers.

Dave Dunmore is a class-one driver. He is also shop steward for the Transport and General Workers Union and a national representative. He sees little need for confrontation between union and management, and, unusually for a trade unionist, he foresees a day when unions won't be needed in Federal Express. 'Federal Express is like a bird taking off. If you want to fly with them, then jump on the wing,' he says.

Enthusiasm for the company is not restricted to drivers. Beverley Megson, a customer services manager, sees teamwork as one of the reasons why Federal Express is doing so well. Her contacts range from some of the biggest organizations in the land to some of the smallest. Dealing with such a wide assortment of clients is stimulating in itself but it pays off when even the tiniest concern recognizes the quality of service.

The whole operation is governed by a huge IBM mainframe. But the computer is treated as a subsidiary tool. Managing director Malcolm Howard says, 'It is simply there to support our people.'

A people culture is at the heart of Federal Express. In Britain it is a young enterprise, and its employees are characterized by youthful attitudes. There is a certain resilience about them. If they fail they get up and start again. Federal Express has a very American personality

121

which it has adapted to fit the British marketplace. The company reflects the best attributes of its enthusiastic parent combined with British pragmatism, and there is a genuine desire by management to sit and listen to what their people say, and to learn from their experience.

Staff benefit from a non-contributory pension scheme and the company employs a full-time pensions manager to answer queries. Each location pursues its own charity activities, which recently included a football match between Leeds staff and Leeds FC old boys. Billy Bremner, Peter Lorimer, Eddie Gray and Bobby Collins made short work of the Federal team, winning 9–1, but more than £600 was raised towards the cost of a local kidney machine.

In America Federal Express, synonymous with founder Fred Smith, was the first company in corporate history to create a $1 billion turnover in ten years, with the benefit of acquisition. Smith spotted an enormous gap in the delivery market in 1973. Starting with a depot in Memphis, a strong commitment to technology and his People First philosophy, he built up a worldwide empire.

Today, more than half the next-day package market is controlled by Federal Express. In the UK Smith appointed Lex Wilkinson as its pick-up and delivery agent in 1985. The next year he bought them out. Personnel director Geoff Hoyle, who has served both masters, says: 'Federal Express knew it was buying a company which treated people well and had a natural affinity towards technology. They believed in us and left us to get on with things.'

MD Howard comments: 'I would hazard a guess that the acquisition of Lex was one of the most successful transfer processes which has ever taken place.' Smith had invented the hub-and-spokes system of delivery. Nuneaton and Higham Herrers are the central sorting depots, or the hub, where the packages are sorted before transmission along the spokes. That saves what Federal calls the double shuffle – bouncing between depots – and makes it easier to offer a next-day service.

'One of our problems is that it seems a very simple concept and process but not when you think of the volume of parcels which we have to move,' says Howard. Some 100,000 items come in and go out every day, so there are likely to be 250,000 consignments in the network at any one time. 'We rely on our people to do their job correctly day in and day out, but we are much more susceptible to human error than manufacturing industry, which is why we place so much emphasis on our People First philosophy,' comments Howard.

Hoyle has a clear idea of what the company wants from its people. 'Competence, a commitment to excellence, capacity for change and a

122

competitive edge,' he adds. 'The organization is characterized by broad job descriptions, autonomy and self-regulation, flexibility to meet customers' requirements and problem-solving expertise. We seek to achieve a sense of moral superiority over the competition, constantly looking for change which improves our position.'

A major investment programme included new depots in Perth, Edinburgh and Croydon, plus another three depots in 1988. At a recent major Federal Express conference in Coventry we met a wide range of company personnel from around the country. The commitment of the staff is unmistakable. Turnover is so low that it is impractical to measure. Employees we spoke to put it down to the competitive rates of pay, annual salary reviews and the profit-related bonus scheme. There is also a genuine feeling among employees of contributing to the success of the business.

Shop steward Dave Dunmore says: 'It is a very good and fair management which tries to see our point of view. Now we have a much more positive approach to people and teamwork. I would not want to work for anyone else. If they are successful I have a good future.'

FITCH & CO.

Fitch is one of Europe's largest design consultancies. Based in central London, the company reported a turnover of £10 million and pre-tax profits of £1.8 million in 1987. It employs more than 350 people.

pay ☐		ambience ☐	
benefits ☐		environment ☐	
promotion ☐		equal opportunities ☐	
training ☐		communications ☐	

Starting with three partners and five employees in 1972, Fitch & Co. has grown into one of Europe's largest design consultancies. This remarkable success has been achieved through a happy combination of missionary zeal and sound business acumen.

Since the 1960s there has been a growing consciousness among retailers, manufacturers and developers of the need for good design. Without pushing any particular style, Fitch has aimed to satisfy and develop this need. Rodney Fitch remains the driving force behind the company. He commands a tremendous sense of loyalty from his people, not least for his visionary proclamation of the concept of good design. 'We see ourselves as standard-bearers for the design world,' says Fitch. 'We see almost no limit to the fields in which design can add value.'

His influence can be seen all around. He designed the fourth terminal at Heathrow Airport, the new galleria format for Debenhams, the revitalized Dillons Bookshop and the recent redesign of Midland Bank. The company is involved in every aspect of design, from repositioning a tired product in the market, to creating a new corporate identity, or styling a new shopping centre. And it is not just commercial work. Fitch is engaged – for free – in charity work for Oxfam, the Heart and Lung Foundation and the V&A. For the staff this means a huge variety of work, a lot of responsibility and a lot of freedom to make what you want of the job.

Mark Landini, division retail director, made this comment: 'Fitch understands what motivates designers; not money but being creative.' Fitch worked with Terence Conran in the 1960s at the time when design was breaking through, and formed his own company in 1972.

The aim was to introduce design to almost any field. The only area which Fitch never covered was domestic interior design. At first the company grew in a haphazard entrepreneurial fashion. It spread its wings across Europe, and found work whenever and wherever it could. One of the longer-lasting connections was with Ralph Halpern and Burtons.

In 1978 management consultants advised Fitch to restructure the company on divisional lines. This included ten main specialisms: retail, printed communication, travel environments, furniture design, leisure environments, corporate identity, shopping centres, product design, packaging and branding, and office design. Since then Fitch has expanded at a rapid rate, culminating in a stock market quotation in 1982.

The cornerstone of the Fitch philosophy is to allow the creative team to determine its own style. This means encouraging staff to take as much responsibility as possible. Landini says, 'You get opportunities to experiment and you are allowed to make mistakes, which are seen as a positive part of the learning process.' From this point of view Rodney Fitch sees the role of management as 'providing a safety net. The work should always be under some control and direction.' Anyone can set out to develop new lines of business. Bill Sermon, a senior designer in the products division, says, 'You know what the opportunities are. If you want it, go for it.' If the designer feels a particular piece of work will be a valuable experience for Fitch, then it can go ahead, even if it does not produce any immediate financial return.

By contrast, overall financial control and corporate development is run from the centre. Everyone can find out what is going on if they want to, but the management attitude is rather that staff do not really need to worry about such things. To some people this is not an altogether satisfactory situation: one employee commented that there was not enough liaison between the divisions. However, there is a company newsletter and occasional briefings on the company's progress.

The ethical stance of the company also bears the hallmark of Rodney Fitch. Fitch will not do any work for tobacco companies, but is quite happy to work in South Africa. In fact, there are not too many things that Fitch will not undertake, but, again, the staff have a say in what they will or will not do. Jamie Asher, aged twenty-three, is a designer in the packaging division. He said, 'If there is no one in the studio who wants to do it then it will not get done.'

Most people see the main benefits of the job as being the work itself, the warm friendly atmosphere, the responsibility and the freedom.

Working for Fitch is also a good stepping stone in an industry with a high turnover. Jamie Asher comments, 'In terms of salary Fitch is not necessarily the best company to work for, but it's the best to have on your CV.'

By and large salaries appear to be slightly below the industry average, in what is quite a high-paying business. As an assistant director you could be earning £27,500 and have a company car by the age of thirty. A designer straight from college might expect to earn around £9500. To some extent salaries are tied to qualifications: a marketing analyst with an MBA can start at £21,500. The back-up staff, and secretaries and librarians, who make up about one-third of the employees, also get slightly below the average for their level of experience. For example, an experienced secretary to one of the MDs earns £12,500. Time and again, however, employees said that they could get far more outside if they wanted to but were perfectly happy to stay with Fitch.

The benefits package outside of salary is meagre indeed. Company cars only start at assistant director level, holidays are the standard 20 days, there are no bonus or share option schemes, and only the standard redundancy package. Rodney Fitch believes that the remuneration for the job should come entirely through the pay packet, and there was no suggestion of dissatisfaction from the staff.

The family atmosphere of the business is prevalent in some of the less tangible benefits. The company is very sympathetic to personal problems, such as bereavement, and an employee is sometimes allowed a considerable time off on full pay. The Fitches give a garden party every year for all staff, bussing them down to their mansion in Wiltshire. They are greeted with champagne, followed by a buffet lunch, with game shows and amusements for the employees' children, cricket for the men, croquet for the ladies, afternoon tea, and a brass band!

The company is full of young people, which is partly a reflection of the design industry itself, and partly a reflection of company policy. Fitch is happy for the company to be seen as the training ground of the industry, and to this end the company offers extensive training for staff at all levels. There are specific training courses for teaching relevant skills which are run by the company itself, some of which are design related, while others are self-assessment courses. There are also outside courses, for example time management and effective presentation. An employee might expect to go on one of these at least once a year. Then there are more general information systems within each division aimed at keeping staff up to date with the latest developments in their field. Finally, at 5 p.m. every Friday work stops and all those who wish to can participate in the 'review'. This might consist of an informal talk on some aspect of the company by a senior manager, or a seminar from someone outside the company.

The company takes in a number of students on secondment, usually from art school, but also from the London Business School.

A high-pressure job in a family atmosphere might be the best way to sum up Fitch & Co. It is not easy to get a job with Fitch, but once you're in everything is done to try and keep you there, and nobody we met seemed eager to go. As Landini says, 'It's like playing for Liverpool. Bolton Wanderers might have a nice strip, but nothing beats being at the top of the first division.'

GLAXO

Glaxo is the UK's largest pharmaceutical company, and employs 32,000 people worldwide. Group turnover in 1987 was £1.7 billion and pre-tax profit £746 million. Glaxo Pharmaceuticals operates manufacturing sites in Greenford, Middlesex, Barnard Castle, Co. Durham, and Ware, Hertfordshire.

pay	☐	ambience	☐
benefits	☐	environment	☐
promotion	☐	equal opportunities	☐
training	☐	communications	☐

Glaxo boasts a product range which includes world-beaters like Zantac and Ventolin, and R&D is a predominant feature of the group's work. It majors on high ethical standards which when combined with its strongly pragmatic nature and largely individualistic culture brings out the best in its people.

The company's origins lie in Wellington, New Zealand, where, in 1861, East Ender Joseph Nathan became a partner in his brother-in-law's thriving merchant business. While the enterprise blossomed their relationship deteriorated. In 1873 the business passed into the sole hands of Nathan, and three years later he opened an office in London. In the 1890s he left the antipodean end of the business to his sons. As the new century dawned Nathan became interested in dried milk production and a new plant was established in Bunnythorpe, NZ. The original name – Defiance – was deemed inappropriate for the infant food market in the UK, and attempts to find a strong product brand resulted in Glaxo.

The Glaxo Co. took a full-page advertisement on the front page of the nascent *Daily Mail* offering parents a booklet and a liberal sample. While early sales were not encouraging, a nationwide summer epidemic of diarrhoea in 1911, together with the First World War, stimulated demand. By 1918 turnover exceeded £500,000.

In 1919 Glaxo took its first tentative steps into research. This led to a refinement and standardization of the quality of the product. By 1923, sales had peaked at £1½ million. Vitamin D was introduced in the dried milk and sales surged again. But something more fundamental was at work. This signified the change of direction to pharmaceutical production. The company next produced Ostelin – vitamin D in glycerin – its first pharmaceutical product. This was immediately taken up by the medical profession, and a series of related lines was thus spawned. Alec Nathan, the founder's son, and Harry Jephcott, a researcher who became general manager of Glaxo House, ran a tight ship. Nathan knew each employee by name and it was a sign of the company's far-sighted attitude to staff that a pension scheme was introduced as early as 1932.

The range of products and geographical targets expanded each year. In 1935 the company moved from Euston to what was then rural Greenford. The new building was purpose-built and included laboratories and modern open-plan offices. A large canteen and recreational facilities were provided. As today, the company sponsored sporting and spare-time activities on site or around the area. Staff were well paid. A skilled worker received £4 for a 48-hour week, a process worker £3 15s and a general labourer £3 10s. Communications are a high priority. Apart from regular team briefings, newspapers and video reports, the company is looking at site publications to complement the group's *Glaxo News* and *Glaxo World*.

The Second World War brought increasing attention to Glaxo's pharmaceutical output. By D-Day in 1944 80 per cent of all British penicillin was supplied by the company. A range of vitamin products and the notorious dried egg powder were among the wide variety of products issued by Glaxo. After the war Glaxo took over a government factory at Barnards Castle, County Durham, for the mass production of penicillin. But an equally significant shift also took place.

In the 1950s Glaxo moved into veterinary work and cortisone production. Allen & Hanbury's – another pharmaceutical company – was bought in 1958 which was to lead to Glaxo's dominance in the anti-asthmatic field. The 1960s saw the pace of acquisition step up and in the 1970s Glaxo saw off a hostile bid from competitors Beecham. As the next decade began, the anti-ulcerant Zantac was launched. This proved to be a massive prescription product.

Glaxo products are traded through three subsidiaries – Glaxo Laboratories, Allen & Hanbury's and Duncan, Flockhart & Co. Current chairman Sir Paul Girolami would like to add more powerful independent companies to his worldwide network and he expects those businesses to perform better than they have done to date. Girolami has actively devolved management from the centre into operating companies, while ensuring that he retains effective control. He is also putting more emphasis on promoting people earlier. 'People should

129

get on to the board not at fifty-five but forty-five,' he told *Glaxo World*. The company provides fertile ground for good decision-making, he says.

He is justified in his belief that Glaxo allows people space to show their worth and run with ideas. The company provides high-quality training to support managers. Some of the courses are run in-house, but most, according to personnel director Bill Proudlock, are fashioned with outside consultants for Glaxo's express requirements. As befits a pragmatic enterprise, no one school of management thought predominates.

The company believes that the individual is responsible for his or her own self-development but that it should provide the best possible environment for this to be successfully achieved. 'We feel that they have a duty to develop their own potential,' says Proudlock. He suggests that behind this concept is the notion that the individual should choose his or her own career path and not feel coerced into moving in any specific direction. 'But we are seeing competitive and turbulent times in business and there will be no medals for complacency,' he says.

The company takes in perhaps 12 graduates a year from the milk round, and perhaps another 20 to 30 by direct entry. There are many long-servers. It is the type of company that people emphatically do not want to leave once they have managed to join. Theo Theocharides, who is based at Allen & Hanbury's in Ware, worked for other pharmaceutical companies for six years before enlisting with Glaxo. He says it is by far the best. 'It was an attractive offer. What I do is visit supplier companies to see if they meet the high standards set by Glaxo.' In this sense Glaxo has become the Marks & Spencer of the pharmaceutical world. It demands exceptionally high quality from its suppliers and enforces its norms with great efficiency. Theocharides also praises Glaxo's training which he says has helped him to become a more efficient negotiator.

Pay is average to above average for the sector, and none of the staff we spoke to had any complaints. Everyone at Ware who offered opinions thought that Glaxo was one of the best payers in the sector, if not the best. Benefits are good. A health scheme exists for all staff, while senior managers get free health insurance. There is a company-wide personal accident policy and subsidized canteen facilities.

The company makes no distinction between staff on grounds of colour or sex. Women have reached very senior positions in the company and continue to make up a significant part of the scientific team within Glaxo. There is no positive discrimination but everyone

130

genuinely does progress on his or her own merit. There is still a paternal hierarchy in the company, but this is due more to tradition than anything else, and it is fading with the passage of time.

Glaxo has established itself as the market leader in the pharmaceutical community. It has dropped its involvement in other areas and is sticking to its core business. The company is fighting hard in an increasingly tough sector but it has lost none of its commitment to its people. A vigorously professional and competitive player, it commands widespread respect for its human approach to employee relations.

GLYNWED

Glynwed is a diversified conglomerate making a wide range of industrial and domestic products. It is based in Birmingham. Some 70 companies comprise the group.

pay ☐		ambience ☐	
benefits ☐		environment ☐	
promotion ☐		equal opportunities ☐	
training ☐		communications ☐	

The name Glynwed tends to conjure up the image of a Welsh village, but Glynwed is a company based in the heart of the industrial Midlands and can boast the sort of success record that makes the bosses of better-known concerns sit up and take notice.

Glynwed's main areas of operation are in consumer and building products, engineering, steel and tubes and fitting. It is the biggest copper-tube manufacturer in the UK, and one of the largest privately-owned steel manufacturers. Glynwed goes for the unfashionable products in the world of manufacturing. Manhole covers, cast-iron pipes, cable clips, steel walkways and tubular fencing – products that most of us take for granted but rarely consider who is producing them.

Some of their products are household names. Aga-Rayburn, Flavel and Leisure are well known to buyers of cookers, fires and sinks, but few customers would associate them with the name Glynwed.

Some 70 companies operate within the Glynwed net. The average turnover is £10 million with perhaps 200 employees in each company, although some may have up to 1000. 'Small is beautiful,' says group staff manager Hugh McCredie.

The group's managing directors are told every year that they are expected to increase annual turnover by 20 per cent. Most of them do. The company has an enviable knack of buying – usually for cash – firms which they then successfully develop.

There is something indefinable about the skills, abilities and person-alities of men who can consistently show a profit in the business jungle. Why does one wheeler-dealer scratch a bare living on a market stall and another turn up with his wares in a Mercedes?

Glynwed's men would be in the Merc. The people who fill the top jobs are grafters with an inbuilt financial acumen. Times are changing of course, and Glynwed reluctantly accepts that those men are a dying breed. It is looking carefully at its graduate recruitment policy – which has been fairly low key up to now.

McCredie, who has spent two years studying the most effective performers in the company, says: 'The virtue that is most valued is purely and simply a track record in meeting targets. Another feature is intelligence, but not necessarily a high level of qualification. There is almost a preference for people who have worked their way up the hard way, although that is perhaps changing a little now.

'There is tight financial control on growth but a very large degree of operational freedom. We know what we are about in running companies even if we are not the most exciting business in the world. We tell people what we want and let them get on with it.'

The buying boom financed by the public's increasing use of plastic credit helped the company's consumer and building products. Although a well-known name, Aga-Rayburn appeals to a fairly select market, but the upmarket Flavel-Leisure cooker and fire business prospered. Glynwed Foundries sought to double its turnover after the complex task of incorporating Brickhouse Dudley into the Glynwed operation.

The West Midlands is (and always has been) the centre of operations but the Glynwed net stretches to Australia, Europe and America.

McCredie adds: 'It is a well-run group of companies. All the managers know we want 20 per cent return per annum and in the last five years most have returned more than that. We are growing all the time, with half a dozen new acquisitions in 1987 and more planned.'

Targets come from the chiefs at head office in New Coventry Road, Sheldon, Birmingham, where 100 managers, lawyers, accountants, computer staff, publicity and personnel departments oversee the massive empire.

Nearly all operations are heavily unionized and within Glynwed there are some 150 bargaining groups. Managers are left to sort out their own union problems but McCredie would find it an unusual year if he heard of more than a couple of strikes. Success seems to breed union–management contentment.

There is a BUPA scheme and a company-wide pension scheme, but almost everything else is left to individual managers – with that minimum 20 per cent return always at the back of their minds.

Branded products have tended to have a higher profile than the group name, but that seems to be changing in recent months. The

133

group has been a little shy in the past but is now making more and more effort to publicize its name – at least in the City.

Shareholders who bought in at the beginning of 1983 have seen their investment multiply in value more than seven times. Perhaps the figures speak for themselves and Glynwed has little need of a huge publicity drive. The word must be filtering through the City that Glynwed has the magic formula.

Training is vital to a company such as this, and apart from the obvious courses offered by individual firms there are two top management courses available. Middle management are encouraged to take a problem-solving and decision-making course, originally developed by the Kepner-Tregoe Organization in the States. At least 400 of the top 1000 companies in the world use the Kepner-Tregoe approach, which looks at four key areas:

• Sorting out priorities.
• Finding out the cause of something that has gone wrong.
• Making choices.
• Avoiding future trouble and exploiting future opportunities.

Senior management have a course developed alongside the Huthwaite Research Group. It concentrates on the ability to work with a wide variety of people and the development of interpersonal skills. Having discovered that up to 90 per cent of a senior manager's time is spent communicating verbally, mainly at management meetings and in negotiations, the course tries to identify which behavioural patterns are most effective on such crucial face-to-face occasions.

A cost-cutting exercise between 1978 and 1983 saw the UK work force drop by 39 per cent, but the employee/sales ratio soared. Selling out in strife-torn South Africa just in time gave Glynwed cash to manoeuvre and look for small acquisitions.

Gareth Davies, a personnel manager, said: 'Rather than buying companies in complete isolation the aim has been to link the lowest-cost manufacturer in a particular sector with the best distributor.'

Glynwed is investing heavily in the plastics market, particularly high-pressure systems, and expanding in the United States. The future looks good.

HALIFAX BUILDING SOCIETY

The Halifax is the second largest building society in the UK. In 1987 the society reported assets of £33 billion with a gross profit of £350 million. Based in Halifax, West Yorkshire, the society has 745 branches around the UK.

pay ⬒		ambience ⬒	
benefits ⬒		environment ⬒	
promotion ⬒		equal opportunities ⬒	
training ⬒		communications ⬒	

There is something uniquely British about building societies. No other country has anything like them. They originated as termination societies, where groups of workers banded together to build each other's houses. When everyone had secured a home they folded. Britain's second largest permanent society came into being at the Old Cock Inn in Halifax in 1852.

The society has been a model of Yorkshire shrewdness and conservatism, prudence and thrift ever since. The Halifax conveyed an impression of a stout, robust, even implacable organization. It would not be hard for those who have never been to West Yorkshire to visualize the society housed in an impressive citadel of solid Yorkshire stone. Wrongly, however, since the Halifax's headquarters is only fourteen years old.

Such was the growth of the society by 1913 that it had the largest asset base of any similar organization, with £4 million under its belt. The Halifax Permanent Benefit Society, as it was then called, merged with the Halifax Equitable in 1928. In 1951 the Halifax commanded 100 branches, 200 in 1969, 300 in 1975 and 745 at the beginning of 1988.

As reflects the innate conservatism of its home county, the Halifax was less willing to follow the gimmickry in which some of its competitors indulged. Until ten years ago the society had only mortgage accounts and savings accounts – both at different rates of interest. Its approach to computerization was characteristic. The Halifax was in no hurry and it waited for everyone else effectively to run trials on its behalf. Then it jumped from the ledger to the sophisticated mainframe in one bound. Equally, the Halifax was slow to make the leap to complicated financial marketing. But when it did, it was a powerful move. The society embraced the Building Societies Act 1986 with tender enthusiasm. Yet, despite its unadventurous approach, the Halifax commands 20 per cent of the entire market – or one in six of the UK population.

Nevertheless, to assess the Halifax on its past record would be a mistake. The range of services which the Halifax now offers is much wider than at any stage in its past. It has moved into wholesale funding, raising £3 billion, and into estate agency with 343 offices. Two subsidiaries – Halifax Homes and Halifax Urban Renewal – have been created to support and develop housing standards in the UK. Its automatic telling-machine card, Cardcash, may possibly be augmented by a credit card, according to general manager David Gilchrist.

The society employs 14,000 people – one-tenth in head office, and the rest in branches anywhere between Inverness and Penzance. It now sees itself as a forward-looking institution, with some justification. Its commitment to high technology is impressive. But, as Gilchrist says, the Halifax also aims to be advanced in its human relations policy.

The society's recruitment policy is designed to find the right people who can be moulded into technicians to serve the Halifax's customers. This usually means someone who is intelligent, friendly, enthusiastic and sociable. Once such suitable people have been found, the Halifax trains and develops them. So successful is the recruitment record that 80 per cent of the managers are drawn from within.

Peter Hutchison, a manager in mortgage administration, is a typical example. He started in head office in 1968 and worked his way up through the ranks, becoming an assistant manager aged twenty-nine in 1981. In 1985 he was promoted to branch manager before moving on to head office.

Graduates appear to find the Halifax particularly appealing, with more than 5000 applicants competing for 20 places, and they obviously like the work. More than 80 per cent of recruits stay with the society, climbing up the ladder in the organization.

Gilchrist says, 'We aim to give people the right skills to attain rapid promotion.' Part of the approach is team-building. Among the courses are subjects such as dealing with people, selling, managing for results, efficiency and team-training. Facilities for training are very impressive.

Training is linked to the appraisal scheme. This gives an accurate assessment of individual strengths and weaknesses, and is also linked with the management development programme. All managers have targets which they must meet, and their achievement is measured against specified objectives. Mike Payne, a personnel manager, argues that while this system is commonly used, at the Halifax it is more effective than most.

Halifax people show a definite direction and sense of purpose. They find their work stimulating and demanding. Especially the men. As yet women have still to make significant steps towards management. Only 40 women have achieved branch managerial status, a majority of them actually working in branches, and the rest at head office. But, when you consider that the Halifax operates 745 branches, it is not very many.

Nevertheless, the society can look forward to a bright future. With an extremely solid asset base, and an alert approach to the market, the Halifax stands at the forefront of its industry.

HALLMARK CARDS

The world's largest manufacturer of greetings cards, Hallmark is based in Kansas City, USA. It European subsidiary is run from Henley-on-Thames, Berkshire, and comprises a number of businesses in the UK and on the continent. The European division employs 2300 people. Worldwide sales for Hallmark are now around $2 billion.

pay ☐	ambience ☐
benefits ☐	environment ☐
promotion ☐	equal opportunities ☐
training ☐	communications ☐

Many companies with multinational management teams strive to be family-style enterprises. They realize the benefits of creating a warm, mutually-caring atmosphere where everyone feels part of a community. They know that when everyone feels that they are working for the same goals as the next person, profitability can only benefit as a result. Some companies try to manufacture an atmosphere of commonality where none such exists. Hallmark did not need to try – it was there spontaneously from the start.

This greetings card company opened in England in the late 1950s. The early years were characterized by a distinctly American approach to the British market and progress was slow. In 1969 the US owners were persuaded that they needed to take notice of the 'peculiarities' of local demands. Since then the story has largely been an unalloyed success. At the top of the European enterprise sits Keith Wheal, a major figure in the greetings card industry. He explains that Hallmark has grown through a process of acquisition. Two major indigenous UK competitors – Sharpe (Classic) and Valentines of Dundee – were purchased in 1980 and 1984 respectively. Photo Production, of Chatham, has also been added.

The European company has businesses in France and Germany, and representatives in several other continental countries. These 2200 people employed by Hallmark in the UK are spread largely between Hallmark UK, Valentines and Sharpes. The company is the acknowledged leader in the greetings card market, accounting for up to 50 per cent of cards sold to retailers.

Wheal says that the greetings card market grows by an annual 1 to 2 per cent. 'In 1987 we grew by 14 per cent,' he says with a warm sense of satisfaction. Hallmark's performance is undeniable. Not only is it market leader but it has also achieved a reputation for quality. Wheal says that the pursuit of excellence is one of the company's primary goals. It is precisely this which wins Hallmark an ever-growing share of the market.

The fundamental values of Hallmark are those of its founder, Joyce Clyde Hall, who established the first major greetings card company in Kansas City in 1910. There is a high ethical stance in dealing with customers, suppliers and staff alike. Hallmarkers shy away from any description of themselves as aggressive operators in the market. But true to the prescription of J. C. Hall, his commercial successors are skilful at locating and exploiting a market for their greetings cards.

Nonetheless, callers at Hallmark's delightful HQ building close to Henley-on-Thames railway station are struck by a gentle friendliness and a degree of earnest determination. Hallmark is a warm but low-key place. People work hard but they enjoy their work. Whether they are card designers, salesmen, retail planners or accountants, they enjoy equal opportunities. Hallmark is one of the few companies in the UK where women genuinely can get on without having to try much harder.

Pat Gardiner, whose job is rather like that of a company secretary, says that she has never been hindered in her career. 'I feel a strong sense of loyalty to Hallmark. I am proud to work here. It is like a family,' she says. When she left to have a baby, Hallmark kept a job open for her. It is typical of the company that senior management are willing to acknowledge that its people have a home life as well as the pressures of work.

People speak warmly about the company's open-door policy. Anyone can approach senior management with personal or business problems and they are listened to with practical compassion.

Hallmark is a fair payer. It is not among industry's leaders but it is certainly comparable with any other company in the greetings card sector. Among its benefits is the rare gift of a day off for employees on their birthday.

There is considerable staff discount on Hallmark group cards, and each Hallmark location has a shop where staff can purchase cards. The company's pension scheme is especially good and is non-contributory. Manager grades get PPP private health insurance. Hallmark sponsors a wide range of sporting activities based on the sports and social club, there is a sumptuous annual dinner dance, which is free for Hallmarkers (with a nominal charge for partners).

David Haenlein, personnel director for Hallmark Europe, outlines how the company lives up to its slogan, 'When you care enough to send the very best'. He says, 'This is our company watchword and people of like mind are those who best develop and thrive while contributing to the organization's continuing success.'

Every support is given to people who want to run with ideas. It is based on an advanced and extremely well thought-out appraisal system. At the recruitment stage Hallmark wants its prospective employees actively to select the company, rather than the company solely selecting them. Considerable effort goes into choosing the correct post for a recruit, and time is spent counselling if an initial posting is not successful.

Since a heavy emphasis is placed on internal recruitment, all posts are advertised within the group. Staff turnover is very low, although some people are wooed away to more lucrative jobs after being trained on Hallmark's excellent sales courses. They are the envy of the industry and the company is justly proud of them. Training overall is good and it underlines how much consideration the company gives to personal development. Haenlein says that Wheal spends a large proportion of his time on personnel-related matters trying to develop new schemes which will contribute to the growth of the staff.

Hallmark is a happy company. Its people are loyal and dedicated. There is little sense of politics or personal chicanery, and, above all, the company radiates an aura of fun.

HTV

The HTV group makes television programmes and provides local television services to Wales and the west of England. In 1987 its sales were £116.6 million, with profits before tax of £11.9 million. The group employs in excess of 1300 people.

pay	☐	ambience	☐
benefits	☐	environment	☐
promotion	☐	equal opportunities	☐
training	☐	communications	☐

The television industry is under pressure. The old Independent Broadcasting Authority structure is creaking at the edges and the present government has said that it wants to put regional service franchises up for sale. The regions described by the IBA were drawn up in the 1950s at the beginning of commercial television and were reflective of contemporary needs. HTV covers two broadly incompatible regions – the West Country and Wales.

'We are really two companies in one,' says a manager. HTV West covers Bristol, Bath and Avon and makes large-scale international drama productions, while HTV Wales is a national service for the principality. It supplies nine hours a week to S4C, the Welsh-language fourth channel, and it is probably the only institution in Wales which tries to promote every aspect of Welsh culture. 'We make the money and the Welsh spend it,' says one manager in Bristol. But the comment is made with good humour – and characteristically so, because while HTV may be enthusiastic, committed, idealistic, it is neither bitter nor back-stabbing.

HTV came on the air in 1968 as successor to Television Wales and West, the original contractor. It absorbed most of the technical and some of the creative staff. 'It was a change of direction and most of the staff took to it like ducks to water. The IBA, which was responsible for appointing the contractor, liked what HTV wanted to do. It was the right direction for the time,' says Derek Clark, controller Bristol.

Patrick Dromgoole, HTV's MD, remembers the early days. 'I arrived two years after HTV had taken over from TWW. We were deeply unpopular with the audience. The public don't like change. The old

141

company, which had lost its licence, was rather liked. I think it was a conservative act. I don't think it was a deep personal identification with their programming or philosophy. We had to get over that. We had to build an attractive persona. We also had to get our staff on our side as a new management.

'The main way I thought of doing that was to get them involved in exciting programming as well as in the regional service. We started drama only for the region. It allowed me to get to know people within the building. And then we started to win prizes.'

The company started spending money on its drama productions because it realized that there was a global market. In recent years everything is pre-sold – the company has someone who is contracted to buy the programme after it has been made.

'We have been able to provide the total job satisfaction of working on major international product, while still being able to live in the region. Then people also work on regional output. So one day they could be on a major drama and the next on the farming programme,' says Ron Evans, director of programmes.

It is the stimulation of the job which is primarily enticing people to work at HTV, if you are a film cameraman on a major international feature, or an editor on a Welsh-language programme for S4C.

The company is very good for women. It has actively sought to employ women in every area, with some degree of success. One-third of the HTV population is female. There are two producers and two programme directors. HTV is running self-awareness courses for its women, and women's groups have been started in Bristol and Cardiff.

A 'well-being' screening aimed at the female members of the work force was launched in 1986. Another one, looking for signs of heart disease in men, is in the pipeline.

Pay is high for the area and there is a Christmas bonus which reflects years of service. HTV also has an excellent contributory pension scheme.

Service to the Welsh community is a major ethic of HTV Wales. It sponsors concerts and readings. It is active in every aspect of the language and the society. Hugh Davies, press officer for HTV Wales, says that the language is integral to the culture of the society. Some 200 HTV staff are engaged every week in providing nine hours of programmes for S4C.

These programmes are now coming up for auction, since the people who run the Welsh fourth channel want to give independent operators the chance to bid for the allocation. HTV is arguing that, while the independents could produce programmes more cheaply, they would not have the quality. Equally, and, as the HTV men would say, probably a graver sin for the language, is the fact that most of the independents are based in Welsh-speaking enclaves in northwest Wales. In contrast, HTV is in the capital and exposing the people of industrial South Wales to the language. In addition, according to Davies, more people speak Welsh in the Glamorgans than in Gwynedd.

The future of the Welsh-language programmes is hotly disputed in Wales and if they are withdrawn from HTV then the soul of the Welsh company will be injured.

'The news programme in English is our backbone,' says Davies. Both in Bristol and Cardiff the news programmes are informally presented. There is a familiarity with the viewer which does not exist in local BBC bulletins.

Ted George, director of engineering at Cardiff, says that more pressure will be brought to bear on the company when the government forces it to accept a higher input of independent production. 'We probably have about three years to get up to 25 per cent, and five years up to 40 per cent. We have had due warning to get ourselves up to a new way of thinking, a new way of working. There is no reason why we cannot make the transition reasonably efficiently. I am not saying that it will not be unpleasant. If, as part of that transition, we have to reduce our programme-making capacity, then people will have to go.

'In this industry which has done nothing but grow we are good at recruiting people. We are not very good at letting them go. We don't know how to handle that. There are several pressures on us. If we lose the S4C contract, that will have a direct and immediate impact on staff in Cardiff. It could easily lose us 10 per cent of our staff. On top of that is the use of independents for our own ITV production. That could be another 5 or 10 per cent. I suppose in the worst case we lose up to 30 per cent of our staff.' This nightmare scenario is one which exercises minds at HTV.

The prospect of such widespread redundancy would be horrifying to this company. What comes across principally about HTV people is how pleasant they are. They get paid well and they enjoy reasonable, but not spectacular, benefits. It is an exceptionally good company for women. But the atmosphere shows all the signs of an enthusiasm for the job which is akin to a vocation.

HEWLETT-PACKARD

Hewlett-Packard is the wholly-owned UK subsidiary of the Hewlett-Packard Company of Palo Alto, USA. It designs and manufactures computers, computer systems, test instrumentation and measurement systems, electronic components, medical electronic equipment and instruments for chemical analysis. The company opened its first UK operation in Bedford in 1961 and now has twenty locations in the UK. Its turnover in 1986 was £357 million. Hewlett-Packard employs 3500 people, and the headquarters are at Pinewood, Wokingham.

pay	☐	ambience	☐
benefits	☐	environment	☐
promotion	☐	equal opportunities	☐
training	☐	communications	☐

When the computer industry experienced its downturn in the middle 1980s, Hewlett-Packard was hit in common with most others. Sales fell by 30 per cent and the company had to think carefully about its business strategy. Salaries were cut by 5 per cent for a few months until the nervous twitch in the income graph subsided and the upward pattern resumed, but to ensure that hardship was kept to a minimum the 5 per cent Christmas bonus was redistributed in monthly payments. The inherent loyalty of the work force showed itself too. One employee even volunteered to give up his company car to save money. Flexibility is a keyword at H-P.

H-P people tend not to move on. In the main they enjoy their jobs and have an excellent pay and benefits package. As you move through the long, low buildings, typical of the Hewlett-Packard style of construction, you meet people who have worked with the company since its early days when growth was less rapid. It's not unusual to talk to people who have worked for the company for ten, fifteen, twenty or more years.

Pinewood is the new headquarters of H-P in the UK. It was purpose-built on the site of an old isolation hospital along Nine Mile Ride on the Berkshire Downs. The atmosphere is redolent of a university campus rather than of an active industrial plant. Inside, the informality of the place is striking. Mike Delany, who runs the top-notch Shell account, says, 'This is a little piece of the West Coast of America lifted up and transplanted into the Berkshire countryside.' But the genuine friendliness and camaraderie conceal a high level of energy. 'There are a lot of workaholics here. H-P gives talented technicians the chance to play with the best equipment available. The door is open twenty-four hours a day so you will find people here at the weekends and late at night.'

True to the American ethic, they work hard and many of them play together. The company likes to give parties or beer-busts when a notable order is chalked up, and it encourages staff to have coffee-break meetings where the all-pervading family atmosphere is developed. The grounds of Pinewood are studded with picnic tables where staff take their lunch or run barbecues. The subsidized canteen offers a presentable full-course dinner for £2, and the free coffee machines dispense real coffee. Each weekday everyone gets free biscuits, fruit or sticky buns – a tradition which goes back to the early days in California.

When the cutbacks came no one was made redundant, but one thing to go was the free food, which saved £250,000 a year from the expenses bill. Training courses were more severely regulated and trips abroad were tested for real relevance to work. Now that sales, and profits, are back on target, privileges have been restored.

H-P is specific about the type of individual it recruits. Peter Ward, who controls personnel, knows exactly who he is looking for to fit the company persona. It amounts to open-minded, articulate individuals who cope well with change. They must be the sort of people who can run with an idea but are team-orientated rather than egotistic. The attrition rate is extremely low. People are pleased to be able to work at South Queensferry, near Edinburgh, where the company employs more than 1000 people.

'You get a feel for the right person,' Ward explains. He is a great advocate, not only of H-P, but also of other non-British enterprises in the UK, whose positive, expansive approach he admires. He applauds their commitment to their business and to their people as a prerequisite for operating.

The founders of the company, William Hewlett and David Packard, wanted their people to have the best facilities, the most up-to-date equipment and the best pay and benefits. They were also great believers in R&D, and shortly after opening in 1961 the UK company had its own R&D section. Two years ago the Bristol plant opened on a plum site next to Bristol University. Managing director David Baldwin

145

fought hard to win approval from California headquarters to base the new multimillion-pound R&D facility in the UK. The division, which is working on the most advanced form of artificial intelligence, has already created links with academics next door. H-P use the university's social facilities, while students are allowed into the company's labs to conduct their research with the very latest equipment.

H-P is also big on employee communications. In 1975 a management meeting was held and a list of concepts central to the way the company should work was developed as follows.

The H-P Way

- Belief in people; freedom
- Respect and dignity; individual self-esteem
- Recognition; sense of achievement; participation
- Security; permanence; development of people
- Insurance; personal worry protection
- Share benefits and responsibility; help each other

- Management by objectives (rather than by directive); decentralization
- Informality; first names; open communication
- A chance to learn by making mistakes
- Training and education; counselling
- Performance and enthusiasm

Employees translate the H-P Way, a kind of corporate code, into their day-to-day work, and it reinforces founders Hewlett and Packard's original belief in their people. It underlines sharing responsibilities and rewards.

Mike Matthews, an Anglo-American who once worked directly for Hewlett and Packard, believes that H-P has taken the best of the American and British approaches. 'There is very much a "can-do" attitude here,' he says. 'When I first worked for H-P in Britain, I noticed among some of our British recruits an attitude of "It may not have been done before so we may not be able to do it". This was mainly in sales. But now I think we have helped British business generally to see how things can be achieved.'

The company gives everyone a profit share which is substantially higher than shareholder payments. H-P has initiated a stock purchase plan giving each employee the chance to buy company shares at 75 per cent of their market price. A company long-term disability scheme, BUPA membership, a lucky dip for holidays in company cottages,

146

open-plan work areas, 25 days' holiday a year and subsidized meals, all combine to make H-P a more than attractive company to work for.

H-P contributes generously to charity. Together with personal donations made by its founders, H-P is one of the top three benevolent institutions in the world. In addition, around £10,000 is raised every year as a result of H-P employees' efforts, which is donated to some ninety different charities countrywide.

The company operates in small, tight units where the bonding is strong, and in part it has the feel of a small business characterized by committed people who enjoy each other's company.

There is a light-hearted, hard-working and positive atmosphere at H-P, and, although the intimate and warm approach would not suit everyone, there is no shortage of people wanting to join this unique and prosperous company.

HORSELL GRAPHIC INDUSTRIES

Horsell is a subsidiary of the Cookson Group. It is a specialist supplier to the printing industry. Horsell employs 800 people, 550 of whom are in the UK. Based at Morley, near Leeds, the company's turnover is £66 million with profits of £7 million.

pay ☐	ambience ☐
benefits ☐	environment ☐
promotion ☐	equal opportunities ☐
training ☐	communications ☐

'They are a very good employer. Working relationships are excellent and the management is extremely approachable. There has been plenty of investment in new jobs and they pay good rates. I would say that most of the staff are very happy here.' Not a member of management talking, but Philip Mantle, a plate preparer, who, until recently, was father of the National Graphical Association chapel at Horsell Graphic Industries. His remarks are all the more surprising because in the last ten years, as the British printing industry has undergone radical and often painful changes, the NGA has frequently been in the news for its turbulent relationships with management. At Horsell, however, there has been an astonishing lack of disruption – only one day lost in over ten years – and this must in part be attributed to the management's forward-looking yet friendly style, and the willingness of both management and the work force to encompass change.

Horsell Graphic Industries is part of Cookson Group plc, one of the UK's 100 largest industrial companies. Through a disparate range of activities, Cookson specializes in the preparation of raw materials, from chemicals to metals, for industry. Their strategy has been to move out of more mature industries and into sectors where significant growth could be predicted. Graphics was a case in point, and in 1985 the group acquired Horsell, a privately-owned specialist supplier to the printing industry.

Horsell Graphic Industries has a history reaching back more than a hundred years, but, far from giving the present management a traditionalist outlook, it has encouraged managing director Mike

Green and his team to adopt a pragmatic and progressive approach. Hence the company's business is now in the preparation of printing plates for the offset litho process (rapidly replacing more traditional printing processes throughout the UK and abroad), chemicals and solvents, and, on a larger scale, plate-preparation machinery.

Despite its relatively small size, Horsell's turnover and profits have been increasing rapidly. In 1978 turnover was just £4 million; budgeted turnover for the present financial year is £66 million, with profits of about £7 million. These growth rates are expected to be maintained well into the 1990s. Sandy McDowell, human resources manager, is responsible for ensuring that the right kind of people are recruited to achieve these targets.

'We are already very well known within the industry as a good employer – our industrial relations record, for example, speaks for itself. However, Horsell has always been conscious that to attract the right kind of staff we have to offer the right kind of incentives – and that doesn't just mean money, of course.' On the other hand, McDowell is keen to emphasize that, in terms of salaries, Horsell are definitely towards the top of the range, not just locally, but for the print industry in general throughout the UK. 'In addition, we offer a performance-related incentive scheme for management, together with a similar bonus scheme for our other staff. Our pension scheme is pretty good, and it will eventually be amalgamated into the corporate Cookson scheme, which should bring additional benefits to some staff.'

Apart from offering relatively attractive remuneration packages, Horsell also pays a great deal of attention to training its staff. A visit to headquarters demonstrates that almost every employee has been put through a tailored programme to enable him (or, more rarely, her) to advance within the firm, rather than having to seek additional responsibility or promotion elsewhere. Ian Harrison, who joined three years ago from the army and is now a charge hand, is a good example. 'Horsell really recognized my potential, rather than just looking at me as I was then. I have been retrained, promoted and made aware that there is a long-term future for me here. Now I come in every day to face new challenges and problems, and I hope that continues.'

Awareness of the company's commitment to developing its people pervades every level and every sector within the firm. While Cookson, the parent company, has only recently embarked on an ambitious management development programme, designed to identify and train the top managers of the future, Horsell has – almost subconsciously – been doing this for years as a matter of course. This, rather than the

149

salaries and benefits offered to employees, keeps staff turnover throughout the country to less than 5 per cent a year. Even in departments such as sales and marketing which, throughout industry as a whole, are more vulnerable, turnover is appreciably low.

Apart from day-to-day management, there is a fairly structured relationship between Horsell and Cookson. The managing director Mike Green and his team present financial reports once or twice a month, and submit annual budgets and three-year plans. 'We formulate the budgets and plans here with no reference to the group, and present them for approval – and so far, they have always been approved.'

Green is not the only one to describe the relationship with Cookson as similar to that between a bank and a profitable client. 'I do tend to think of myself as a Horsell employee and for much of the work force the only change they noticed when Cookson acquired us was that we were investing more in the business. So I suppose we do tend to think of them rather like a bank, although they would undoubtedly interfere more if we were not getting the results.'

Like any employer, however, Horsell does not have a spotless record. The print industry is changing, and the company acknowledges this, but there is still a lack of women in management positions, with sales and marketing being the only division making a serious attempt to rectify the male-dominated profile.

Another area of concern for some Horsell employees is the occasional lack of communication about the changes taking place in the company. The entry of Cookson on the scene made little impact on the running of the company, but some workers still feel that the change of ownership was not sufficiently well explained, and that a more formalized internal communications structure would allow the work force to voice their concerns in a more open manner than at present.

IBM

International Business Machines is by far the world's largest computer manufacturer. It dwarfs all the other computer makers. Based in New York state, its influence is felt worldwide. The UK operation, whose headquarters are in Portsmouth, employs 18,000 people at various sites across the country.

pay	☐	ambience	☐
benefits	☐	environment	☐
promotion	☐	equal opportunities	☐
training	☐	communications	☐

When we asked if we could visit IBM as part of our research, the company was cautious. We explained that both the American and Canadian editions of the *100 Best Companies To Work For* had featured IBM in glowing terms. Their reaction was to say that if these books had perceived IBM to be a good employer, we had all the material we needed to write up the UK version. IBM, they said, was essentially the same company anywhere around the world.

There was a great deal of truth in this. IBM – or Big Blue as it is also known – has a personality moulded in cast iron which is apparent wherever the New York corporation positions its factories. It would not be afraid – IBM is never afraid – to admit that it assumes its mantle of market leader with ease, pride, some arrogance, determination and shrewd analysis. After all, IBM is a dominant market leader in the computer and office systems market. In comparison its nearest competitors – however good as companies – are referred to derisively as the seven dwarves. IBM is a multinational in the truest sense of the word – governments listen when it speaks, countries roll out the red carpet when its development people come calling.

The company was started by Thomas J. Watson. He wanted a place where individuals could take a pride in their work and identify their interests with IBM's. He invented what the Japanese later came to call quality circles – but he did it in the 1930s. He was ahead of his time in many ways. [Supervisors were replaced by managers and made to feel that they had a place in the organization.] He contrived to end the clear demarcation between white-collar and blue-collar staff. The

151

company was also ahead of the field in introducing salaries for everyone instead of hourly payments.

The three guiding principles of IBM established years ago were: respect for the individual, high-quality customer service and excellence in everything that the company does. Central to these beliefs was a commitment that no one should ever be laid off. This remains true today and the company will move heaven and earth to prevent anyone from being made redundant.

At headquarters in Portsmouth the five guiding principles of IBM are set out on presentation boards, which constantly remind staff of what the company stands for and what it expects of them. It is a homogeneous environment. It is the prime example of a company where people congregate as a community – many eat, sleep, breathe IBM.

As one would suspect, IBM is a single-status organization and generous with its benefits package. Holidays rise to 25 days, there are eight public holidays and five IBM days, which are an added bonus. Heavy emphasis is given to the open-door policy, which means that you can appeal to the highest levels within the company if you believe you have been improperly treated.

There is a housing assistance plan to help people buy their own property, various pension plans, fair sickness benefit plans, universal BUPA, travel accident insurance plan, IBM group life assurance, a discounted household insurance plan, a share purchase plan for stock in the parent company in America, a savings plan, various corporate awards, a tuition support plan, and discount purchase plan. The company also encourages the growth of IBM clubs wherever the company may establish itself.

The company is looking for people who will put down roots with the organization, move from department to department – perhaps even overseas – and progress within IBM. The aim seems to be to create a wholesome, positive and enriching environment supplemented by excellent pay and benefits, so that staff will not want to venture to competitors. The organization suits many people admirably – notably the bulk of the 18,000 who work for IBM in the UK. It combines the virtues of a highly specific culture, supportive organization and one where the individual can rise. IBM wants its people to have the best in the work environment as well as personally. Training is very good, if perhaps reflective of the specific nature of the organization.

Watson always showed considerable concern for the education of his people, and the diversity of courses available to IBM illustrates a continuing company commitment. IBM also pays for individuals to pursue particular study interests.

The company is highly concerned about secrecy. It is dubious about anyone who is not a lifelong friend or an IBM staffer. It is not keen on the media and spends large sums of money on protecting its research from competitors. IBM people tend to socialize with other IBM employees in IBM clubs. They even marry IBM people.

There is a powerful drive towards communicating business goals internally and there is a wealth of publications which seek to inform.

Some people who work for IBM now, or who have worked for the company in the past, say that it suffers from some of the big organization blues. Bureaucracy can be a factor which stifles initiative, individuals can get lost along the way, and there is a feeling that sales run the organization. In fairness to Big Blue, it does attempt to redress these problems and deals with them by confronting them as issues.

In 1987 the company recruited 90 graduates from a wide variety of disciplines such as business, law and economics, but another 59 were pure arts subjects. In one year recently IBM failed to recruit any graduates at all. For that it was badly criticized in the personnel sector. Recruitment professionals say that eventually the company will lose one entire tier of management. In typical fashion the company shrugs off the suggestion.

IBM is not everyone's cup of tea, but it is a winner. The sort of ambitious people whom the company tends to attract like to work for an organization who is on the top of the pile. On its present form, IBM needs have no worries about attracting them in the future.

ICELAND

Iceland plc is the head of a UK chain of retail frozen food outlets. In 1986 its sales were £116.4 million and its pre-tax profit £5.1 million. It employs 2700 people in over 160 outlets, and in its main office complex on Deeside Industrial Park.

pay	☐	ambience	☐
benefits	☐	environment	☐
promotion	☐	equal opportunities	☐
training	☐	communications	☐

Iceland Frozen Foods was founded in 1970 with only £60. Today, Iceland, fully listed and with more than 160 shops nationwide, claims to be worth nearly as much as its geographical namesake. The company was the product of two hard-nosed and energetic business-men. Neither Malcolm Walker nor Peter Hinchcliffe had any financial training, but with vision and, above all, the simplicity of their approach, they have created an enterprise which is lively, vibrant and demands a perennial loyalty from its staff.

It is this capacity to inspire startling dedication from its people which has been a mainstay of their dynamic success. In its first nine years, the company made its living selling loose frozen foods, but at the end of the 1970s opened its own coldstore. They moved into the freezer-centre market and the Iceland of today was born.

Walker describes the company culture as the foundation stone. A unique style of management, financial controls, a dedication to excellence and an attention to detail are common to all their concerns. Walker explains that 'Noddy Systems' were developed – so simple that even Noddy could understand them. A direct approach is also a mainline contributor to style. The company stamp carries not a traditional For Immediate Consideration but the exhortative Do It Now.

'We are not a company of Rolls-Royces, flagpoles and foundations,' says Walker. Though the car park at Iceland's long, low, redbrick headquarters at Deeside is packed with Rolls and Porsches. The head office is a smart but not ostentatious building. There is a sense of purpose and teamwork about the place, and a buzz that something exciting is happening or about to happen.

All office doors are left open. Everyone is on first-name terms and staff are encouraged to approach senior managers with well-thought-out ideas. No patience exists for timewasters, and the pair's success has not been without its ruthless edge. Janet Weinstein, personnel director, says that morale is very high, and explains that Iceland staff are expected to offer total commitment. This often means working exceptionally hard and for long hours, but the staff seem to carry this off with a degree of cheerfulness and zeal.

Weinstein says that the directors encourage the staff to come to them with any substantial grumbles. Staffers do telephone senior management with their gripes and there is a real willingness to settle problems in a fair and amicable way. One employee complained about the company's policy of not paying overtime, even though they are given time off in lieu.

Much of the apparent enthusiasm can be explained by the youth of the company. The average age of staff is twenty-six. Relatively young people are in positions of authority, and reach dizzy heights in the company at an early age.

As the company continues its headlong expansion, the opportunities for promotion are substantial. There are many instances of people who have been taken on at lowly positions and have subsequently worked their way up the organization very quickly. District managers, who are expected to know each of the employees in their area by name, have a continual brief to look out for young people with talent who can be promoted.

As Iceland is such a young and committed company, great care is taken with recruitment at senior levels. Applicants for the top jobs are put through a gruelling schedule of assessments which includes psychometric testing. To date only one recruit to the top level has failed to make the grade.

The simple, so-called Cut-the-Crap approach is further manifested in everyday work. Weinstein comments: 'Nobody is on a pedestal. We're all here to do a job.' Managers in the shops remove their jackets and muck in when a delivery comes in. At head office everyone is free to poke their noses into everyone else's business.

Steve Blanchard, a warehouse manager, said, 'It is very unpolitical here. People are honest and open-speaking. It is easy to put ideas into effect.'

This pragmatic style is extended to the layout of the shops. The initial 'blue' design was functional, and encouraged the shifting of maximum volume in a relatively pleasant environment. The more recent 'red' design, apparent in the company's acquisitions, reflects

155

the move of the enterprise up-market. Eventually all the shops will share a common design. Each store uses only a handful of staff. You would be lucky to find more than eight people in each of the outlets, including the manager. The nature of the operations means that staff costs are tiny in comparison with Sainsbury and Tesco shops, and turnover is negligible compared with elsewhere in the retail sector.

Communications are a high priority. In this area the videocassette is used as the basis for disseminating information to staff. 'Iceland TV' is a weekly transmitted programme which is watched by all staff. There is also a company newspaper, and the company runs team briefings on a traditional Industrial Society model. News makes it from the boardroom to the shop floor in less than two days. It can be sooner if the lorry drivers' network is working at full speed.

The benefits package is relatively good for the retail sector – which has been known to be bad although some of the major retailers are paving the way towards improvement. Holidays amount to four weeks, increasing to five weeks; all managers get BUPA; everyone is entitled to free life insurance, and to a 10 per cent discount on Iceland goods.

Pay is average for the industry, and is not a source of grievance for the staff. It is the quality, drive and the success of the enterprise which keeps people working for the company. Iceland promotes a concept called zero-defect, which means getting everything right first time. People are proud to be working for Iceland since they consider it to be a dedicated and highly profitable company.

The grading structure in the stores operates on three tiers – manager, supervisor and full- or part-time staff. It is a six-day working week, which the company says discriminates against women rising particularly far in the management of the stores. Women can succeed but they need to be able to demonstrate perhaps slightly more energy and dedication than men. In head office there are more opportunities, but Iceland is not a company which women should look to as providing an easy ride to the top.

The organization is ruthless in weeding out people who are going to slow the pace of its development. In 1987 five people were made redundant, but that was the first time that such a sweeping move had been made. It caused some disquiet among staff, but Weinstein says that if the company is going to grow at such a strong pace then it cannot afford to carry dead wood.

Despite this, everyone who spoke to us during the course of our research found the work both fulfilling and satisfying, and a sense of humour prevails at Iceland which is a powerful bonding factor.

156

Iceland is growing at a rapid pace each year. In 1982 the company snatched the St Catherine's chain of foodstores from under the noses of the Bejam group. These 18 stores in the southwest were losing money but the Iceland directors saved the St Catherine's group in a few months, and added to their own prestige while doing so. Their aggressive approach to development means that they will be opening stores to complete their network around the country. Scotland is, as yet, barely tapped, so the company still has some way to go.

Walker and Hinchcliffe have established a potent force in the retail business. Their staff are 100 per cent behind them. With a combination of incisive, forthright and ambitious leadership, the Iceland directors have created exciting opportunities for a work force with the energy to keep pace with them.

ICI

ICI is one of Britain's largest companies. It is engaged in many industrial activities centring on its pre-eminence in the chemicals sector. Turnover in 1987 was £11.1 billion with pre-tax profits of £1.3 billion. The group employs 127,800 people, more than half of whom are based outside the UK.

pay ☐		ambience ☐	
benefits ☐		environment ☐	
promotion ☐		equal opportunities ☐	
training ☐		communications ☐	

'ICI has a love of scientific excellence. We make the best and others recognize that, but we don't assume we're going to win. We go out and look at what is wanted.' So says Anne Ferguson, corporate marketing and publicity manager. It is the sort of thing you might expect a PR person to say, but what makes it different is that it is true.

Since Imperial Chemical Industries was created in 1926 it has been spurred on by a love of innovation and inquiry. In its early days the company operated five divisions – alkali products, metals, explosives, dyestuffs and general chemicals. Its corporate title then indicated that it aimed to find markets anywhere within the British Empire. From its inception the company was one of the largest in the UK, and it grew steadily through the age of plastics to the status of world pathfinders in the 1960s. ICI is now divided into many businesses. Among them are: Agrochemicals, Fibres, Electronics, and Chemicals and Polymers.

ICI has always been a forward-looking employer. It was one of the first companies to consult its staff and to promote a real sense of cooperation between management and employees. A share option scheme was introduced in the 1920s and ICI launched a magazine which reflected staff views.

The ICI message has always been clearly spelled out: most people know what ICI is and broadly what business it is in, and even its competitors acknowledge ICI's superiority at image-building. The way it conducts itself, its style, its performance and its direction are seductive. Undergraduates regard ICI as the company which most of them would like to work for.

The company encountered its rough patch after the second oil crisis at the turn of the last decade, but it is now aiming itself with characteristic enthusiasm for the 1990s. 'We are extending the range of our manufacture, looking to move more outside the UK and looking at the market to see what the end users want,' says Adrian Auer of ICI's finance department. 'We have faced the problems of the early 1980s and have done very well. The eye won't come off the UK but we are looking at Japan and the US.' Following the purchase by ICI Paints of Glidden Paint Company in the US, the group's intention is to look more aggressively for acquisitions there.

The positioning in the market has changed in the last few years. 'We are much more customer focused – ICI is very strong on presenting its image,' says Auer. The centrepiece of this movement was the upgrading of the famous roundel which symbolizes ICI the world over, and this also served to signify a more purposeful company. A booklet has been issued to all staff reinforcing the message that ICI is a world-class company. At the same time television advertising was booked to build a greater international awareness programme.

ICI manufactures in 40 countries and sells in 150. Among its products are beta-blocker pills, taken by 12 million people, ski jackets (50 per cent of all those bought are made with ICI fibres), dyes which are used in one-quarter of all jeans, and stockings – a third of all women in Europe wear ICI fibres. ICI is also the biggest paint-maker in the world.

The group employs 55,000 people in the UK. John Simpson, graduate recruitment manager, says, 'We are professional, not cut-throat; efficient, but we don't ask for the last drop of blood.' He says that staff turnover is not a problem which affects the company. Graduates will come for the ICI name and its training and some will leave after two to four years. After that they generally stay for good.

Graduate entrants come in at £9600. A Ph.D. would entitle you to £12,700 to £13,770 outside London. Senior staff earn £30,000 or above. Bruce Davis, a senior project engineer at ICI Agrochemicals, says, 'Overall the salaries are good. Perhaps not so good for the southeast but getting better.' He has been with the company for fourteen years and notices the change in direction. 'The company has become much more entrepreneurial while trying to update its image,' he remarks. He says that prospects are good within the company but that there is heavy reliance on the individual. 'As long as you are seen to contribute and act as part of a team you will be noticed. It's put on the individual's doorstep.'

Sue Howe, a secretary in head office, feels that the company has changed dramatically in the last five years. 'We were overmanned, now it's sleeker.' Maureen Maclean, an administration officer, was encouraged by management to take legal courses and now works in the legal department. 'If you are interested to move up the ladder and will take the time out to study, you will make progress – there's real encouragement to go on training.'

John Edgar, a senior PR officer says, 'Twenty years ago it was a household name – the people were more Civil Service. But despite the change the company is still very relaxed. Management maintain good relationships with staff. There's approachability. They are paternalistic in a good way,' he says.

ICI is one of the great companies of the UK. It is viewed with pride and respect by those people who work for it. They see themselves as fortunate to be employed by ICI. Yet the atmosphere, while always calm and professional, is lighter-hearted than one might expect in such an august agency. The company offers good pay and excellent benefits, but it attracts people mainly because it *is* ICI.

INVESTORS IN INDUSTRY

3i – Investors In Industry – are venture capitalists: they supply money to industry. Based in Waterloo Road, London, they have offices around the country. In 1987 the 3i group produced a turnover of £194.6 million with pre-tax profits of £66.4 million. It employs 755 people.

pay ☐		ambience ☐	
benefits ☐		environment ☐	
promotion ☐		equal opportunities ☐	
training ☐		communications ☐	

If a small businessman wants to raise capital, he generally has only two points of call. One is obvious – the local High Street bank. The other is the regional office of 3i. Investors In Industry is the largest venture capitalist agency in the country.

Headquarters are in a sombre-looking building opposite a side entrance to Waterloo Station. The reception area is spartan – almost unfriendly – but as you approach the lifts a splash of orange, red and purple in a wall-hanging suddenly reveals that there is more to 3i than meets the eye. It is that sort of company. 3i is full of surprising twists and turns.

The literature, which is plentiful, is innovative, highly colourful and distinctive. 3i is an initiator, an organization which stands at the front of new ideas.

'We are the largest operator in the venture capital market,' says Robin McIntosh, head of personnel. 'Our common thread at 3i is a commitment to the job to provide risk capital, or equity capital, to small and medium-sized businesses to enable them to grow. We are all enthusiastic for our sector. We want to do as much as possible.

'Many business people have given up their jobs to start a new enterprise. They are tremendously brave. Some will succeed and some will fail. We are dealing with their dreams. But we have to strip the reality away from their dreams and ask, "Is this person capable of running this business?"'

3i has 25 offices across the country and five overseas. It has two large bases – London and Solihull. The other bases usually employ no more than 20 people, each of whom is highly motivated and competitive in their marketplaces.

'We try to devolve as much responsibility as possible to the local man,' says McIntosh. 3i wants its local people to be proud of their patch, the businessses they are supporting and the company. 'We take on very few first-degree people,' says McIntosh. 'We prefer people who have done something with their degree. Perhaps they have spent two or three years in industry, become a chartered accountant, or got themselves an MBA.

'At this stage we recruit investment controllers. It is their job to market 3i, to identify investment opportunities, negotiate with client companies, persuade senior people within 3i to accept their ideas, put together final investment schemes, see them through their legal stages and monitor progress subsequently,' he adds.

It's quite a task, but it is no more than some of the jobs 3i people will have held in industry. McIntosh says that the company wants people who have style and personality. 'They should be outward-going people, strongly self-starting, self-reliant. Judgement is another quality we look for. If someone came to us with a good academic background but did not make an initial impact, then I doubt we would take them on. They must be bright, open, enthusiastic, friendly – but not too friendly – and professional.

'We are an organization that expects 100 per cent commitment from our people. Second best, 90 per cent, is not acceptable. Throughout the company, from the top to the bottom, you will find people who display this sort of commitment to the job.'

Nigel Olsen, general manager, says, 'This is an individual's business. The size of the deal does not necessarily make it economic to involve a team and you don't get it done any quicker. It's much more expensive. But you can plug into an accountant, a lawyer, an industry expert, somebody who's done that sort of thing before. The quiet retiring type isn't going to be much use in this sort of business.'

Olsen says that deal-flow is quick, and that if recruits prove themselves they can move up through the organization fairly rapidly. 'They can get some independence and personal authority in the field. I think this is very important.'

Pay is as high as most City institutions but is not topnotch. It is reviewed annually for most employees and twice a year for investment controllers. Young recruits can expect rapid pay rises. Graduates in 1988 came in at £13,000. Soneone who joined in 1986 in Birmingham started at £9000 and got a rise after six months to £12,000. Within the year he was on £15,000. This sort of increase is typical at 3i.

There is a companywide profit share which is paid to everyone, regardless of their position, at a percentage of their salary. For example, in 1987 everyone received 7 per cent of salary. 'With 3i you'll always be paid quite a good salary,' says Joe McGrain, a London director. 'What keeps me here is that 90 per cent of the deals I see done here are better than our competitors.'

Beyond this there is a non-contributory pension scheme, BUPA membership, cars for investment controllers and above, house purchase loans, season ticket loans, discounts on the products of 3i suppliers and customers, personal insurance and membership of City sports clubs.

While women make up almost half of the 3i establishment, you would be lucky to find one near the top. Women are finding greater opportunities within 3i, but at the moment these are solely in marketing and personnel.

Investors In Industry is a positive organization which enjoys widespread respect throughout the financial and industrial community. As the institutions broaden out, 3i is well placed to prosper. 'We are very keen to expand in Europe and in the United States,' says finance general manager Don Clarke. He admits that 3i is losing market share in the UK. Most of its competitors are staffed by people who have been trained at 3i, the so-called University of Venture Capital. However, 3i is by far the largest organization in the market and is actively reviewing salaries to draw in the good people and keep them.

JEWELLERS GUILD

The Jewellers Guild is a wholly-owned subsidiary of BAT Industries. Its turnover in 1988 is scheduled to reach £42 million. The business operates from a head office in Stanmore, Middlesex, and a warehouse in Acton, west London. In summer 1988 the company operated 80 shops, mainly in London and the southeast. It has 800 employees.

pay	▭	ambience	▭
benefits	▭	environment	▭
promotion	▭	equal opportunities	▭
training	▭	communications	▭

At first glance the Jewellers Guild might seem an unlikely candidate for inclusion among the top 100. It is a relatively small operation which was opened at speed by its two principals after persuading BAT, the parent company, to go boldly where it had never gone previously. In short, Jewellers Guild is a one-off.

David Stephens, its managing director, and David Rothschild, sales and marketing director, were two managers at Argos (another BAT subsidiary) who saw an opening in the busy jewellery market. 'Argos had already established jewellery counters in its stores but we wanted to go off alone. BAT wanted the new venture to have a separate identity and so the Jewellers Guild was born,' says Rothschild.

Given the go-ahead in May 1984, the first six shops were opened in September; at breakneck speed by any description, and some mistakes were made. But one of the salient characteristics of this company is its integrity, and the two founders quickly learned to improve the efficiency and direction of their enterprise.

However, the Jewellers Guild's great merit stems from the revolution it has generated in the jewellery business. This trade is notorious for its staff being paid as little as the operators can get away with, and where the owner – not the customer – is always right. Stephens and Rothschild turned traditional values on their heads. First, they made their stores inviting places in which to shop; second, they recognized that to get good staff you need to pay well and offer excellent benefits. Stephens is a personnel professional by training, and always realized

164

that a business runs according to the quality of its staff. 'I had a Saul on the road to Damascus experience after reading Professor Ardeanis. He argued what I now see as common sense. If you treat your staff well they will repay you and the business a thousand times over,' says Rothschild.

Their main competitor is Gerald Ratner, who in the same period acquired H. Samuel, Ernest Jones, Watches of Switzerland and Terry's. Generally, Ratner took his stores somewhat down-market, while Stephens and Rothschild moved theirs a notch upward. In some stores Ratner pays slightly higher than Jewellers Guild, but across the country JG comes out as the better payer, and all staff get a 15 per cent discount on stock.

Caroline Pierce, an assistant manager in the JG Sutton branch, says, 'I worked in the local branch of Ernest Jones for six months before coming here. The atmosphere is entirely different and the pay is much better. I know many people in the jewellery trade who would like to work at Jewellers Guild if they could get the chance.'

Pierce helped open the Epsom branch and was impressed that the atmosphere of the stores was light and friendly. 'We work hard but we enjoy it because there is a sense of unity,' she adds. The shops are spacious. Rothschild says that they were designed to encourage people to feel easy about walking into a jeweller's shop and browsing.

'We strive hard to get the balance right between being helpful but not being pushy. Our staff are trained to ask the customer if they want help but not to turn on the hard sell.' It is this more relaxed mode of customer service which has won the company a lot of business and the appreciation of its staff. Turnover in staff is negligible, unusual for any part of the retail sector.

Andy Smith, manager of the Sutton store, has been with JG since the start. 'I opened the Hounslow shop, moved to Oxford Street, and after a period of sickness was allowed to come back to run Sutton.' What Smith doesn't mention is that during his five months' absence the company kept him on at full pay. It is precisely this kind of gesture which ensures staff loyalty.

Every store gets a visit from at least one of the two principals every three months. They also call in to present spontaneous prizes to stores or individuals who have hit and surpassed their sales targets. A Saturday girl who hits target might be surprised by a bunch of flowers arriving midway through her shift. 'This shows her that we are pleased, but it also demonstrates to the rest of the team that they can win prizes as well,' remarks Rothschild. One woman received a gold-plated hammer for relentlessly beating away at her targets, and managers often win gift vouchers for restaurants or the theatre.

Stores are divided into five divisions according to size. Sales targets are based on size. If a manager consistently makes target, then reaches the target for the next division, the shop is lifted up to the next level, where the manager has a bigger budget and more staff. Go For Gold was a recent promotion where a week's wages was paid to each member of the store which won the league for a period of sixteen weeks. Three main bonus schemes are in operation at any one time, each providing prizes for managers and staff alike.

A career structure was built in at an early stage to give staff, including management trainees, professional targets to aim for. Pierce, who says that she has not been held back in her career because of being a woman, wants to be a manager, and her colleague, Claire Wallis, presently a management trainee, wants to be an assistant manager. 'I worked at Mothercare and the department store Allders. It's totally different here. Everyone is so nice,' says Wallis. She recommends the training, which is personal, largely store-based and especially tailored to maximize sales in a friendly, quality environment.

The company opened 29 shops in 1987 and aims to reach 250 outlets within five years. Currently achieving a 2 per cent market share, JG wants 11 per cent within the same time-frame. Rothschild says that as the enterprise develops he and Stephens will inevitably spend more time visiting stores, but he realizes that another tier of management will need to be introduced between area managers and the principals.

The obvious benefits to the staff come from their pay package, participation in the BAT share scheme and the 15 per cent discount on JG goods, but the potential in job satisfaction is unusually high. Stephens and Rothschild have built a business where people can contribute directly to their own career structure and to the development of the company. They have created an enterprise where the pay is high in a sector which generally treats its employees like cannon fodder. But most of all they have created a sense of pride and ambition for their people which no other jewellery chain has previously achieved.

JOHNSON WAX

Based in Ascot and Frimley Green in Surrey, Johnson Wax is the UK subsidiary of the American cleaning giant S. C. Johnson. It employs 600 people in the British Isles, and turnover in 1987 was £66 million. Profits were £3 million.

pay ☐	ambience ☐	
benefits ☐	environment ☐	
promotion ☐	equal opportunities ☐	
training ☐	communications ☐	

Most of Johnson Wax's cleaning products are known the world over. It manufactures Pledge furniture polish, Sparkle window cleaner and Glade air fresheners. S. C. Johnson is one of the largest privately-owned companies in the world and it is still controlled by the Johnson family, under current chairman Samuel C. Johnson, with a fair degree of paternalism.

Founded in 1886, the Johnson empire now stretches across more than fifty countries and employs more than 12,000 people. Johnson Wax has been the UK outpost since 1914, and is the oldest foreign plant. It has the largest case-volume operation of anywhere outside the States. Yet the UK company employs only 600 people, including those at its European headquarters in Ascot, its research and development centre and UK base at Frimley Green, near Camberley in Surrey. The Frimley site houses the UK manufacturing and distribution side, as well as the sales, marketing, export and administrative facilities.

Dick Posey, who left the UK in 1988 after two years as managing director to take over the Latin American business, describes their relationship with the parent company: 'Although we agree annual targets with our European HQ, which in turn agrees its overall strategy with the USA, we run ourselves autonomously beyond that. The company's overall policy is to be highly responsive to each local market, and to introduce new developments which meet the needs of its consumers. I suppose you could say that while this is probably the most rewarding relationship one could have with a parent company, it does sometimes make it difficult to coordinate operations beyond one territory. On the whole, though, we find that the degree of independence we have makes us far more successful in the long run.'

167

Financially, as far as UK operations are concerned, this strategy has worked very well. Current turnover is about £66 million, profits are £3 million, and growth since 1985 has been healthy. However, this has not always been the case. For years S. C. Johnson operated a worldwide 'no lay-offs' policy, and the UK subsidiary was one of the first to break with this tradition. In 1984 it began to restructure itself and, in management's view, redundancies were inevitable. However, employees agree unanimously that these were necessary to allow the company continued success, and the commitment to staff was such that the changes were fully explained and redundancy terms were extremely generous.

The same was true when Johnson Wax acquired Brillo in 1986. 'We offered all 150 Brillo employees jobs with us here in Frimley Green,' says Dick Posey, 'as well as a valuable redundancy package. We employed out-placement consultants to help those leaving the company to find alternative employment, and I was very pleased that in more than 97 per cent of cases they were successful in relocating the employees. On reflection, maybe we were a little too generous – I lost some very good people who I badly wanted to stay with us!'

Johnson Wax is quite open about these redundancies – a reflection of its management philosophy, which is dedicated to commercial success achieved through the goodwill of its employees. This, in turn, is accomplished not only through a policy of rewarding employees with generous remuneration packages, often performance-related, but also through open discussion of targets and goals and how they are to be achieved, at all levels within the company. While the guiding philosophy comes from the USA, implementation is left to the UK management, and this ensures that its style is appropriate to the British people it employs.

John Hume, director of personnel and public affairs in the UK, explains the remuneration system. 'We start from the assumption that people work better when they have more to do, and that those we recruit recognize that this is a company which gets things done and is committed to growth. The fact that we have achieved a 300 per cent increase in volume turnover during the last four years must mean that our employees understand that. They know that we employ fewer people but of a higher calibre, and that we have to pay them better to keep them.

'Apart from ensuring that our wages and salaries are consistently in the upper quartile of the market, we also have a profit-sharing scheme which applies to everyone who has been with us for over six months. For employees who have been with us for ten years or more, this scheme can guarantee them between 20 and 35 per cent of their annual salary, depending on their seniority, while someone who has been with us for five years, for example, can expect at least 12½ per cent.

'In addition, everyone's salary is directly related to their individual performance. We have an appraisal system through which every employee is assessed against previously agreed goals, and this takes place at least once a year, or more frequently depending on the individual concerned.'

Johnson Wax is similarly forward-thinking in the benefits which it provides for its employees. There is a non-contributory pension scheme to which all employees working 20 hours a week or more are entitled to belong, and the company has made strenuous efforts to present the details of the scheme in a concise and simple way. There is also an optional health-care scheme providing a wide range of medical treatment, for which employees contribute £2.25 a month. They can also choose to have their families covered for an additional 50p a month.

In fact, the health of its employees is of prime concern to Johnson Wax. Apart from the health-care scheme, employees and their spouses are given regular medical screening checks, and in the last couple of years a well-equipped gym has been built on the premises, which all employees can use during their lunch hours and outside working hours. In addition, there is a rigorous smoking policy which was introduced in 1987 to 'provide a smoke-free environment for those who want it' – and for those who want to give up smoking, counselling is provided by Johnson Wax's occupational health nurse.

'Although many of these policies are relatively new to the company, we have always had a tradition of looking after our employees very well,' says John Hume. 'For example, the profit-sharing scheme was first introduced in 1917, although of course we have made changes since then!'

Cars are provided for middle and senior managers. The company decided that instead of offering any car within a given price range, a total of only six models would be available. However, to make up for this limited choice, the cars are comparatively luxurious.

This relatively high level of benefits has been achieved despite the fact that the company is not unionized. 'Apart from negotiating with the management on pay and working conditions, which our employees consider to be excellent anyway, very often unions perform a communications function instead of the management,' says Hume. Employees at every level in the company agree that they are kept well informed by management and are made to feel involved in developments within the company.

Johnson Wax works hard at disseminating information about progress and targets to its staff, and is constantly making changes to improve the procedure. Apart from an informative monthly newspaper, *Waxwords*, which has news of new products, advertising campaigns, personnel developments and the company's active community relations programme and charity fund-raising, there are also quarterly meetings, attended by all staff, at which any matter relating to the company's performance and policies can be discussed. The company's commitment to these meetings was shown recently when management realized that although a free-for-all discussion session allowed a great deal of openness in theory, many people were in fact reluctant to speak out. Now the work force is organized into groups which meet before the meetings, and a spokesperson is nominated to raise any issues put forward.

In general staff turnover is very low – one manager claimed that in his department, with over thirty people, nobody had left to join another company during the past two years. Johnson Wax develops its staff not only through promotion but also by recruiting people for long-term development and with an eye on their future within the organization as a whole, rather than within a specific department.

Kim Benton, a personnel assistant who is responsible for the administration of the graduate recruitment programme, summed up the type of person Johnson Wax look for. 'We want people who can point to their achievements and will want to succeed all the way through their time with the company – and this applies not only to our graduate intake but to every level within the company. There is no such thing as a Johnson Wax clone, but I would say that one characteristic of everyone who works here is that they are willing to take on assignments and run with them – and they work well in a commercial environment. And I think that drive is what creates such a good atmosphere – the contribution you make to the company is always recognized and appreciated.'

KODAK

Kodak Ltd is the UK company of Eastman Kodak, which is based in Rochester, New York. Kodak employs 7200 people mainly in Hemel Hempstead, Hertfordshire, and Harrow, northwest London. Its turnover is £661 million and its pre-tax profit £73 million.

pay	☐	ambience	☐
benefits	☐	environment	☐
promotion	☐	equal opportunities	☐
training	☐	communications	☐

If you think of Kodak's quaint 'We Have the Clicknology' slogan the main factory in Harrow will come as no surprise. It may be the British branch of the world's biggest photographic company but the whole place reeks of Box Brownies. Even the receptionist has been with Kodak for forty years and you can feel a tradition going back to old man Eastman who invented the holiday snap one hundred years ago.

But Kodak is changing. Wages are high with experienced shift workers earning £15,000 a year for a 42½-hour week. Since the 1970s most employees have joined trade unions in place of the in-house staff associations. At management level Kodak recruits 60 graduates a year and joined the milk round in 1986.

Some 1800 middle managers are in the £12,000–£25,000 pay band. Benefits and perks are not spectacular, although the Kodak Recreation Societies do have a yacht at Lymington and a fishing lake in Hemel Hempstead which any employee can make use of. In 1987 Kodak discovered the joys of the company car.

More importantly, Kodak is no longer a meal ticket for life. Many of the staff now retiring joined immediately after the war, following in the footsteps of their fathers and grandfathers before them. According to Dave Ford, company industrial relations manager, 'It used to be like the railways before the war. You worked at the rail or Kodak because you wanted a lifetime working for one company very often doing the same job.' That security has gone. In the last ten years the work force has been halved but with little acrimony between company and staff. What did come as a shock was the 1986 directive from Eastman Kodak's Rochester, New York, headquarters to cut 10 per cent off staffing and 5 per cent off costs immediately.

Up until the mid-1970s Kodak behaved as if it owned the British photographic market. The company museum served as a shrine to George Eastman. Kodak Ltd produced and processed most of the films needed in the UK and worried little about the threat of cheap imports or the need to export; after all, they would only be competing with other Eastman subsidiaries.

By early 1986 the recession of the early 1980s had come and gone. Kodak had shed 7000 jobs and decided that they were quite slim enough. With business booming a new recruitment video was put together under the slogan 'We've done the pruning, now we're going to plant the trees'. One hour after the video had been completed a hurricane from Rochester came roaring out of the woods. Eastman Kodak, under stock market pressure, issued a directive to all its subsidiaries to make more cuts. In Britain another 700 jobs had to go.

The company coped with that crisis. It put together such an attractive package that the voluntary redundancy schemes were over-subscribed. 'There were 261 workers in my shop,' says one shop steward. '261 wanted to go.' Redundancy was not so popular in the north. The Manchester distribution centre closed and the Kirkby, Liverpool, plant (which produces photographic chemicals) was cut back. At the 18-storey Hemel Hempstead headquarters the marketing and PR departments were not so badly hit, and at Harrow the cuts were made by axing support staff rather than front-line production workers. Outside caterers were brought in – and food is not as good as it was. Many ex-Kodak staff now find themselves working for contractors in the same kitchens for two-thirds of their previous wages: a backhanded compliment to Kodak's pay.

The new 'greenfields' plant at Annesley near Nottingham takes bulk product from Harrow and packages it in the familiar Kodak boxes. The site is ten times as big as Harrow and no one would be too surprised if Kodak centralizes its downstream operations in the Midlands some time in the 1990s.

It is difficult to overestimate the shock of 1986 to the whole company. Even industrial accidents increased by 50 per cent that year. Kodak medical staff attribute this to increased anxiety, especially since the number of accidents has now returned to normal. It certainly reminded everyone that Kodak Ltd is just a subsidiary of Eastman Kodak Company in the United States. Although it had been changing it took the Company Cost Improvement Programme of 1986 to make everyone realize that Kodak was no longer Mr Eastman's family firm. If the company could no longer promise a job for life it had to make itself attractive in other ways.

Worldwide Eastman Kodak employs 120,000 people and has a turnover of more than $12 billion. On a crude ratio of sales against employees the British operation is now twice as 'efficient', as well as being more profitable than the Eastman norm, but managers are aware that on this basis Fuji is two and a half times more efficient and Konica six times. Kodak is attracting new types of workers: people from the Asian community who want to work hard, save fast, get out and set up their own businesses; managers who insist on rewards today. Company cars were restricted to the top 100 employees but that leapt to 400 in 1987.

Many production teams work in the dark dealing with light-sensitive films, which is maybe why they recruited a personnel chief, Dave Ford, who used to work down a coal mine. Even managers on £30,000 a year can find themselves on shiftwork. Flexitime is not an option but there is no clocking in. Office staff can work staggered hours. Some managers on over £20,000 claim they rarely need to work more than their statutory 37½ hours or take work home. Others work a 50-hour week. The new catchwords are 'quality' and 'team-work'. Kodak boasts that nearly a century ago George Eastman personally recalled a faulty shipment with the words, 'Nothing is more important than the value of our name, and the quality it stands for.' In practice this approach to quality control persisted until recently. 'Throw away the bad' as Tim Fisher of quality control puts it, 'rather than don't create it.'

Teamwork is part of the new total quality control process. Kodak takes each production team away for a couple of days to play games and learn to work together. Management has had to learn to listen to the work force, as Dave Ford explains: 'Surprise, surprise, you find that people who are running the machines have a better idea of what's causing the problem than the technical people.' One casualty of the teamwork drive has been the suggestion scheme. Kodak feels individual rewards for ideas would be disruptive. Instead managers hand out Parker pens to good teams.

Total recruitment is about 600 a year. New technology has de-skilled some of the craftsmen's jobs but there are still craft apprentice-ships. It takes two years to become a fully-fledged process worker or three years to become a craftsman. At the moment they are all men, although Kodak soon expects to appoint its first female apprentices. Historical restrictions on shift working have kept women off the shop floor, but that too is starting to change. Kodak explains that this has a knock-on effect with the number of women in management. A shortage of female science graduates is also blamed.

173

Pay has stayed high and the bonus system is particularly popular. For a manager on £20,000 it might mean an extra £1000 at Christmas. Free BUPA membership is another new benefit. There is also a site ambulance and a 24-hour health centre with an SRN and a toxicologist. The company is unusually supportive of employees with personal problems. All vacancies are advertised internally and promotion from within is the norm.

Kodak may no longer be 'special K' but it still pays better than most and will not dump you the first time you make a mistake. Graduates are recruited with an eye to taking top positions in ten years' time. Compared to Mr Eastman's days there is a better chance of moving within the company and earning rewards quickly.

KOMATSU

Komatsu is a Japanese construction equipment manufacturer. It employs 300 people at its site in Birtley on Tyneside. The plant's production is expected to grow to accommodate another 100 people during 1989.

pay ▭		ambience ▭	
benefits ▭		environment ▭	
promotion ▭		equal opportunities ▭	
training ▭		communications ▭	

Amid all the publicity surrounding the march of the Japanese into UK industry one company is regularly quoted. Not Nissan or Sony, but Komatsu. The name may be unfamiliar, but it is the world's second largest maker of construction equipment. When the press wants an expert on the influence of Japanese thought on British industrial practices, they telephone Dr Clive Morten.

Morten is the director of personnel and was the first person taken on by the company before it opened on Tyneside in August 1986. Such was the influence that personnel policies were going to have on the factory that Morten's appointment came before anyone else's in the management structure.

'My first task was to go to Japan and see how they do things there. And then work out how to adapt my findings to a UK situation,' says Morten. The idea he resolved was human resource management. This is the basis of the success of Komatsu. It rests on the twin Komatsu principles of quality and employee involvement.

The company was founded in Komatsu City on the north coast of Japan in 1921. Since its inception the company has been dedicated to quality. Within Komatsu it takes on almost biblical reverence. Commitment to that goal has spawned countless devices, techniques and mechanisms. Total quality control (TQC) is one example. 'In this company the most important people are those who produce the goods,' explains Elaine Hall, a personnel officer. TQC was devised to achieve the goal of complete quality in production.

Each worker is encouraged to look upon the next worker in the chain as his final customer. So the work must be in tip-top condition for the next man to receive it, and he too must then ensure that his work is good enough to pass the exacting design standard.

175

Everyone is treated with equal respect. Each person's view is regarded as valuable. Involvement is another key Komatsu message. Every member of the staff is briefed on a daily basis on the company's performance, changes in production, personnel news and anything which is relevant to his job or his sense of belonging to the team. This is done by the team leader who is briefed by his managers. The supervisors brief their teams once a week, and the production manager talks to everyone once a month.

Morten concedes that two-way communication is an art form which Komatsu has yet to get right, but they are working at it. 'We have to educate briefers to remember that communicating is a two-way process, and the briefees that they should not be afraid to speak out. Their previous industrial experience may have been negative and so it is understandable that people feel unsure of themselves.' Komatsu can be quite a culture shock. Tyneside was notorious for its prehistoric industrial relations. Stepping into single-status, communicative, highly-informed, opinion-seeking and, above all, quality-seeking Komatsu with a traditional attitude could be surprising.

'Status does not figure in my approach. You cannot think in terms of status, only in functional terms,' says Morten. This strictly pragmatic approach also tends to lead to addressing business goals in decidedly frank language and coming to a common solution. One aspect of this approach is found in Komatsu's commitment to quality circles.

The factory is run on five principles, or the five Ss: systems, scrutiny, spotless, shipshape and safeguard. Each of these qualities is plugged relentlessly, and no one is able to forget them. The company has also set up an advisory council on to which employees elect representatives. The council is composed of staff from all levels and management. It is not like a works council where people have their own entrenched positions. Everyone talks freely to improve the direction of the company. It cannot decide policy but it does influence the direction of the company.

The factory is unionized but with a single union – the Amalgamated Engineering Union. Everyone works exactly the same number of hours – 39 a week – and there is a company pension scheme to which everyone contributes. PPP is available to anyone who wants it.

Ron Hudson, a production engineer and a member of the employee council, says, 'It is a joy to work here. You are not constricted in any way.' He likes the flat management structure, which means that there are few middle managers who get in the way. Personnel manager Elaine Hall says that the speed with which the company was set up means that some policies have yet to be fully implemented. But, she adds, 'For the first time I am really happy in my career.'

Morten says the company came to the area with a commitment to women, the disabled and the unemployed. 'Half the three hundred we took on were previously unemployed and so we are making progress there. We have changed attitudes towards taking on disabled people. But we have failed 100 per cent when it comes to getting women to work on the factory floor. We have tried and we will keep trying,' he says.

Nevertheless enthusiasm is an obvious factor at Komatsu. People like the company and welcome the opportunity to play a greater role in how their company makes its decisions. Not everything is right yet by any means, but Morten's people have come a long way in a short time. They have an eager and supportive work force who are keen to make the product. Komatsu is set to grow, and if it continues to extend the hand of trust and cooperation to its work force it will no doubt prosper.

JOHN LEWIS

The John Lewis Partnership is one of the foremost retail partnerships in the country. It includes several department stores and the Waitrose chain of supermarkets. It employs more than 30,000 people in the UK. In 1987 their turnover was £1.57 billion with pre-tax profits of £63.3 million. Its headquarters are in Oxford Street, in central London.

pay ☐		ambience ☐	
benefits ☐		environment ☐	
promotion ☐		equal opportunities ☐	
training ☐		communications ☐	

The spirit of John Spedan Lewis hangs in the airy shopping halls of John Lewis and Waitrose. It pervades every aspect of the structure, organization and policy of the group. It underlines every judgement made within the company, and is the force behind the partnership's continuing success. An indomitable character to say the least, he was the beneficiary of his father's enterprise.

In 1864, John Lewis senior opened a drapery store in Oxford Street, a few yards down the road from Peter Robinson where he had worked as silk buyer. As a coming-of-age present, Lewis senior gave his sons Oswald and John Spedan a quarter share each in the business. The founder had also developed links with Peter Jones in Sloane Square, and when the old man retired Lewis took over that store as well.

Spedan felt it unjust that the profits which he, his brother and his father had derived from the business were so out of proportion with the income of the work force. At that stage the combined salaries of all JL workers were less than the profit enjoyed by the directors. Spedan, himself influenced by radical and liberal social thinkers of the Victorian time, decided to find ways of making the business more worthwhile for his staff. In 1914 his father gave him control of the loss-making Peter Jones. This was the opportunity he had waited for. He set up staff committees and told the shareholders that he was extending ownership to the staff. It was a hard pill to swallow.

Six years later the staff were rewarded for their efforts not with a profit share in cash but in preference shares. In 1926 Oswald handed

178

over his 25 per cent to Spedan, so that two years later when John Lewis died Spedan was in total control. In 1929 he created an employees trust to which he sold his own shares in the company in return for a £1 million loan repayable over thirty years. It was the first of two trust signings which effectively created the business as it stands today. The second was in 1950.

All staff became partners, and today if you hear tannoy messages in the store for partners, these are for the staff. Although John Lewis plc is quoted, it is ultimately controlled by the trust. It has what appears from outside to be a complicated structure. All policy decisions are made by the 180-strong central council, composed of one-fifth appointees and four-fifths elected from the 30,000 partners. The former are selected by current chairman Peter Lewis, a nephew of Spedan. These are drawn in the main from management.

The remainder are elected across the patch and campaigning is actively encouraged. The candidates use the staff magazines, notably the rather old-fashioned *Gazette*, for manifestos. The trust is run by Lewis and three others who can combine to remove him. The plc is run by five directors nominated by Lewis, plus his deputy, and five nominated by the council. The chairman, while in control, must be accountable annually for all his activities.

Democracy is the life blood of John Lewis. It can be inefficient, it can be frustrating, but it does genuinely seem to work for this company. It is remarkable how happy JL employees appear to be. They exhibit a remarkable friendliness and freshness in dealing with customers. Staff at John Lewis stand apart from assistants in other High Street department stores.

They are encouraged to write to staff newspapers about any problem they may have, and it is guaranteed to be printed, unless – a highly unusual step – the chairman uses his veto. The culture overtly dates from the mid-1950s and the concepts of retailing can be traced back to the founding days.

John Lewis and Waitrose are some of the toughest fighters in their trades, but this does not undermine the partnership's commitment to honesty, value, clear market positioning and a wide selection of stock. So precise is the company about its tenets and so ruthless is it about pursuing them that it is highly successful. Customers can be assured of the highest quality when visiting a John Lewis Partnership enterprise both in goods and service.

In the John Lewis stores a somewhat old-fashioned atmosphere is created by the dated and largely basic design format. There is an air of tradition, and to some extent the flavour of retailing as it used to be

179

before the pressure increased in the sector. There is a mixture of informality and low-key quality reminiscent of most department stores before the 1960s design revolution.

As is common to the style of the company, both John Lewis department stores and Waitrose supermarkets are expanding at a measured pace. The company remains wedded to the High Street as the principal focus of shopping in the twenty-first century, and out-of-town developments are limited.

At present the partnership operates 21 stores and 80 Waitrose supermarkets. In addition there are warehouses, textile production and computer centres. John Lewis is not committed to growth for its own sake.

In laying down the foundations of the business Spedan Lewis used the now often-quoted words: 'The supreme purpose of the John Lewis Partnership is simply the happiness of its members.' The ultimate goal, before achieving high profits, is a contented partnership enjoying its work and benefiting from it.

Pay is average to above average for the retail sector, which is one of the meanest areas of British industry. But as a partner each member of staff receives a partnership bonus. This varies from year to year and is an annual share of the profits calculated in relation to pay. In recent years it has averaged 18 per cent, but in 1987 it was 24 per cent. This is paid in cash.

Additionally a staff discount scheme exists which allows 10 per cent off most department store goods, rising to 20 per cent after three years' service. At Waitrose the discount is 5 per cent rising to 10 per cent after three years. The partnership has a holiday camp where its staff can take a break. There are three country clubs and a hotel. Sport is heavily featured and partners are supposed to take their leisure seriously. No doubt Spedan Lewis thought it was good for the soul.

The partnership subsidizes a wide variety of sporting activities such as squash, sailing and golf, and leisure interests such as music, parachuting, yoga and drama. Individual branches have a plethora of clubs espousing almost every leisure pursuit. The commitment of John Lewis to the welfare of its people is excellent, and, though somewhat paternalistic in its thoroughness, demonstrates a fine appreciation of the fact that life does not begin and end behind a counter.

The partnership draws from a wide base for its recruits. It is difficult to get into the company. On the shop floor John Lewis could fill any vacancy several times over, such is the demand from assistants at competing stores. At the graduate level intake is diverse. The company

180

takes on candidates for management in several areas within the whole business.

One of the great attractions for graduates is the early promotion which trainees enjoy. Appointment as a section manager should follow ten months of intensive training, with promotion to departmental manager within two years of joining.

The magic of John Lewis is its slightly old-world charm, high-quality service and its remarkable management structure. Set against this is its stark retailing philosophy which puts JL in competition with the best in the country. The decision-making process within the partnership is somewhat cumbersome, and it is remarkably shy of publicity, but it remains one of the great retail success stories of the last hundred years.

LITTLEWOODS

The Littlewoods Organization comprises businesses which include retail chain stores, catalogue selling and an interest in football pools. Based in Liverpool, in 1987 the group reported £80.2 million profit on a turnover of £1946 million. The company employs 36,000 people.

pay ☐	ambience ☐
benefits ☐	environment ☐
promotion ☐	equal opportunities ☐
training ☐	communications ☐

'I had no qualifications when I came here. Littlewoods has made me what I am today.' Marie Spencer, food manager at the Littlewoods store in Liverpool, is testimony to the diligence and commitment of the Moores family, who created, developed and still own the Littlewoods Organization. Spencer, and people like her, are the heartbeat of the company which runs 114 retail stores, catalogue-shopping businesses, printing and, perhaps most famously, the football pool partnership. Spencer is a lively and articulate Merseysider who rose from Christmas temp through the ranks of the store to become departmental manager with 82 people reporting to her.

She is clear-sighted about the group which commands spectacular loyalty from its people. 'It is a family. Littlewoods has been my life since I left school. I came here fourteen years ago. Some of the people I work with have been here much longer – twenty-five or thirty years.' Littlewoods managers have an enviable capacity to spot people who will get on and train them for the task.

The company started as the brainchild of the founder Sir John Moores, now ninety-two, and two partners. While still working for another company, the trio established the pools business in 1923. They were keen to avoid interest from their employer and adopted the family name of one of the principals. But the football pools was a slow starter and Moores' partners developed cold feet. So Moores bought them out and it became a truly family enterprise. Littlewoods is now the largest treble-chance promoter in the world.

In 1932 they started the first catalogue home-selling business which today embraces Littlewoods, John Moores, Janet Frazer, Brian Mills,

Peter Craig and Burlington. The first chain store, at Blackpool, was opened ten years later. It is impossible to consider Littlewoods without the drive and initiative of the Moores family. It was their vision which created the group, and their commitment to their people which encouraged it to prosper.

But in the late 1970s and early 1980s the family's charisma was no longer enough. Turnover and profits flattened. The reins were drawn more tightly. Training, which had been a primary facet of the business, was cut back. Staff today remain nervous of the memory. Management changes failed to find the right combination to unlock the secrets of improved profitability.

Senior managers commissioned policy changes only to leave before they could be implemented. The immediate and residual impact was a confused work force. But in 1985 a new team took the helm. Desmond Pitcher, frustrated at Plessey, became chief executive. He immediately detected powerful bonds of loyalty which hold the company together, and distinguish Littlewoods from many of its competitors in the retail sector. It was a source of corporate good will which, if properly handled, could be the foundation stone of Littlewoods' revitalization.

Among his first moves was the improvement of the group's communications network. Bob Irving, executive assistant, explains that this has two channels. First, with the unions, and second, directly with the work force. In 1972 the company agreed to full unionization. Usdaw, the shop workers' union, and SATA, for management grades, were acknowledged as the representatives of the work force. Consultation with unions takes place at all levels – from organization on a national scale to the individual store.

Employee communication comes in the form of a group newspaper, an annual employee report and team briefings. The briefing mechanism is well oiled. Executives meet on Monday, essential messages are relayed to the shop floor the same evening, and non-essential information during the Tuesday morning training sessions.

Pay and benefits are above average for the retail sector. An Oxford Street sales assistant in January 1988 was earning £6800, and a store manager, depending on size of outlet, started on £16,000. He or she – there are ten women store managers – can earn up to 30 per cent bonus, though 10 per cent is more usual.

Ron Wright runs one of the largest stores, which is at the Arndale Centre in Manchester. He has 300 staff who report to him. 'The company rewards hard work,' Wright comments. 'You make your own bed. There are plenty of opportunities if you are prepared to work for them. But you need ambition, determination, an ability to absorb pressure, and, above all, you must love the work.'

Wright was at teacher training college in 1973 when he decided that he wanted a commercial rather than academic future. He enlisted as a trainee manager in Birmingham and began what now looks like a textbook rise through the company. Stints as departmental manager in places like Derby and Wandsworth were followed by rapid promotion to assistant manager in sites such as Romford and Swindon. Stays in Bradford and Woolwich preceded promotion to manager in 1978. Scunthorpe was Wright's first store, followed by Exeter. He opened Oxford and the Metro Centre on Tyneside. Those who have no appetite for travel, beware!

Some 50 per cent of store managers are given company cars, and all managers and their families are offered PPP medical insurance at the most expensive cover. They also enjoy the same 15 per cent staff discount on all retail goods and up to 33 per cent on most catalogue items which are available to all staff. Every store has a staff restaurant which offers an acceptable full-course meal for between 30p and 40p. Head office staff at the JM Centre pay slightly more. The food is varied and adequate. In the group's 46 catalogue shops, which are considerably smaller than the chain stores, staff receive Luncheon Vouchers. Store managers have their own dining rooms.

Between store managers and the board is a tier of regional managers. On average a minimum of twelve years' service is needed before the group will consider a candidate for a regional managership.

With a 75:25 female to male ratio, the company is acutely aware of its responsibility to improve the promotion prospects of women. This policy is enshrined in an equal opportunities code of practice and is supported by a unit devoted to creating equal representation for women, ethnic minorities and disabled people within five years. This is an optimistic target, but the company really does appear to want to do something about the white male preponderance in senior positions. Some 50 per cent of all staff in training for management grades are women, and Littlewoods boasts an above-average rate of women returning to the company after pregnancy. Maternity benefit is statutory at present, but proposals for extending and improving it were about to be put on the table when we visited.

Desmond Pitcher's appointment as group chief executive was symbolic. It characterized the company as a unified team heading in one direction. Pitcher is clear about corporate objectives. He wants Littlewoods to stick straightforwardly to its mainstream business, and to exploit a larger percentage of its existing target market. His analysis of the buying public is nothing if not precise. He visualizes families, harder hit by pressures on their incomes, wanting good-value products at a reasonable price. Mum, Dad and the kids all dress alike, they spend more time together and they are proud of their house like never before. 'We are reaching 20 per cent of our target market, so we have another 80 per cent to tap,' he says.

Nor will Littlewoods be taking bold steps into America. 'Our business is here in the UK,' says Pitcher. Europe is more of an open book, but even so he reckons that the proposed harmonization of the EC in 1992 is something which will, in fact, take ten years to complete. So Littlewoods is concentrating on the UK, opening new stores every year and expanding the home-shopping (catalogue) business. The home delivery service which supports the catalogues is proving popular.

In the meantime several high-tech projects are underway. Shop TV, an interactive video format, and teleshopping are being investigated. Dave Raywood, a former data-processing graduate from Leeds University, is looking at a number of technology-based initiatives which could revolutionize retailing as we know it.

Raywood also lectures at an intensive 14-day residential management training course structured with Manchester Business School. This rigorous package gives Littlewoods managers detailed training and problem-solving experience, and is being hailed as a major move forward in the already noteworthy training programme of the company.

At the shop-floor level a customer-service training scheme called Putting People First is having remarkable effects on staff morale. Some members of the shop-floor staff are being put through the two-day course, and this has produced an extremely positive response from them.

These developments characterize the Littlewoods which retains its persona as a family company but which is conscious of the nature of its competitors. For the first time in a decade the group has clear strategies. Its ability to realize improved profits is becoming apparent and the future looks good.

LOGICA

Logica is an independent computer software, systems and consultancy house. It employs 2600 people worldwide, 45 per cent of whom are based in the UK. In 1987 sales reached £110.7 million. Headquarters are in London.

pay	☐	ambience	☐	
benefits	☐	environment	☐	
promotion	☐	equal opportunities	☐	
training	☐	communications	☐	

Logica was founded in 1969 in the front room of a private house. Among the small circle of people present at the birth was current chairman Philip Hughes. The aim was to create a company which promoted high technical standards and to reach a position of prominence in international markets.

Today Logica is one of the largest companies in the UK software markets. It has offices in 13 countries and is running projects in more than 50 countries worldwide. Some 54 per cent of its work is done in the UK, with the rest of Europe accounting for 30 per cent and the USA 8 per cent. Custom-built systems – both hardware and software – bring in 61 per cent of turnover and consultancy 29 per cent.

Such is the impact of Logica on its people as well as its marketplace that one employee, John Ford, comments: 'If you work for Logica, you've made it – you're where it's at.'

This passion for the company is common among Logica employees. They praise the combination of ruthless dedication to standards, commonality of excellence and friendliness which has forged the company into a market leader.

Roger Cocks, a consultant, was encouraged by friends to join Logica in 1981 having graduated in computer science. 'The job is no sinecure. You must keep aware of developments. There's no shoulder to cry on.' Tracy Norton, five years with Logica, is another devoted fan. 'I could earn more elsewhere but it is not the salary which motivates me but the mobility – the variety factor. There are opportunities to work anywhere in the world.'

There is strong emphasis on making your own breaks. 'Opportunities are within my grasp and people will give them to me – you make your own career,' says Norton. This is one of the familiar traits of the Logica character. A willingness to carve out your own niche by dint of personality, expertise and drive. A Logica person is one who is assertive but personable. Chairman Philip Hughes acknowledges these perceptions and points to Logica as an individualistic culture. 'We enjoy what we do, and the company is driven by what the staff want to do,' he says.

Recruits are tempted into Logica by its already considerable reputation, its innovative style and pleasant working conditions. They are attracted by its roster of clients which includes Bay Area Rapid Transport in San Francisco, Nederlandse Gasunie in the Netherlands, the BBC in London, American Express, Thorn-EMI, H. J. Heinz, Ansett Airlines, Ford, the New Zealand Dairy Board and the Iraq National Oil Company.

Logica's approach is to throw newcomers in at the deep end – but not unaccompanied. It will make sure that the recruit is accompanied by experienced swimmers. There is no period of initial training. The two main project areas are consultancy and implementation. Consultancy usually involves a couple of people working on a project and producing recommendations to a client some months later. Implementation can involve teams of fifteen or more on a working system and the task can last for several years. It can be completed at Logica or at the client's offices. After this is finished staffers will be moved on to a new project.

Logica regards on-the-job training as the most productive, but it boasts a catalogue of training schemes which enhance the worker's knowledge of the company, professional skills and personal development.

Sally Howes joined Logica in 1985. She was inducted in her first week to Frontiers, which is an interactive system for real-time analysis of weather conditions. 'I joined Frontiers in my first week and was immediately involved in general system support. After nine months I was promoted to project manager. I gained experience in agreeing and planning work with the client.'

Non-computer graduates are trained in structured programming. Logica also uses information-gathering, time-management and effective-presentation techniques. There is special emphasis on software training. And the company has evolved an internal project called SESAME which enhances effective softward production. Esther Marsden, once a secretary and now a WP trainer, says that the training throughout the company is particularly effective. 'The training courses

187

are giving me the opportunity to develop myself. The opportunities are there for promotion but the competition is hot.'

Logica, in common with other software houses, has commissioned surveys of salaries in the marketplace. It emerged as on a par with the rest. Salaries do not seem to be a problem for Logica people – it is the company's style and approach which attracts them. In a fiercely competitive field Logica keeps pace with the leaders but is not usually out in front. Salaries are reviewed annually and are related to individual performance.

A senior manager earns £40,000, and a senior project manager £30,000. Graduates enter the company at £10,000 and after five years they could expect to be on about £20,000, but all of this hinges on manager assessment.

Benefits include four weeks' holiday a year, but rising to five weeks after five years. The company operates a pension scheme which is employee-contributory. As an alternative to the pension scheme, Logica also has a contributory scheme with a building society for housing. It also offers health and life assurance, and a disability pension.

Logica is a major contributor to the graduate recruitment round each year. It takes 200 graduates from a wide assortment of disciplines. Non-graduates, principally on the non-technical side, come from electronics companies. They might be ex-British Telecom engineers or from manufacturers. But one-third of entrants work in the software field and are computer science graduates. The company also takes on mathematicians and chemists.

On the management side, the rapid growth of the company means that some senior people are drawn in from outside, but generally posts are filled as a direct result of internal promotion.

Logica is keen to encourage its own people and aims to breed more in the Logica mould. It remains an attractive company for software writers and developers, specializing in a uniquely creative approach to its business.

LWT

London Weekend Television is a programme contractor for the London commercial TV region. It broadcasts on two and a half days a week. Its turnover in 1986 was £157.8 million with pre-tax profits of £13.7 million. The company employs 1700 people at its headquarters on the South Bank of the Thames in central London.

pay	☐	ambience	☐
benefits	☐	environment	☐
promotion	☐	equal opportunities	☐
training	☐	communications	☐

London Weekend Television was formed in 1967. It was created to fill the gap left by outgoing programme contractors in the London region. The early days were tough and not uneventful. The original group combined a mixture of television personalities from the BBC and ITV and senior behind-the-scenes executives from both services. Among the initiators were David Frost, Michael Parkinson, Jimmy Hill, Aidan Crawley, Michael Peacock, Frank Muir and Michael Burton. They wanted to call the company Thames, but were pipped to the post by another group. The team began with lofty ideals and a determination to change the viewing habits of the television audience. The result was a schedule which was uncommercial by anyone's standards. Typical was a Saturday peak-time concert by Yehudi Menuhin.

Financial problems followed in 1969 and a whole tranche of BBC men left LWT. But concern that the then Independent Television Authority might revoke the contract was unfounded. A major cash injection from a now notorious Australian media figure called Rupert Murdoch helped the company get back on its feet. Murdoch soon became frustrated by his inability to exert control and went almost as soon as he came. He was replaced at the top by John Freeman, and Brian Tesler, the current chairman and managing director, moved in as Freeman's deputy. This was a significant turning point for the company – and it has never looked back. Freeman is still warmly regarded by many employees at LWT. They say that it was his wise and good-natured leadership that created the business which is so successful today.

189

LWT is now enjoying an extension until 1992. In the last batch of contractor assessments the IBA granted LWT more air time at the expense of the weekday programmer Thames, and in 1987 LWT began all-night broadcasting with the Night Network series.

In 1972 LWT moved from its early base at Wembley and occupied purpose-built premises on the South Bank. The LWT tower is a landmark in central London – one which the company has used in its publicity from time to time. Its black and white layers stand out among the more bizarre aspects of South Bank architecture.

With its liberal programming and equally generous staffing attitudes LWT is a happy company. Industrial relations problems have been scarce, with the notable exception of the 1979 national TV strike. People like it so much at LWT that the chances of getting in are pretty remote. Those places which do exist are several times oversubscribed. On top of this the government-sponsored move to independent production means that LWT, like the other major companies, will not expand but slowly reduce its staffing.

The company is characterized by its long-serving employees. The personnel department has calculated that by 1989, the year of the company's twenty-first birthday, it is possible that as many as 285 staff will have been with the station since it opened, and the bulk of these were with LWT's predecessor Rediffusion. What keeps them there is the knowledge that they are working for one of the best TV companies in the world, the high standards of pay and benefits, the friendly atmosphere and the challenging nature of the work. While the station is dotted with programmes and personalities which do not appear to change, there is a constant quest for new ideas, material and programmes.

The principles which guided the pioneers of the station are still broadly adhered to today. The company is meticulous in its commitment to equal opportunities. One per cent of staff are from ethnic minority backgrounds. When the company was based at Wembley it was as high as 6 per cent. About one-third of the staff are women. Roy van Gelder, director of personnel, says that the company is opposed to employing the children or spouses of employees, except on rare occasions when appointments are in two entirely separate departments. Some members of staff have a different view. They quoted us examples of whole families in the bosom of LWT and some where jobs passed from father to son. They say that this causes few problems. If anything it adds to the convivial atmosphere of the company.

Everyone is on first-name terms and no separate dining facilities exist for senior management. Everyone mixes. The main meeting points are the canteen, the bar and the restaurant which is open to everyone.

Benefits include a profit-sharing scheme, which has been running for three years. Five per cent of profits are distributed in the form of shares to everyone on a *pro rata* salary basis. Managerial grades get private medical insurance, assisted car purchase and a TV and a video recorder. Union members are paid overtime and the more senior members also get a TV and a VCR. Everyone is encouraged to watch LWT. The 7 per cent contributory pension scheme is extended to the entire staff. The company doctor calls twice a week for anyone to consult and all staff can visit the LWT physiotherapist. The company also sponsors golf, squash and badminton clubs which are managed by employees.

Most vacancies are filled internally. They are advertised on the promotion boards which hang in every department. The selection is made competitively, even where a seemingly obvious candidate exists.

LWT runs a generous early retirement scheme. The company encourages staff to retire at sixty and many people have chosen to do so. Considerable advance help is provided to help retirees adjust to their new life style. For the last three months they work only three days a week, and in their last month only two. LWT stays in touch with them through outings twice a year – in the summer and at Christmas.

LWT is committed to open-door management. Staff are free to approach senior managers about problems, ideas or queries. Every eight weeks a management board meeting is held. This consultative committee liaises with shop stewards and the management association, and information is thus passed rapidly up and down the company. The downwards flow, however, is sometimes not as effective as it might be. Communication systems are slightly more informal within LWT than an outsider might expect, but they produce a staff magazine called *In Vision*. 'This is not used to lecture the staff,' says van Gelder, and, significantly, it does have an independent editor.

Simon Kershaw, a senior sales executive, has been with the company for four years. It is longer than he expected to stay with one company. Jane Stuart, with LWT for fifteen years, is the group sales manager. She enjoys the friendly atmosphere within the company and likes its style of communication. Joyce Coughlan, a group administrative assistant, came from the banking sector thirteen years ago and hasn't been tempted back. The sales department is more or less out of the internal spotlight. It doesn't make programmes, although indirectly it pays for them. 'We work hard here,' says Kershaw, 'but everyone mixes well. No one is stand-offish.' Sales people within LWT say that they are extremely well paid and they believe that they are better off than almost anyone in the sector. All three employees say that the management are entirely approachable, especially in a crisis – which is when, in other workplaces, normally equitable relationships can turn frosty.

Training is controlled for day-to-day purposes by group managers, and the quality varies widely as a result. While some formal training does exist, it is more likely to be arranged within an employee's home department on a less structured basis. Stuart cites a women-in-management course as a good example of a more formal training programme. Three or four people normally take this each year. Two people might go out to a seminar on work in industry or on public-speaking courses.

Stuart is a representative on the company's equal opportunities committee. She is supportive of LWT's record. 'I have never had to fight for equality for women. LWT does not hold women back. Everyone is treated fairly and the company is more interested in an individual's ability to do a job rather than his or her sex.'

The company's caring streak is well illustrated by a young proba-tioner who discovered she had cancer. The company was especially supportive when she told them that she needed time off for chemo-therapy treatment. She was kept on full pay. She was told not to come into work if she didn't feel like it, and her job was kept open for her until she was able to return full time.

This is typical of the company's generosity to its people. Craig Pearman, head of sales, says that the distinguishing factor of the LWT approach is its humanity. Formal bureaucratic procedures are deliber-ately kept to a minimum and most contact is face to face. People who are passed over for promotion are spoken to in advance of the announcement to explain why they did not make it. Pearman says that everyone is told to speak out which means that grievances are often settled before they build up into explosive problems.

LWT's personality is lively, bright, human and happy. It makes programmes which its staff believe are, in the main, first class. It has a responsible attitude towards its community, both as a television station and as an employer. It is a cosmopolitan team with a more liberal and laid-back approach than other TV stations, but the image belies the dedication, quality and inspiration of its staff. Above all, it is a fun place to work.

LOWE, HOWARD-SPINK & BELL

Lowe, Howard-Spink & Bell is an advertising agency. It is based in central London. Turnover in 1986 was £214.5 million with pre-tax profits of £7.3 million. The company has 2000 employees worldwide.

pay	▭	ambience	▭
benefits	▭	environment	▭
promotion	▭	equal opportunities	▭
training	▭	communications	▭

Passion is the watchword at Lowe, Howard-Spink & Bell. If you want to succeed here, then you need to be extrovert, self-conscious, elitist and have a total belief in your work. 'It is no good being creative if you cannot stand up in front of a client and sell your idea,' says deputy chairman Tim Bell. It is a remarkable organization. It was started by Frank Lowe and Geoff Howard-Spink in 1981. Lowe is an *éminence grise* in the industry. He has the power to attract people and make them want to work for him.

'I don't like the idea of serving companies. It should be a mutuality. You get something out of it and they get something out of it. But the great thing about our business is that you can motivate people to do the very best they can,' says Lowe.

He started the business with two principles in mind. 'The idea that you can't be big and do good ads, that Aston Martin and British Leyland don't go hand in hand, I've never really accepted as a concept. The Japanese have proved that you can do it. You can have good quality and still be big. Second, advertising does have social responsibility. It pounds out from the television. The method is as important as the message. 'You can do good work and grow. And do work that enriches rather than impoverishes people's lives,' he says.

The business was carefully planned. It was formed in 1981 when Lowe and Howard-Spink left CDP with the accounts of Unilever and Whitbread. In 1984 the company made a reverse takeover of an American agency which gave them the General Motors account. During the same year the company was floated to fund capital expansion. The following year Tim Bell came on board and the international network was constructed. Another agency, Allen, Brady & Marsh, and a PR company, Good Relations, were drawn in.

Lowe says that when they created a new agency with a strong international presence opportunities to do so were slim, and they become fewer as each year passes. Bell adds, 'Saatchi was the first company to utilize the share quote and the price/earning ratio to make acquisitions. All they did was copy what the Americans had been doing for the last twenty years. But it had never been done in Britain before.'

Lowe has created a disciplined agency with tight controls on advertising. Nevertheless, he still emphasizes the emotional rather than rational side. 'Passion. Without passion there is nothing, passion to want to do something fresh, passion to create something new.'

The sort of people who can create in the way that Lowe describes are generally not graduates. 'I think to be genuinely creative you have to think in an undisciplined way. An academic education teaches you to think in a disciplined way. Highly-trained minds often find eccentric creativity almost offensive. These people tend to get frustrated,' says Lowe. A large amount of advertising copy is ungrammatical and might therefore be anathema to a tidy mind.

Lowe himself, and several other senior executives in the industry, started as a messenger boy and worked his way up. Luck, and being in the right place at the right time, plays a part in it. Administrative people, such as traffic controllers, can move into creative jobs like copywriters, if they happen to be the only ones in the office when a client needs something urgent. If they are good they might get a break.

The agency draws in people in three areas. School-leavers who go into despatch and traffic or become secretaries; the creative people who work on the accounts; and a few graduates who work in executive planning. There is no graduate recruitment scheme akin to Shell, ICI, JWT or Unilever, for example.

The industry and the company are both comparatively young, and the opportunities for making a name are therefore considerable. Bell says that it is still an individual's business, that ultimately it is down to the individual to prove himself. Lowe, Howard-Spink & Bell expect their people to come up with the goods, and to leave if they don't. Advertising is a volatile business and this agency sees no reason to put job security before creativity.

Pay is high for industry as a whole, but only fair for the sector. Salaries are lower in those agencies which have a good reputation because people are keen to work with key people at the top. 'Strangely, you seem to get more if you move around an awful lot,' says Trevor Kennedy, art director at the agency. He was drawn there in the early days by Lowe's charisma. 'Frank was CDP. So the potential and the accounts were there. It was only small then but it seemed to me it was doing the best work.'

Benefits in advertising are notorious: free holidays, TVs, videos, flights on Concorde, lunches and dinners. Things are not quite as rich as they were ten years ago, but this agency indulges in them as much as any. 'Every ad agency's car park looks like the starting grid at Le Mans. We're no exception. People expect serious cars,' says Bell.

It is a good place for women. The industry is more meritocratic than most, and this company certainly takes no notice of gender in making appointments. Women have reached board-level appointments in major subsidiary companies of the Lowe, Howard-Spink & Bell group.

All the training in the group is confined to what you pick up as you go along. It is real on-the-job stuff. 'We don't give people a career. We give them a job,' says Bell. Every day is an opportunity. An opportunity to prove that you should be given a chance, or that your work is better than the next guy's. It is competitive. It is tough. No one is going to do you any favours. Ultimately your only loyalty will be to yourself. But if you turn out work which the client likes – and, more importantly at Lowe, Howard-Spink & Bell, that the company likes – then you can achieve a good deal of creative satisfaction here.

MARKS & SPENCER

Probably the most famous retailer in the UK, M&S employs 61,000 people in 263 stores and 18 satellites. The company also has operations in Europe, Canada and the Far East. Turnover in 1988 was £4.5 billion with pre-tax profits of £501 million.

pay	☐	ambience	☐
benefits	☐	environment	☐
promotion	☐	equal opportunities	☐
training	☐	communications	☐

In *Personnel Management* at the end of 1984, M&S's centenary year, the company's president Lord Sieff recalled how Marks & Spencer had always been at the forefront of good industrial relations. 'During the deep recession of the 1930s we were a moderate but successful business. When Simon Marks and my father Israel Sieff were visiting our store in Kilburn, they thought one of the sales assistants was ill. They discovered that her father and two brothers were out of work. She shared her salary with her family and none of them had enough to eat. They immediately installed dining rooms, rest rooms and kitchens in every store so that good meals could be provided at a nominal price.

'Today this is hardly unusual, but fifty years ago it represented a revolutionary step forward and led us into the whole area of looking after our staff's welfare – medical and dental care, chiropody and hairdressing, and eventually non-contributory pensions and profit-sharing.'

M&S is not only a first-class retailer with enviable product lines and systems. It is also an understanding and considerate employer, and one which is revered throughout industry. When conducting the research for this book, we were often told defensively by other retailers, 'Well, of course, we're not Marks & Spencer.'

The company has often broken new ground when it comes to employee relations. M&S was one of the earliest companies to introduce team briefings throughout the business – bringing staff up to date on new policies, the opening of new stores, and suggesting improvements. Staff are also encouraged to offer their views.

When devising his six guiding principles for the company, Lord Sieff devoted one to 'fostering good human relations with staff, customers and suppliers'. This alone seems to sum up the whole M&S ethos, but in addition the company is a tough-minded and exclusive retailer demanding high quality from its suppliers.

M&S is especially good at talking to its people. Managers walk the floor and chat to staff about any aspect of their work. Even at the most senior levels people with finely-tuned communications skills are recruited. M&S is an object lesson in how to talk to employees.

Andrew Webster, personnel manager at the prestige Marble Arch branch, says, 'We put an awful lot of emphasis on the people side of the business. If we were interviewing someone who had strong commercial skills, but wasn't particularly strong in the people area, then we would not be interested at all.'

It is hard to find fault with M&S. It displays all that is positive about paternalism. Not only does the company pay exceptionally well, its list of benefits compares with the best in British industry. The company gives fast promotion and provides a wealth of training courses to help enhance and motivate its staff.

Gemma Carmadie, a full-time deputy supervisor, recalls how she was keen to join the company when she was sixteen. 'Everybody knows that M&S have a good name as an employer.' Carmadie enlisted as a temporary seasonal worker in men's knitwear. She was rapidly promoted every few months until she reached her present position. 'I was really shy, but they sent me on a week's course. That really brought me out of myself. We had to act out real-life situations and interview people on the street about their favourite TV programmes,' she recalls. The purpose of this course and scores of similar ones is to make staff more positive about taking decisions and meeting people.

Many assistants are recruited in a similar way. Adam Gilbert, who is training coordinator for the ground floor at Marble Arch, joined in 1984 as a Youth Training Scheme recruit. 'They are a very fair firm, and if you have the potential there are possibilities all the way up.'

Judith Mackenzie, who worked in personnel for several years but is now a press officer, says, 'It is a very good company for women. We employ a lot of women on the shop floor. When you are a staff manager the majority of your staff – probably 90 per cent – are female. There is an opportunity to work up from the shop floor if you are not a graduate,' she says. This is certainly borne out by the number of women who reach relatively senior positions in the structure.

Some suggest that M&S is paternalistic but not in the pejorative sense. 'I think we were,' says Mackenzie, 'but I don't think you can say that today. When it was much more a family business, yes, it was paternalistic, and there are some very good remnants of that which still remain in the company. But we are no longer so small nor a family business. Things change very rapidly in a business like this. The attitude remains the same but you can no longer call it paternalistic. Staff welfare does remain exactly the same. But now it is company policy rather than one man's decision.'

Webster says that the company now puts a lot of emphasis on self-help. 'If someone comes to us with a problem we encourage them to help them to help themselves. We will ask them, for example, if they have thought of this course of action or that way of approaching the problem.' The company is nonetheless very generous when confronted with genuine staff distress.

Ronnie Jacobson, press and public relations executive says that the company invests large resources in training. 'We have a training department with sixteen people who are responsible for disseminating training material of every sort for everybody who's involved in the business. They produce training videos. Most stores have a separate training room so they can go and practise how to work the latest till, or see the latest training video.'

For shop-floor staff M&S is an excellent employer, with good benefits, superb pay, fine training and a tremendous atmosphere. Managers check daily to see how they are doing and are encouraging and supportive when they perform well. Middle management also offers good opportunities, and there is an invigorating and stretching climate in which to work.

Marks & Spencer is probably Britain's best-known good employer, and it represents the royalty of retailing. A vibrant company, with a tough commercial edge, its commitment to people is hard to match.

MARS

The Mars Group in the UK is composed of eight companies which are engaged in food production, export and electronics. The group employs 6500 people in the UK. Turnover is £1.3 billion.

pay	☐	ambience	☐
benefits	☐	environment	☐
promotion	☐	equal opportunities	☐
training	☐	communications	☐

A handful of companies in this book would be contenders for the best employer in Britain. One of the companies which the chosen few would have to beat is Mars. Not because the Mars Group pays 10 per cent more than anyone else, or because its products include the world's leading chocolate bar and the top-selling cat food. Mars makes a much greater statement about company management than simple items of personnel policy or systems of corporate management.

Mars is one of the most perfectly balanced enterprises we have encountered. It believes that its attitude to its people should be as important as its commercial activity. With superb quality products and excellent people, it will come as no surprise that Mars is a highly profitable company.

The business was founded by Forrest Mars Sr, who set up in England in 1932 after leaving his father's company in the United States. He brought with him the recipe for the Mars bar. It was an unusual product in the highly competitive chocolate market, but such was its success that it was followed by Milky Way and a series of other products which were to lead Mars Confectionery to assume the mantle of leading chocolate producer in the UK.

It was also the foundation for a business which today includes Pedigree Petfoods, Masterfoods, Four Square, Thomas's, Mars Electronics, Information Systems and Effemex. Pedigree Petfoods produces Whiskas, the biggest-selling cat food, and Pedigree Chum, the brand leader in dog food.

'We are a brand business,' says George Greener, Mars Confectionery's general manager. 'We totally believe in brands. We take the long view in the marketplace. We never make any own-label products. We work very hard to make sure that our brands satisfy genuine consumer wants.' Whether it is Yeoman's mashed potato, Pal dog food or Aquarian fish snacks, the same rigorous attention to what the customer wants is given in every Mars plant.

'If you get the right brands and the right people you make money, and that's the way to run a business,' says David Fish, director of personel organization. It is wholly pragmatic. Mars is clean, simple, straightforward and orderly. The whole atmosphere is one of openness. Nobody has any commercial secrets from anyone else. Everyone knows how much the next man is earning. And there are, quite literally, no doors, since everyone, including the managing director, works together in an open-plan setting.

'We work very hard in terms of manpower planning. Our people are as important as our physical assets. We do not see them as short-term assets either. We do not lay people off,' says Mars. He understates the loyalty which senior management in Mars have managed to engender in their people. The staff are genuinely happy. 'A ballot at Pedigree Petfoods voted against admitting unions by 91 per cent. The company would have failed in its people policy had there been a vote in favour,' says Leslie Simmens, Pedigree's managing director.

Shassin Mohammed, a machine operator at Slough, says, 'We have a very good atmosphere. It's like a family here in the bay. We are all very good friends. We like to help one another.'

Mars is uncluttered by structure. There are five zones of managers. Each job has a precise function and each is paid within a set maximum and minimum. The company represents a quintessential meritocracy. People rise on merit and performance. Everyone, including the managing director, clocks in each morning. A good time-keeping allowance is paid at the rate of 10 per cent of pay daily for people who clock in ready for work on or before time.

Pay is worked out by making an in-depth assessment of the market and pitching the basic pay 10 per cent above the average. The lowest zone comes in at £200 a week. If a worker here completes five modules which improve his skills his pay goes up to £250. 'We are looking for professional people with a pride in their job at any level. We try to create an environment where they can improve what they are doing and themselves.'

The management development programme is remarkable. 'A lot of companies will talk about it but don't actually do it. We take people on and they have skills when they arrive. But all the time we are looking at people to give them a broader business perspective. People are encouraged to move across functions and units [operating companies]. This is real on-the-job management development by putting associates [Mars workers] into different jobs with different people, different sets of problems and it is something which seems to work,' says Fish.

Roger Chatterton, personnel and organization director of Pedigree Petfoods, points to some differences between Mars Confectionery and his company. 'We are in different businesses. Confectionery is supplying one customer. We are supplying two – the pet and the owner. This means that there are certain differences in the way that we operate the business – how we market and how we sell.

'Pedigree is slightly more self-confident. We do pay well and we have advanced equally policy practices. If we opened a waiting list then we would be flooded with applications.'

The backbone of the Mars Group is made up of 'the five principles'. The business is wedded to quality, responsibility, mutuality, efficiency and freedom. These guidelines underpin the Mars approach to its people, its customers, its suppliers and the community. For too long Mars has kept quiet about its superb employee relations. It is a story which deserves to be better known.

MERIDIAN

Meridian is Europe's largest computer-leasing company. It was formed in 1987, the product of a merger of UK and Swiss interests. Meridian employs 700 people worldwide, 150 in the UK.

pay ⬜		ambience ⬜	
benefits ⬜		environment ⬜	
promotion ⬜		equal opportunities ⬜	
training ⬜		communications ⬜	

The birth of Meridian was one of the great computer industry stories of 1987. Europe's largest computer-leasing company was formed when the Swiss-owned conglomerate Inspectorate Internationale merged the separate leasing operations, United Leasing and CPS. Ian Orrock was named chief executive and he immediately made it known that Meridian would grow fast and aggressively through acquisition.

Meridian's largest competitor was IBL, but it was facing financial difficulties and the threat it posed to Meridian never therefore materialized. The company known today as Meridian is the product of the merger of IBL with Meridian. In October 1987 61 per cent of IBL's shares were sold at 41p each, making a total cash bid of £29.4 million. Meridian gained IBL at a substantial discount.

With the merger behind them, the staff at Meridian pulled themselves together in quick order and began working towards a projected turnover of £750 million. Merging IBL with Meridian paid dividends in many ways. Talents were complementary, client lists were boosted and, most notably, the worldwide operations fitted snugly. Meridian's pre-merger strengths lay in the UK and US, while IBL was stronger outside these markets. IBL added operations in five countries new to the Meridian network – including Spain and Portugal. In addition IBL had a ready-formed systems maintenance division, a sector which Meridian was planning to move into. On the other hand, IBL was planning to move into the disaster recovery areas, where Meridian already demonstrated proven strength.

Orrock must have smiled from ear to ear when he saw what was available to him. But the problems of settling down the three businesses into one, and achieving profit forecasts, dictated a brief period of digestion and introspection. According to financial director Karen Merrinam, Meridian is going through a period of consolidation, evaluation and building up of operations to achieve its maximum potency. 'We are in a unique position, as the largest computer-leasing company in Europe,' says Merrinam, 'and we are also looking to the Far East and Asia, as well as to plug any gaps that we have not filled. Leasing is a cash-hungry business. We have built up our operation so that we can start to generate cash ourselves.'

The rapid growth caused Meridian to move its UK headquarters out of the West End in 1987 to a larger site in Ealing. This helped to accommodate new staff absorbed from the IBL merger. The combination of two companies operating in the same market sector led to remarkably few redundancies. Orrock was quoted in the trade press at the time as saying that his business was growing and it was still very short of people who know the computer-leasing sector.

The computer-leasing industry, like any other leasing concern, is subject to a highly concentrated level of commercial pressure. Far more than in other sectors, companies need to be alert to the latest moves of their competitors. They aim to keep flexible controls over staff terms and conditions to stay ahead of the opposition, but they also need to be careful to avoid price-cutting wars which could damage revenue growth.

The IBL merger was not the only shake-up to occur in 1987, but it was an accurate reflection of the speed at which this sector is moving. The characters of the computer-leasing companies and the personalities of their chief protagonists are vibrant and mercurial. The industry itself is only fifteen years old, and this is another important influence on Meridian. 'The company is not aggressive but firm,' says leasing manager Tony Morey. 'Computer-leasing companies were regarded as cowboys in their early days but this one isn't. There is a good service to clients, with a longer-term view in client relationships than the vast majority of competitors.'

A young organization can escape from the traditional approaches to employment. Within Meridian 61 per cent of all expenditure including salaries is staff-related, and 5 per cent of that figure is committed to staff training. Each member of staff receives an average of ten days' training a year: some on an internal basis, and some externally. There is an induction course for new employees.

Financial controls within the company are through separate divisions, operating as individual profit centres. Each division is performance-targeted in relation to the financial profitability of the company, and aims to improve profitability are related directly to staff in terms of incentive packages.

Individual staff are set their own performance targets within their job role. Each employee has a performance review twice a year, in order to see how they are progressing and to outline areas of improvement, or to see if some kind of training is needed. According to FD Karen Merrinam, there is a strong commitment to the philosophy that individual performances contribute to the whole. 'We like to make our people feel that they can contribute to the business.'

Remuneration within Meridian is based upon individual performance. There is no official salary-grading structure within the company. 'People don't discuss their salaries, but they know that if they work hard, they get paid well for doing it,' says Merrinam. As an employer, Meridian aims salaries at a point within the upper quartile of comparable rates within the industry. There is a definite policy of not wanting to be the top employer in terms of salary, as this is seen as tying staff to the company for financial incentives only.

There is a bonus scheme operating if deadlines or targets are met. Sales staff salaries are in direct relation to the levels of business that are written. There is no bonus scheme in operation, however, for junior members of the company. Management accountant Matthew English believes his employment package to be very competitive. 'If I was disappointed, I think the company would respond, but you must prove your worth daily and weekly. A lot is expected of you – it can be exhausting, but stimulating. People don't make excuses for their jobs – they just do something about it if they are not happy. A few people do leave. If you can't take pressure, you are going to struggle in this company.'

The basic employment package also includes both pension and life insurance schemes, and a 10 per cent international travel discount through another subsidiary company within the Inspectorate group. All staff, their spouses and children, are members of the Private Patients Plan. Some 30 per cent of the staff have a company car.

Within Meridian in the UK, about 18 per cent of the employees are managers; the rest of the work force perform sales, clerical and administrative roles. There is a definite drive to keep overheads lean, and avoid a top-heavy management structure. The attrition rate is low – the company in the UK losing only five staff in 1987 despite the acquisition and the move to Ealing.

'We get people involved in the company, and to take responsibility for their own area, so that they feel that what they do matters,' says Merrinam. 'We take time to make sure staff are aware of what other areas of the business do.' Both weekly and quarterly meetings with departmental managers make sure that reports on recent events are fed back quickly to staff. 'I feel there is a much greater chance of having an input into sorting problems out here,' comments field sales manager, Ros James. 'I feel part of it, not just an employee. I hope that won't change as the company grows.'

Meridian, as reflects a modern industry, has no bias in favour of any group of employees, and is an equal-opportunities employer. The work force has a 50:50 ratio of women and men. Although staff are given a written job description on joining the company, it changes from review to review as the employee, the job, and the company, change. Besides one woman member on a board of three, there is a woman manager (as well as three men managers) at the 40-strong general services division based in Warwick, and five of the eleven-strong management team in Ealing are female.

The atmosphere within Meridian could well be summed up by account manager Ross Cunliffe. 'Meridian is a quick-witted company, nimble on its feet. If you accept responsibility and make decisions people applaud. If you get it wrong, you are kicked around the car park!' Even so, Cunliffe enjoys working for Meridian, because he feels he is paid well, and that his job is personally challenging. 'I like working to targets and beating them. That is typical of most people that work here.'

METAL BOX

One of Europe's largest packaging companies, Metal Box employs 26,000 people. Turnover in 1987 was £1.1 billion with pre-tax profits of £82 million. Headquarters are in Reading.

pay ☐	ambience ☐
benefits ☐	environment ☐
promotion ☐	equal opportunities ☐
training ☐	communications ☐

'You must have heard this story,' says Brian Smith, chairman of Metal Box. 'Two trekkers in the forest came face to face with a bear. One of them slowly takes off his walking shoes, puts on his trainers and places his knapsack on the ground. "What are you doing that for?" asks the other. "You can't run faster than the bear." "I don't need to run faster than the bear," he replies. "Only faster than you."'

'The bear' has eaten over half of Metal Box in the past ten years, but it would appear that what remains is running pretty fast nowadays. Metal Box is a medium-sized multinational with a turnover of over £1 billion, and a very large number of factory sites. The main business of Metal Box falls under the general heading of packaging. Perhaps it is best known as a manufacturer of tin cans for food and for drink, which are slowly being replaced by plastic. This change has forced Metal Box to reorganize almost constantly, closing down outdated plant and developing new product lines. At times during the 1970s and early 1980s the company seemed to be drowning rather than waving.

Smith's arrival from ICI in 1986 breathed a new spirit into senior management, a spirit which they are now being urged to convey to the shop floor. Essentially, Smith came in and told managers to raise their heads from the gutters up to the stars. 'When I was younger a football team would play to a set pattern. You'd never see a winger in midfield or a fullback in the other side's half, but look at teams nowadays – much more fluid. We want to motivate people to move around the pitch too.'

The psychological impact of this change in attitude cannot be overstated. From a position where managers were always on the defensive, always being asked to cut back, they were suddenly asked to expand: to think up new areas for possible investment. In short, they were asked to be entrepreneurs, not managers. All the senior managers we spoke to were full of praise for Brian Smith's innovations.

The group is divided into five broad operating categories:

UK Packaging, which makes up about half of group turnover and operates in food, beverage and general packaging
Packaging International – operating in Europe, Africa, India and the Middle East
USA – packaging and security printing (e.g. chequebooks)
Central Heating – manufacturing and selling in the UK and Europe
Engineering – building packaging machines

Smith's first innovation was to sell off the corporate head office and reduce central staff from 600 to 100. Prior to his arrival the senior management of each division were based at head office, so they were immediately sent off to individual operating units of each division. He was keen to see strategic planning as well as day-to-day operations devolved as far as possible to the operating units. 'We think the head office function should simply be the creative end of the personnel department,' says Smith.

Much of what remains of head office is dedicated to compiling the 'Agenda for Change', investigating areas such as strategy, market responsiveness, quality, innovation, and associating these with the human resources of the company, through recruitment, training and promotion. In principle, the agenda is defined by the management and personnel of each operating company, with head office acting only as coordinator. To this end Smith has been systematically meeting the top 200 managers in the company and asking for their observations as to how the quality and performance of the business can be improved. He has instituted six-monthly meetings for them all. With the amount of reorganization already achieved, Smith is now considering whether it is time to change the corporate image.

To see how all this feverish reorganization is taking effect one has to consider the basic personnel structure of the group. Beneath the top 200 managers there are another 900 executive staff, each with an individual assessment and reward package. Most other employees are skilled or semiskilled engineering workers. Take incentives as an example: formerly, only the top 200 managers received a bonus related to profitability, and that was at a fixed rate. First they introduced variable rates depending on performance of the individual, and now all the executive staff are being put on the variable-rate bonus. However, letting the system work through to the factory floor is difficult. One manager told us that he has been unable to persuade his immediate superior that such a scheme was feasible.

Another insight into the changes within the group came through visiting their brand-new 'Lamipac' packaging factory. Lamipac is a plastic package that can be used to store food at room temperature for up to two years. It is this kind of material that is replacing the tin can. Ray Fazakerly, the manager of the factory, has been with Metal Box for twenty-five years. He started off as an apprentice and has worked his way around a large part of the company. He summed up the recent changes: 'We now have a better working relationship with the employees: the old systems are gone and we are breaking down barriers.' For instance, the factory has a team meeting on a regular basis to discuss progress, including profitability. This differs from the Industrial Society's concept of the team briefing in operation in the rest of the company, which is more restricted in terms of the questions which can be asked. Paul Ramsay, an engineering union convenor who has been with Metal Box for nineteen years, says, 'Team briefings are a waste of time, but I like the team meetings because we get a lot of information. Whatever shift you're on, people always turn up at the team meeting.'

As far as pay and benefits are concerned, the company says that it aims to be competitive rather than at the top of the range, and this is probably a fair appraisal. A semiskilled worker will get around £190 a week and a skilled worker about £220. Like everyone in the company, they get a pension and an SAYE share option scheme. Paul Ramsay described the company's pay and benefits as 'not bad for this area'. On the executive staff you might start on around £9500 per annum, rising to £15,000 by mid-twenties, £20,000 by early thirties and £40,000 by late thirties if you reach senior management. However, as the company tries to become more performance-orientated, the range in terms of age and salary is becoming quite wide.

One of the strongest aspects of Metal Box is its training which covers an enormous range of activities. The company sponsors around 60 individuals through university at any one time, including one year at Metal Box on £5500 net, plus expenses, and an annual bursary while at college of £1575. Newly-employed graduates are sent on a two-month induction course which involves moving around the country to various manufacturing sites and being asked to identify and solve particular problems on the factory floor. It also includes a week-long

208

endeavour training course involving rock climbing, abseiling, orienteering, and so on.

For a company which has always enjoyed a good reputation as an employer, has been through severe traumas in recent years, and is now trying to change itself, Metal Box gets ten out of ten for effort. Brian Smith plays down his own role in all this. 'The days of the "battleship" company with the Admiral sitting on the bridge are gone. Today, companies have to be more like a fleet of frigates working together on a joint mission.' This may be so; but at Metal Box it is clear that the current Admiral is playing a large role in shaping that mission.

MFI

MFI is a furniture manufacturer and retailer. It employs 5834 people in the UK. Turnover in 1987 was £420 million, with a pre-tax profit of £46 million. Headquarters are in London.

pay	☐	ambience	☐
benefits	☐	environment	☐
promotion	☐	equal opportunities	☐
training	☐	communications	☐

'I've bought stuff from MFI,' boasts one senior staff member, 'and I've had no problems with it, touch wood – well, chipboard.' Sometimes even MFI managers forget that it is trying hard to shed its old image of the 'if you touch it, it falls apart' bargain basement. The brash 1950s Brentford Nylons style advertising has finally been buried, and the company's 'Take A Look At Us Now' campaign is encouraging customers to come back into new, livelier stores. They now sell carpets and lighting as well as complete bathrooms but it will take time for the message to get through. Meanwhile MFI is still the butt of many a comedian's humour.

Mullard Furniture Industries invented the flatpack idea in 1964, originally using mail order and then opening up their own stores. Anyone could take home a table or chair in a kit and assemble it themselves. Since then MFI has grown into a company with a £420 million turnover. It is the biggest furniture retailer in Europe and is expanding worldwide – originating products in Siberia which it sells in Philadelphia. By 1982 it was attracting takeover speculation and it soon became part of the Asda giant supermarket chain. Five years later Asda needed cash fast and sold off MFI in Britain's biggest management buy-out. Some 350 of MFI's top staff demonstrated their faith in the company by buying it for £750 million.

MFI has ten times as many stores and ten times as many staff as it did fifteen years ago. Since the buy-out managers have been reluctant to move on, but new openings are still creating plenty of opportunities. There is a limit to the number of full-size MFIs any one country can take. Ideally a site should be in a community of at least 100,000 people, but most of those already have an MFI so the company is getting round this in three ways.

First, it is expanding internationally – setting up operations in the United States, the Middle and Far East and Australia. MFI has a register of all languages spoken by staff and is preparing for the Single European Market of 1992. MFI's main supplier Hygena is now part of the group and has stores in France and Spain. Second, it is opening cut-down MFI 'fitted' stores and mini-MFI advance-order-only 'boutiques' which would slot into any High Street. Third, it is widening the range of products it sells. MFI sees its competitors as being not just furniture stores but every other retailer: 'We are selling against compact disc players and the lot.' MFI realized that selling kitchen furniture without cookers or fridges meant that 'we were selling holes'. Now you can buy white goods at MFI as well.

'People think there are only two jobs in retailing,' says an MFI personnel officer. 'Check-out operator and fashion buyer for C&A.' MFI's policy is to 'get the best, train the best and retain the best'. They are looking for people with strong, outgoing personalities. Staff have to prove themselves on the shop floor before they can get promotion. Some 80 per cent of managers come through the business. There are incentives in the form of bonuses and competitions throughout the organization. The directors quote Napoleon's saying about a field marshal's baton being in every private's knapsack. They can point to regional managers who started out as warehousemen.

MFI spends millions of pounds a year on training. At the same time it is also encouraging a graduate recruitment programme and along with other major retailers, such as BHS, Marks & Spencer, Dixons and the Co-op, has backed a new degree course in retail marketing. There is even an MFI chair in retailing at Manchester Polytechnic.

MFI has more than 4000 full-time and nearly 2000 part-time staff. Those working on the tills and in the warehouses earn around £7500–£9500 including store bonus. This can be about 10 per cent of wages. Salespeople on the shop floor earn around £16,000 a year and managers between £16,000 and £24,000. MFI deliberately runs on low staffing levels, which can cause problems when people are ill but they believe that up to a point 'the less people you have the more gets done'. School-leavers with 'A' levels are encouraged to spend a year on the shop floor before going on to the management training scheme. MFI recruits 60 management trainees a year, mostly from the shops but also graduates straight from college.

Second-year managers are sent on week-long courses at Ashridge Management College and MFI is setting up an MBA in retailing with the Open University. Deputy managers qualify for a car and at twenty-four a management trainee could be managing a store with a turnover of £5 million a year. Head office offers other opportunities for promotion and MFI is considering setting up an accelerator programme to attract graduates who specifically want to aim for senior management positions.

MFI sends all its staff on a two-day residential customer-care course. There is also a continuing cartoon strip in the weekly publication *HOB* to reinforce the message. *HOB* is a cheerful mixture of sales reports, competition winners, safety and product news, complaints and accolades from customers.

Few women are in management grades. It seems to be easier for women to make progress in head office where there are 16 female department managers and now also a director. There are only three managers out in the stores.

MFI is competition-crazy. Every year there is a High Flyers competition. All the staff of the winning branch plus their spouses get a four-day break in the sun and staff from neighbouring stores have to fill in while they are away. There are in-house Masterminds, complete with black leather chair and spotlight, and other competitions between offices and warehouses. Over 100 MFI staff win breaks abroad with their partners every year. Nearly 90 per cent of the employees turned up to a National Sports Day a couple of years ago.

Benefits include 20 per cent off MFI products, full BUPA cover, and legal support for litigious employees. MFI still thinks of itself as a young company, but 111 people joined the Ten-Year Club for long-standing employees last year putting a strain on the supply of £200 silver salvers and plaques.

MFI is preparing to go public in 1990 and a share-participation fund is being set up to encourage more of the staff to feel they own the company. It is still expanding fast and open to keen school-leavers looking for a career, as well as to graduates wanting a grounding in the retail industry. Managers rarely work more than 45–50 hours, but retailing is not a career for someone who values weekends.

The company image is still a problem. When MFI and Habitat opened stores near each other in the home counties recently, MFI had problems competing for quality staff. But MFI's product has improved and its reputation is changing. Managers are clear that they want to be seen as 'the Marks & Spencer of the furniture business'. Head-hunters already chase MFI's managers and rival companies have asked MFI to train their staff. The in-house design departments are being asked to produce glamour products such as record sleeves.

Perhaps when the company hits the market with the predicted capitalization of over a billion pounds, employees will no longer confess that 'I don't mention who I work for at parties'.

3M

3M – Minnesota Mining & Manufacturing – employs 4500 people in the UK spread between headquarters in Bracknell, Berkshire, and manufacturing in various locations, especially South Wales. The company is the wholly-owned subsidiary of its American parent of the same name. The company manufactures and markets coated abrasives, notably Scotch tapes and 3M notelets. The company does not publish UK figures but its parent reported $8.6 billion sales in 1986.

pay	☐	ambience	☐
benefits	☐	environment	☐
promotion	☐	equal opportunities	☐
training	☐	communications	☐

When Thomas Peters and Rober Waterman compiled their influential text *In Search of Excellence*, they devoted eleven pages to discussing the contribution made by 3M to innovation. Above all else 3M revolves on creating new ideas. The ubiquitous yellow adhesive notelets were just one product of the company's enthusiasm for an idea. An eleventh commandment – Thou Shalt Not Kill A New Product Idea – exists at its St Paul headquarters, Minnesota, and, although the innovation fever is somewhat more controlled at the Bracknell headquarters of 3M UK, there is certainly no absence of creativity and originality.

The company started in the mining sector. In 1902 the business was founded in Two Harbors, Minnesota, but unfortunately its mineral deposits at Crystal Bay were almost worthless. In 1905, after a move to Duluth, 3M started making sandpaper. Five years later it moved again to settle in St Paul. Cloth abrasives were introduced in 1914, and in 1919 annual sales reached $1 million. In 1925 Scotch masking tape was first devised, and within four years the company joined with other groups in the sector to launch Durex Abrasives in the UK. Two years later the first adhesive and coated products were brought on to the market. In the early 1950s Durex was renamed 3M and Scotch audio tape was created. In 1965 global sales reached $1 billion. Throughout this period and up to the present day 3M introduced new products in a wide variety of areas. The four main areas of business are industrial and consumer; electronic and information transfer; graphic technology; and life sciences.

In its booklet 'A Profile of the Company', 3M UK suggests that its approach to corporate development is based on small units which are largely autonomous, encouraging initiative and making a permanent contribution to the community. Mark Smith, 3M UK career and organization development manager, says, 'We do encourage a climate of innovation. In fact, I was at a CBI conference when, completely unsolicited by us, one of the speakers mentioned 3M as a company which not only has the ability to innovate in terms of products, but also to create markets.' As many as 25 per cent of current 3M products were not on the market five years ago. 'We're very proud of that,' says Smith. 'It's a very strong thrust.'

Innovation creates its own set of structures. 'We are a worldwide business. But under that total umbrella there are many different businesses. The range of our products includes the production of Scotch videocassettes, which everyone has heard of. Then we are talking about light water chemicals for fire extinguishing in plane crashes, and fluoro chemicals for carpet protection. We are also selling reflective materials for road traffic signs. Now these businesses are worldwide concerns. There is strong linkage. The man running the videocassette business in the UK is utilizing resources which may be in other parts of the world. So there has to be a worldwide business strategy. But that does not dictate. It's a strategy built up from the bottom,' Smith says.

Jack Heritage, who has been with 3M for nineteen years as a business planner, says that after four years with Sainsbury's and five at Lucas the immediacy of decision-making is remarkable. 'You are encouraged to function and think as an individual. I still think it's true that we operate as individuals. There has to be some corporate culture – not imposed upon you but as a backdrop against which you can work.' He says that the downside of the culture is that there is some duplication or triplication of effort which can be unproductive.

Ken Woolley, engineering design manager, says that the small autonomous groups which work on projects do enjoy a genuine sense of freedom. 'As much responsibility as possible for operating the equipment is given to the operators themselves, with some guidance from local supervision.' Woolley adds that the company is looking for ways to make the work more stimulating. 'You have got to think of new ways to do your job, all the way from the operator to senior management. And you get a feed of information percolating down through the organization.'

Communication is one of the company's strong points. It seems it has an easy facility with words and setting out in clear language the direction of the various business activities. 'It is one of the hardest things to do in a multinational corporation – free and frank communication. We are not brilliant, we're learning all the time. You try to recognize that it is the only way you can get trust, understanding, cooperation,' commented Woolley.

3M people at any level talk about anything other than pay or conditions, and not because these are bad. Quite the contrary. 3M is one of the best payers in the country. David Smith, a project engineer, says, 'I suppose everyone complains about salaries but 3M pay better than most. We are in the higher bracket of salary payers.' Salaries are reviewed annually.

Training is high-quality and virtually continuous. In all the business units training is coexistent with commercial and research activities. The company uses several external consultants, but Time Manager is used predominantly.

3M is a smashing company. It is integrated without being overwhelming. People are committed to quality and innovation, but always with an eye to commercial application. There is a genuine freedom of communication, and senior management listen when staff put forward good ideas. Last year business manager readers of the American magazine *Fortune* voted 3M among the most admired corporations in the States. To that accolade they can add being one of the best employers in Britain.

MOTOR PANELS

Motor Panels is a division of Rubery Owen Holdings, a UK group with activities overseas. Motor Panels employs 900 people and produces cabs for commercial vehicles and tractors. Turnover for Panels and its subsidiaries is £35 million. It is based in Coventry.

pay	☐	ambience	☐
benefits	☐	environment	☐
promotion	☐	equal opportunities	☐
training	☐	communications	☐

Motor Panels operates in what must surely be the roughest, toughest area of British industry. Sandwiched between Europe's strife-torn steel mills and Britain's strike-prone car industry, Motor Panels still manages to operate – often on a knife edge, but always with flair, imagination, foresight and downright determination.

It is not an easy company to work for. Motor Panels has no patience with the sort of attitude that used to prevail in the car industry, but if you do your job the rewards are there for the asking. Prolonged industrial action spurred the Coventry company to take a good look at its industrial relations. The result is a model for British industry.

Motor Panels is a division of Rubery Owen Holdings which has interests in France, Holland, India and Italy and joint ventures with Rockwell. It includes Motor Panels (Coventry), three subsidiaries and three associate companies. Customers include Rover, DAF, Enasa, Foden, Ford, General Motors, Iveco-Ford, Jaguar, Komatsu, Land Rover, Leyland Vehicles, Massey-Ferguson, Rolls-Royce and Volvo.

Managing director is Merrick Taylor, and on first sight he would appear more suited to a job in the theatre or public relations. Taylor started his career as an apprentice with Rover. In 1966 he came to Motor Panels as PA to the managing director. A year later he became technical director. He was elevated to the MD's chair in 1973 and took the company to the position of Europe's leading independent designer and manufacturer of truck cabs with 25 per cent of the market. At the heart of Taylor's business philosophy is a belief in excellence.

In practice this is worked out in quality circles. By pooling the creative talents of designers, production people and shop-floor staff, and inputting capital, Taylor has created a business with 25 per cent of the UK market. He has found the right combination of keeping his people happy and making money. In short, everyone knows what everyone else is doing, and they are all pulling in the same direction.

Their attitude towards lorry drivers is indicative. 'A cab is a home from home,' says Greg Horne, Taylor's personal assistant. People who work for Motor Panels have friends or relatives who drive lorries, and when they return from long trips any moans will filter through. Shop manager Ken Williams says, 'The British are the most conscientious people in the world. The British are these guys and their relatives. If they hear lorry drivers say their cabs are no good, they know the buyers will go elsewhere and their jobs are at stake.'

Apart from the emphasis on quality, the company has decentralized its decision-making. Each manager has genuine responsibility for his work force. It operates a vigorous absenteeism policy, tempered with a degree of understanding. Recently, one man was consistently absent. He was called in for a chat with his boss. The man was facing considerable financial problems. His boss helped him to sort them out and now he scarcely has a day off sick.

The company has gone through a metamorphosis in industrial relations, taking the risky step of appointing a senior union convenor as industrial relations officer. Coventry is traditionally at the centre of union activities where the word confrontation is writ large. Motor Panels negotiators succeeded in finding the magic formula. While there was an element of take it or leave it in the negotiations, this style appeared to work and relations are positive.

Works convenor Jack Starkey joined Motor Panels in 1963. He spent sixteen years as a shop steward in the press shop and has seen both bosses and new ideas come and go. Now he views the future with special confidence. 'It is a good atmosphere. We are on first-name terms with the management and they are all reasonable in their approach,' he says. Starkey went through the rough spell, which was blamed on militant shop stewards, but he is now content that the present arrangements of job flexibility and training are working well. 'They are hard at times in negotiation. The company is not going to give us everything we want, but at the end of the day common sense prevails and both sides come to a sensible agreement. They always explain why they cannot meet a particular claim.'

The company operates a one-year agreement with the AEU, T&GWU and the National Society of Metal Mechanics. Nine shop stewards represent the 400 shop-floor workers at the plant. Anyone made redundant in past years is the first in line when new vacancies are on offer.

The stability and future prospects at Motor Panels are its best points, according to Starkey, but some improvement in the general tidiness of the shop floor is badly needed.

More than 80 per cent of the company's projects have been developed internally from prototype. Motor Panels has developed a simplified form of cab assembly – the Cube Principle – which brings together six sides of a box. This negates the need for expensive and complex assembly jigs and allows the cab to be welded with six or eight spot guns. More usual techniques would require some thirty such operations.

Motor Panels is not a gentle or comfortable place to work. It calls on its employees' resilience and dependability. Its determination to achieve the very best is obvious at the slightest glance. Yet it is the same desire to work for the best in the field, which also drives chemists to work for Glaxo and physicists for British Aerospace, which sends high-quality assembly men to Motor Panels.

NATIONAL FREIGHT
CORPORATION

The National Freight Corporation is an employee-owned transport and distribution group. It employs 28,000 in nine divisions. In 1986 its turnover reached £750 million, showing pre-tax profits of £48.7 million. Its headquarters are in Bedford.

pay ▢		ambience ▢
benefits ▢		environment ▢
promotion ▢		equal opportunities ▢
training ▢		communications ▢

At the beginning of 1988 National Freight Corporation received press coverage for some unusual problems. The organization had been spectacularly successful since it began life in 1982. But at the start of 1988 its directors wanted to go for a stock market listing. For most strong-performance companies a flotation on the stock exchange would be relatively simple. But for NFC its structure presented a real dilemma. National Freight is 83 per cent employee-owned.

One of the question marks over the proposed £500 million float was the double-voting right enjoyed by employees. 'We hope that the Exchange will agree that a guy who has all his life, his money and his employment in the company should have a greater say in who controls the business,' chairman Sir Peter Thompson told the *Evening Standard*.

It is this unusual structure which sets NFC apart from other companies in this increasingly competitive sector. 'NFC will maintain its commitment to widespread employee control, it will have a participative style associated with first-class results orientated package.' This is the NFC 'Business Mission'. It emerged from the strongly demoralized and poor performing nationalized company which became the subject of a unique form of privatization in 1982.

Since then, NFC has achieved major advances in morale, commitment, and profits. One staffer told us: 'Before 1982 people were not very well informed and did not want to be; now it's like a big family.'

Even so NFC is a bewildering collection of companies – more than fifty – operating in road transport and distribution. There are nine major divisions: BRS group, distribution, property, special services,

Pickfords, Lynx Express, Pickfords Travel, Tempco Union and NFC International.

This *mèlange* is managed from a large modern head office in Bedford. Sitting in his office there, deputy chairman and finance director James Watson identifies the four main areas for expansion. 'We want to expand NFC International with a particular eye to Europe, contract distribution for supermarket chains, the travel agency concentrating on the US, and, finally, property development.'

The track record to date in the first five years is impressive. Profits have mushroomed from £4 million in 1982 to £48.7 million in 1986. And the company is looking for groupwide growth of between 15 per cent and 20 per cent.

NFC employs 28,000 people in locations across the UK. Among the 70 per cent who are shareholders, those who bought in in 1982 have seen their profits increase fiftyfold. By any standards it is a remarkable achievement. But it also shows in what a desperate state the company was before the employees took over. The structure has been a positive force in galvanizing employee attitudes. Jacky Connor, a marketing assistant at National Carriers who has been with the company since 1985, sums up the prevailing attitude. 'When I bought my shares I did feel more of a responsibility towards the company.'

The NFC work force is probably one of the best informed in the country on how shareholders operate and what movements in the market mean for their own stakes in the company. The information department spends most of its budget on explaining issues related to ownership.

NFC shares are not traded on the market in the usual way, in order that control is retained by the employees. Shares can be bought and sold on one of the four account days in the year. The price is set by accountants Ernst & Whinney on the basis of the price of comparable stocks in the transport sector.

The first account after Black Monday saw a considerable drop in the price of NFC but that did not deter anyone from dealing. Owning the company means that employees can, and do, demand accountability from the management. Senior executives seem to regard this as a task to set about with great enthusiasm. 'In a democratic company like NFC success comes through keeping people informed,' says Andrew Parkhouse, communications manager.

Parkhouse sits on top of a department which produces a quarterly magazine for shareholders, a company magazine for all employees and newsletters. The company is divided into eight regions. Each region is addressed quarterly by a member of the board. An annual national

221

employee report amounts to an exegesis of the report and accounts. The company also produces several leaflets explaining share ownership.

Informing the work force is not treated as a solely statutory obligation. Watson argues that it is the essence of the enterprise. 'NFC can perform better because it has a committed work force, and to maintain that commitment the work force has to be kept fully informed, not just as employees but as owners.' NFC have an almost religious dedication to communication.

Another facet of the total employee involvement in company affairs is the training policy. 'We expect 80 per cent of our executive board to be home grown. We consider that everyone who joins us has the chairman's baton in his knapsack,' said Watson.

Pay at NFC is average for the sector, but with 70 per cent of staff on dividends the picture looks slightly rosier. A graduate can expect to earn £9000 a year on day one. After five years he or she could expect to be on around £20,000. But non-managerial grades are on significantly less. A secretary with two and a half years' experience earns £5000 and a packer at Pickford, after five years at NFC, only £5500.

Holidays are single status at 25 days a year. Staff also benefit from a discount on Pickford removals and holidays. There is a contributory pension scheme which is unusually high: $7\frac{1}{2}$ per cent of salary. NFC does not provide private health care, and sickness benefit is standard and without frills. Canteen facilities at HQ are fair and the company is trying to raise the quality of food elsewhere in the company.

Industrial relations are generally very good, as might be expected with a strong employee ownership. Redundancy payments are set at above state provision and limited attempts are made at replacement opportunities. Benefits are negotiated on the basis of agreements which have stood for more than fifty years.

More recently a graduated bonus scheme has been introduced. This is aimed at improving profitability in individual profit centres. If a centre reaches its targets, then a 10 per cent bonus is paid. Outperformed targets are rewarded with bonuses which increase *pro rata* to 30 per cent of salary.

The 10 per cent scheme is not guaranteed though, and its payment depends on a number of factors. A company profit scheme provides an average 2 per cent of salary on meeting general group targets. This has been amended recently to allow payments up to 15 per cent.

The makeup of NFC varies enormously from office to office and centre to centre, and the corporate culture is not allowed to mask the

222

NATIONAL FREIGHT CORPORATION

personalities of the sites. This means that working experience of NFC varies radically from site to site.

It should not be a surprise to anyone that NFC management have not yet got the whole picture perfect. In 1982, it was in a mess. Recovery in some areas has been a slow process. But improvements are being made all the time.

In the past NFC has never had a particularly strong profile in the community. Steps are now being taken to rectify this. A whole programme of different support activities is being put into motion. Among them are sheltered housing, and a support scheme for retired workers.

Few companies have everything right. Even fewer have to cope with a backlog of poor performance – both in profits and human relations. NFC is attempting to make sense of its business, and management are achieving major gains every year. If all goes to plan, in five years the company will be lifted out of a tangled confusion into a finely woven future.

NATIONAL PANASONIC

National Panasonic is the wholly-owned subsidiary of Matsushita Electric of Japan. It employs 900 people at its plant near Cardiff, which today makes TVs and tuners. In 1987 the group had worldwide sales of $10.15 billion and pre-tax profits of $889.1 million.

pay	☐	ambience	☐
benefits	☐	environment	☐
promotion	☐	equal opportunities	☐
training	☐	communications	☐

'When you go out into town and you see a Panasonic television set, you think to yourself, I made that' – the proud words of Janet French, a line supervisor at the National Panasonic plant near Cardiff. Her enthusiasm for the product is mirrored by her dedication to the company.

Panasonic people show remarkable commitment to the Japanese company which started producing colour television sets in 1976. Susan Hafizi, senior floorwoman, recalls the early days. 'There were only 25 people when I first came here. 130 of us all joined on the same day. It's a young company and we've grown with it.' She says that the commitment to quality is a main aspect of the work. 'They like you to stay after work and hold line meetings to discuss how the work has gone today, and how you might improve quality.'

An assistant in production control, Stephen Parry, says, 'On a line of 20 people you are all working on your individual piece but you are all pulling together to meet that day's targets.' French agreed. 'Everyone on the line gets on well. The company keeps us informed and I know if I tell them that we must get an extra 300 out the same day, at the end of the day we will have got the 300 out.'

It is that same enthusiasm which encouraged Konosuke Matsushita to launch his first business in 1918. In 1925 he registered the name National and manufactured his first torch. His conviction that the flashlight would become a household item pushed him into mass production. Maintaining the quality but keeping the price low resulted in widespread demand for the product.

Matsushita was a remarkable man. He held views that were decades ahead of his time. In 1932 he talked to his work force about the mission of a manufacturer. This was to overcome poverty. Businesses are not meant to enrich merely their owners but the whole of society.

The following year, as part of a twenty-five-year mission to put his ideas into practice, he introduced a seven-point code to his staff. The code called for spirit of service through industry, of fairness, of harmony and cooperation, of striving for progress, of courtesy and humility, of accord with natural laws and of gratitude. And it is with spiritual insight and dedication that he pursued his objectives.

These seven watchwords remain the guiding principles of the Matsushita businesses today. The company's commercial and human relations philosophy, as set out by Matsushita, is at all times to be objective, to trust your employees, to recognize that everyone is an asset and to find the right balance between the spiritual and practical aspects of life.

His thoughts underline every activity of the Cardiff plant. Every Monday morning there is an assembly at which everyone in the factory is present. They can see the managing director and top officials, and hear how the company is doing. The organization is avowedly single status. There is one dining room only. David Fowler, personnel director, says: 'Our market philosophy is one of building up a close relationship with our dealers. We sell a quality product and on our shop floor you will see posters about quality, cleanliness and tidiness. So the emphasis on the product range is always on quality. Many of our competitors will sell in the mass market to big institutions. We don't. We try to sell on the market philosophy of after-sales service, technical back-up and service to the customer.'

The employees play a major part in that. 'I think the key expression in our relationship with all our employees is one of involvement, getting employees involved with the company,' he says. Parry comments that 'We are encouraged to make suggestions on improving efficiency. You get a good feeling if your idea is taken up and it is helping the company.'

Meetings are part and parcel of working at Panasonic. Everyone attends a meeting at the beginning of the financial year where the next three-year plan is explained. Section heads will hold group gatherings to explain a change in the line or a production quota. Panasonic believes that everyone should be as fully informed as possible to carry out their jobs.

Training is another major facet of working at the plant. Much of the training is on the job. Some floormen and women are flown to Japan to understand better how the company does things.

225

Promotion from within is a cardinal rule. 'Many people here started in fairly lowly positions and have achieved quite high levels. Some of the British UK directors started as technicians and foremen. You don't get that quite so much with British companies,' says Brown. 'It doesn't mean that we don't recruit from outside. We do for specialist needs, but increasingly we try to support our manpower by developing people internally as opposed to taking people externally.'

The organization has a no-redundancies policy. 'Earlier we did have a downturn in the music centre business, but we absorbed all those people and obviously we knew we would be expanding.'

Pay is very good – and not only for the area. There is a wide range of benefits which are almost comparable with an American multinational. Among them is a product discount of 30 per cent off the shop price of any Matsushita product imported into the UK or made here, a 3 per cent contributory pension and a high-quality subsidized canteen.

A significant majority of the work force is made up of women and the company takes good care to inform them about their rights, especially in the maternity area. But women are not in senior positions of management – yet. 'Five or six years ago women got the little jobs because the men wouldn't do them. But as time has gone on and we have proved ourselves, more women have reached more senior positions,' says one woman on the shop floor.

National Panasonic runs a spotless factory. Its communications are legendary, its methods innovative. As the company grows its ideas will have wider influence in people management throughout industry.

NISSAN UK

Nissan UK is the wholly-owned subsidiary of the Nissan Motor Company of Japan. It employs 1100 people at its site in Sunderland, Tyne and Wear, where cars are manufactured.

pay	☐	ambience	☐
benefits	☐	environment	☐
promotion	☐	equal opportunities	☐
training	☐	communications	☐

The flood of Japanese investors into the UK reached a high-water mark when the Nissan Motor Company moved into Sunderland. Suddenly the national press woke up to the novel techniques of these Oriental masters of high-quality, low-cost production. But as always attention focused not on the truly innovative aspects of their personnel management but rather on the array of Japanese foods available in the Nissan canteen alongside the traditional English meat and two veg. Some more adventurous correspondents, sniffing a story, devoted feature pages to the physical workouts and exercise programmes bolted into the working day at many Japanese factories.

Too little interest centred on single-status policies where managers could genuinely manage and workers could feel proud of the job they were doing. Self-respect had been restored to the workplace. In the pitted industrial landscape of the northeast, a job in itself was precious. A job in which individuals were encouraged to contribute and play a part in the entire process of car manufacturing was treated with a powerful degree of scepticism. The tale had been told before. The difference was that Nissan meant it: more than that, it is essential to the company's way of doing business.

Nissan is one of the most intensely studied of all the Japanese businesses which have been set up in the UK. In December 1987 the *Sunday Times* reported that Japanese businessmen were investing a total of $4 billion in the UK. The largest of their concerns is Nissan, which aims to be producing 200,000 cars in Sunderland by 1992 with a work force of 3500. Fresh attention was generated when Nissan announced the latest phase of the programme. The *Daily Mail* compared the lot of a Nissan worker in the UK with his counterpart in

Japan, but a comparison with the average worker in each of the British car factories would be more telling. The Nissan worker is better off. This is all the more remarkable considering the impact of the 1970s recession on the northeast. Some companies collapsed completely, others were reduced to a shell, and some – like Vickers Defence Systems (pages 344–6) – hammered out new worker–management accords.

Nissan could have picked anywhere in Europe; and certainly several countries pressed for their favours. Locally-raised finance and health support from the government encouraged Nissan to decide on Tyne and Wear. Toshi Yasuda, corporate manager for Europe, told the *Sunday Times*: 'We feel welcome here and that's important. You cannot operate in an unfriendly environment.'

The company quickly established that it had more of a statement to make about employee practice than press-ups and raw fish. 'The policies in action at our Sunderland plant are a mixture of all that's best from Europe, America and Japan,' says personnel director Peter Wickens, reluctant to give all the credit to his Japanese masters. 'The Japanese have no monopoly on good management and the agreement we achieved here with the Amalgamated Union of Engineering Workers owes more to the work of British and American companies than it does to the agreements reached between Nissan and the Japan Auto Workers Union. We have also consistently said that success depends not on the wording of the agreement but on the underlying management philosophy and the working practices which the philosophy generates,' Wickens told the trade journal *Personnel Management*.

Within two years of conversion from greenfield site to purpose-built car plant, Nissan UK employed one-third of its projected work force. By 1992 the company may have developed on to three adjacent sites, into one of the largest auto manufacturers in the country. The company claims that 60 per cent of its components are manufactured locally and 40 per cent imported from Japan. Local observers, however, claim that 35 per cent UK product is nearer the mark. Regardless of this, the plant should be on target for 80 per cent local production by the early 1990s.

The investment is long term. The parent company does not expect to make a profit from its UK subsidiary before the early 1990s. But like all its other projections this has a fair chance of being achieved. Policies and planning are what set Nissan apart. Wickens says that these are arrived at by drawing on a number of influences. There are three main components to Nissan's management philosophy: creating the right atmosphere, a commitment to quality, and flexibility in every aspect of work. To ensure that this is achieved, Nissan management keeps every other employment practice even simpler. Everyone is on common terms of employment, all staff are salaried and any worker can get promotion. The structure limits the number of job titles which are available, since only six different grades exist.

Underpinning it all is the concept of *kaizen*, which in essence means improvement, and is extended to all aspects of work. It is ever present within the factory and everyone understands it, and it is the motivating force behind any decision or action. Improvement should be built into every job, and every individual should seek new ideas and find ways to improve his approach to his task.

On the shop floor the manufacturing staff work in teams to build the cars. Each group is headed by a team leader. The leader is the focal point of the group and the permanent link with the upper tiers of management. The team leader is totally responsible for his people's attitude to their job, and for achieving targets. He is obliged to know everyone's specific task.

A five-minute meeting at the beginning of every shift is the normal time for disseminating company news, profit forecasts and target projections. Management sees these meetings as key motivation builders. Prior to meeting his group, the team leader will himself have been briefed by his manager. Most teams number up to fifteen people. The key recruiting agent for the team is the leader. He will pick individuals to complement the strength of the team and structure it to a carefully blended composition. He is expected to plug any deficiencies in its unique matrix of skills.

Good communication and commitment mean that workers are now much less dubious about the motives of the proprietors. A good example of this is the body shop, where 90 per cent of the changes which have been made came directly from the workers themselves. *Kaizen* allows workers a direct interest in improving the place where they work and in improving the profits which, if the owners have their figures right, will ultimately spring from the business.

Workers' involvement extends into the area of quality control. Overall responsibility for getting it right first time rests with the manufacturing staff, and they are left in no doubt that quality is sacrosanct. A worker is taught to regard the next man down the line as the final customer. This breeds an attitude of supplying only the best throughout the factory. The commensurate benefit is that an individual feels that his work is worthwhile and it adds to his self-esteem when he gets it right.

Flexibility is also important. There is no point in joining Nissan unless you are willing to turn your hand to anything within the factory. On a day-to-day level, this also means that responsibility for the jobs which accompany the manufacturing process, such as tidiness and maintenance, are left in the hands of the individual worker.

The arrival of Nissan in the northeast has caused many traditionalists to rethink their ideas. No longer could they adopt rigid 'them and us' attitudes. Nissan has effectively abolished them. Union representation is a thing of the past. While the company has signed a single-union agreement with the AEU, only 25 per cent of the staff are members. Nissan has its own company council, elected by the work force, which appears to meet the needs of its staff. Many workers prefer this to a trade union.

Few workers could complain about their free trips to Japan for intensive training courses, and in addition the company arranges courses at a local technical college to develop the skills which are needed to bring the plant up to full capacity. A graduate recruitment plan is now in operation to find jobs for graduate trainees.

The human impact of Nissan has emerged. People without work are now in jobs, and above all they are in jobs which they enjoy. Pay and benefits are average for the sector but the level of contentment would be hard to match. It is an exciting and democratic company, but a demanding place to work. By 1992, when it should be at full stretch, Nissan will be a dominant force in the UK economy.

NORSK HYDRO

Norsk Hydro is the wholly-owned subsidiary of a Norwegian company which has interests in petrochemicals,
light metals, oil, gas and fertilizers. The latter represents
the largest part of the UK business, which is based in
Levington, near Ipswich, Suffolk. The group worldwide
reported £4.7 billion turnover in 1986.

pay	☐	ambience	☐
benefits	☐	environment	☐
promotion	☐	equal opportunities	☐
training	☐	communications	☐

One of the largest businesses in Norway is Norsk Hydro – a diversified
company which is predominantly interested in chemicals. Its businesses in the UK are varied, but the largest, most striking and most
significant is the fertilizers concern.

The core of the division is the old Fisons Fertilizers company which
Norsk took over in 1982. At that time Fisons operated twelve sites
around the country and employed 4000 staff. By 1987 Norsk Hydro
Fertilizers was based at two locations and had 1000 staff.

The rationalization was fraught with pain and difficulty but Dr
Jonathan Fox, head of personnel, says, 'We have rebuilt from ashes
with a great team.' The process of modernization was achieved with
the introduction of new technology and the acceptance of voluntary
redundancy. The redundancy package was exceptionally generous.
Norsk also lowered the retirement age to fifty with full pension rights.

Just as important was the negotiation of a single-union agreement,
completed in 1985. Previously, there had been five trade unions. The
new accord swept away many of the vestiges of the old company. Out
went pay agreements, staffing structures and most of the personnel
policy. It was a key step to recreating the company.

The revised organization pays everyone on a 1600 hours a year
basis, makes salary payments monthly, does not credit overtime but
gives time off in lieu. There is a powerful increase in training.
Interestingly, the company has also become much more efficient. In
1980 Fisons produced 1.2 million tonnes of fertilizer. Today Norsk
Hydro produces an identical amount with a quarter of the staff at one-
sixth of the locations. Overheads have been halved.

'We recognize that this is a fairly static market and one which is tied up with the politics of the environment. Chemical plants are a sensitive issue which is why we have spent £5 million on emission control,' says Anthony Brooks, marketing and sales director. 'We may increase our market share as companies go out of business, because we have high standards.'

Brooks argues that the reorganization of the company will have a noticeable effect on business. 'We have come to the end of a major restructuring. We have not just seen the problem and dealt with it in the short term. We have tackled it from the fundamentals and when times get better we will not go back to our old ways.'

The remedy for failure was a tough one but the company has pulled around. Robert Chippendale, who joined Fisons from Unilever, says, 'I personally believe that if Norsk or someone else had not taken over Fisons it would have broken up. Norsk have done a tremendous amount for the people and for the company. As far as the rationalization went it was as successful as possible – some people were inevitably hurt. But the company spent a lot of time talking to staff, explaining what was going to happen.'

Chippendale, who moved from the head office site at Levington Research Station to Immingham in 1986, says that Norsk have invested £80 million in the fertilizer business. 'Hell, we have got to make it work. There's a commitment now which wasn't there when Fison were in charge. It's a thrill seeing the development.'

Paul Green, a plant manager, joined Fisons in 1975. 'Because of the competition from other European companies, Fisons was living on borrowed time. Fisons was phosphate based while everyone else was producing nitrate-based products. Now we are on nitrates. We've gone through a lot of change and made good progress. People are fully committed and feel part of the company, not just a number.' Green makes another point: 'The company's not quite there as far as profit is concerned but that's not surprising when you think what they inherited.'

People talk excitedly not only about the quality of the organization since the change, but especially about the training schemes which are available. Sue French, a personnel officer at Immingham, comments, 'Everybody on site is being retrained so that everybody can do everything, even down to the cleaning lady.'

Norsk has created impressive training facilities at Levington with video-recording equipment for mock presentations. All staff take part in the training programme and everyone must be retrained in the

Norsk way of doing things to understand the management changes which are taking place.

Chippendale says that the retraining programme was exceptional. 'For a year we attended one day a month – this was a marvellous way to get to know everyone.' There are eight days of compulsory training each year. Training falls into three broad categories: understanding the business, improving skills and adding to general education – for example, adding languages.

Fox explains that the pay and benefits structure has also been revised. 'Our philosophy is a single-status company with the same benefits for all.' Hay/MSL rates the salary as medium, but no one appears to mind too much. Benefits include 24 days' holiday, PPP medical insurance for all, and a share option scheme for the worldwide company. Every job is individually rated for pay purposes, and people earn points according to responsibility and seniority. Pay is rated against this points structure.

The company has also greatly improved its communications policy. Updating meetings are held with managers once a month and group meetings once a week. These are used to disseminate information, but also to listen to ideas coming from the body of the company. In this much more positive environment creative thoughts are encouraged.

Norsk has come a long way in a short time. From an ailing fertilizer company on the brink of collapse it has turned into a thriving business with a clear idea of how to treat its people. Despite the difficulties, long service is common. This can only be encouraged by the radical improvements introduced by Norsk management.

PARKER KNOLL

Parker Knoll is a furniture and textiles business, based in High Wycombe, Buckinghamshire. It is largely a family-owned enterprise. In 1987 the company produced sales of £63 million and a pre-tax profit of £6.8 million.

pay ☐		ambience ☐	
benefits ☐		environment ☐	
promotion ☐		equal opportunities ☐	
training ☐		communications ☐	

'When the factory burnt down in 1970 it was the making of the company. The next day everybody turned up and started clearing up. Nobody complained about the conditions or asked for more money – even the wives of factory workers got involved. The spirit was incredible. From then on there was a new attitude towards management in the company.' These are the words of Martin Jourdan, chairman of Parker Knoll, which might best be described as an extended family of furniture and textile companies.

The business has grown up around families. Martin Jourdan is the great grandson of Frederick Parker who founded the company. His uncle Harry was chairman until 1945, and was succeeded by his grandfather and then his father. Brother Tom and cousin John Arnold are also on the board. John Kitching is managing director of Parker Knoll Textiles, a business started up by his father. William Raymaker runs K. Raymaker Ltd, the curtain velvet manufacturing business, founded by his brother-in-law. Monkwell (textiles) was acquired last year and is managed by Richard Gloyne, who took over the business from his father, and the president of E. Lock, the furniture-maker, is 'Uncle Bert' Lock, now a sprightly ninety-three.

'I don't necessarily want us to be called a family company,' says Jourdan. 'Nepotism is not a good thing, but the company does create a certain attitude of mind. The people who work here are not employees, they're people.'

This approach has certainly been infused throughout the whole company. Jeff Wallace, in charge of their computer department, has worked for seven other companies over a period of twenty-seven years and has now been with this company for three. 'Of all the companies I've worked for Parker Knoll is far and away the most friendly. This is the first company I've worked for that my wife has ever been invited to see.' Derek Williams, a warehouseman who has been with the company for twenty-two years, had a similar story to tell. 'I wrote off a company van a few years back, and the first question my manager asked me the next day when I came in was "Are you all right?"'

One of the factors which allows Martin Jourdan to manage the company in his own way is the structure of ownership. The families own virtually all of the voting shares and the other 90 per cent of the shares are non-voting. 'I have a proprietorial attitude to the company. I only own 1 per cent of it, but I have control of it. This allows us to uphold the history and the pride of the company. I believe that it's people who make things happen.'

One of the most striking aspects of Parker Knoll is the length of time people stay with the company. Nearly two-thirds of the staff have been with the company for more than five years, and about a quarter for more than fifteen years. In the words of Pete Moseley, a union convenor at Parker Knoll Furniture who has himself been with the company for thirty years: 'Everything here is done by mutual agreement – the works manager's door is always open.' Moseley has been involved for some time with negotiating improved benefits for shop-floor workers. One of his more recent successes was the 100 per cent sick pay for workers, as opposed to the 33 per cent norm in the industry. His present target is to get profit-sharing on to the factory floor.

Each business in the group has been run separately up until now, but things are beginning to change. Martin Jourdan has been so successful at getting other family firms to 'join us' – his term for a takeover – that he's beginning to think some fluidity between divisions is required. Currently each subsidiary negotiates its own pay and benefits; each is managed quite loosely from the centre, outside the annual budgeting procedure, and there is no movement of staff. If there is a gripe among the work force, it is that there is very little information passed around about group performance.

The growth of the company is reflected in its financial performance: turnover and earnings per share have more than doubled since 1983. The business tends to generate sufficient cash to enable it to look around for new acquisitions, although management would be very unlikely to make a bid that was not agreed. A mistake was made when the company acquired Nathan Furniture a few years back, and one of its factories had to be closed during the recession. This was done in typical Jourdan style: he laid off the entire management. 'I went to Worcester and spoke to almost all of the hundred and fifty work force, since it had been my decision to close down the factory. Some were pretty aggressive, but several people said they were grateful that, thanks to the takeover, they had got a year's employment that they would not have otherwise had.' Most people felt they had had a pretty fair deal. Apart from this, the company adopted a no-redundancy policy, which meant a considerable amount of short-time working agreed with the unions. In the end it was not necessary to make anyone redundant.

No one would accuse Parker Knoll of being a great payer. It is not a high-paying industry, and, as Peter Lacey, a foreman in the furniture factory, put it, 'People on the shop floor say they never give away a lot.' Almost all salaries apart from senior management are in a range of £7000 to £11,000. There is a fairly slim benefits package and a standard pension for most, save those on the shop floor at Parker Knoll Furniture. Apart from that, the best thing is the SAYE share option scheme, from which a large percentage of the work force have made a pretty penny.

Martin Jourdan is currently working on a mission statement for the company which he plans to base on the Johnson and Johnson credo. 'We must provide competent leadership and our actions must be just and ethical. We must do this with confidence, love and dedication.' The way this is carried out may change in years to come, for instance by the introduction of a group personnel department, but there can be little doubt that the fundamental style will not change while Jourdan is in charge. Parker Knoll might not be everyone's kind of organization: those people who do not like Jourdan's style of management are not going to enjoy working for Parker Knoll. However, if you judge a company by the experience of the people who work there, you would be hard pressed to find a better.

PATERSON JENKS

Paterson Jenks is a manufacturer of spices and herbs, and a food brokerage. It employs 860 people including 360 who are self-employed. The company is based in High Wycombe, Buckinghamshire. Sales are £80 million with pre-tax profits of £5 million.

pay ☐		ambience ☐	
benefits ☐		environment ☐	
promotion ☐		equal opportunities ☐	
training ☐		communications ☐	

The PJ group is composed of Paterson Foods – which produces Schwartz Spices, sauces, gravy mixes and relishes; Jenks Brokerage, dealing in beverages, chemists' goods, animal feeds and DIY products; and McCormick Industrial – which manufactures blends and seasonings for fast-food restaurants and hotel chains.

The most exciting moment recently in Paterson Jenks's event-studded life came in 1984 when America's McCormick & Co. bought them out. An earlier merger in 1974 of Paterson & Jenks was the catalyst which transformed these formerly sleepy companies. However, in the early years of this decade the company had closed four out of five of its Paterson Foods plants in Scotland and cut its work force there by 400 to 150. There is still a certain sensitivity in the company about the closures, but the new automated lines and modernized Glasgow plant have contributed to the revitalized profits.

'We are now actually manufacturing more in one plant today than we were in five plants a few years ago,' says Cameron Savage, the group's finance director. 'Job security for those who work here is now assured.'

The full impact of working for an American master has yet to be enjoyed by the staff at the company's four plants at High Wycombe, Thame, Ellesmere Port and Glasgow. PJ already contributes 30 per cent of McCormick's worldwide profits. Pay and benefits are not bad but do not compare with other American multinationals. 'It's a unique company, servicing a wide range of manufacturers while still manufacturing itself,' says Bob Keefe, marketing controller. 'Staff–management relations are extremely good. People work hard of their own choice and the atmosphere is quite informal.'

Benefits are generally average to better than average for the sector. The pension scheme is highly regarded within the company. BUPA is extended to senior staff. Sick pay entitlement grows with each year of continuous employment, and some staff are entitled to 26 weeks on full pay. There are also company sports and social clubs, and very good subsidized canteens where you can buy a decent meal for 50p.

Mary Harris, company car administrator, who joined on £3000 in 1983 and earned £10,000 by 1988, says, 'I am very appreciative of the company benefits, which, for me, means a company car.' Desriann John, customer services clerk, was also enthusiastic about the company perks. 'I think the benefits package is very good. It's much better than anything my friends are getting and they're in similar sorts of jobs.'

Since the takeover by the Americans, 30 new jobs have been created – particularly in marketing. There's a strong loyalty among the staff despite the difficulties which they had to face earlier. Nearly 20 per cent of staff have been with the company longer than ten years and turnover in staff is negligible.

'We are not concerned with how many "A" levels a person has, especially if he or she has been working for a number of years. We look at people's thinking processes. We want to know if a person can form a view, express it clearly and then defend his position,' says Vernon Cunningham, director of personnel. 'Much information flows from division to division, so an ability to communicate is vital. Above all we are looking for people who are performance-orientated. Those who just get by in their jobs may not last very long here.'

The company has no formal communications media. It does not, more or less emphatically, believe in team briefings. There are presentations to the staff by video but communication is predominantly one way. However, a good staff grapevine distributes information fairly rapidly.

Management claim there is good opportunity for advancement within the organization. Staff are divided on this, but it does seem that Paterson Jenks is a good company for initial career steps. The company is growing, which means that the number of jobs will advance. Cunningham says, 'Advancement is not an entitlement. We do not promote merely on the basis of length of service.' Employees are encouraged first to take on more responsibility in their existing job before applying for advancement.

Christine Wypyski, senior stock clerk, thinks there are good opportunities. She has been offered two promotions in two years, but has had to turn them down for family reasons. Peter Brown, a manage-

238

ment accountant, says, 'There are very good opportunities here. It is a small company growing rapidly.'

Myra Kempson, sales ledger supervisor, has a different perspective. 'There is nowhere for young people to go as relatively young people are in management jobs.' Desriann John says that she has applied for every relevant position open. 'There is nowhere for me to go in my department.'

The company is making progress in the equal opportunities area, and, while they are not Marks & Spencer or Thomson Holidays, Paterson Jenks can boast that they have fifty women in management positions. Among them are two deputy heads of sites, brand managers and the head of marketing. There is some chauvinism on the part of male managers, but the trend is now going in the right direction.

Paterson Jenks is a warm company to work for. It is a friendly place where people genuinely seem to get on with one another and take pleasure in their work. We were struck by the spontaneity of the staff and their dedication to the aims of the company. There was a real sense of movement since the 1984 takeover. The company's improved commercial performance has generated a better human relations performance. Management have paid attention to building up staff confidence after the traumas of the early years of the decade. 'We have put a difficult period behind us,' says Savage. 'We are now very healthy.'

PEARSON

The Pearson group of companies is highly diversified. It includes the *Financial Times*, Penguin Books, Royal Doulton and Madame Tussaud's. It employs 23,000 people worldwide and reported a turnover of £952 million in 1987. Pre-tax profits for the same year totalled £152 million.

pay ▭		ambience ▭	
benefits ▭		environment ▭	
promotion ▭		equal opportunities ▭	
training ▭		communications ▭	

Pearson may be an unfamiliar name to a broad band of the general public, but its subsidiaries include two national institutions, a world-famous publisher and a china manufacturer of international repute. It is principally known for its publishing: the *Financial Times*, Westminster Press, the *Economist*, Penguin Books and Longman are among its assets. It has a 21 per cent stake in Yorkshire Television and wholly owns Madame Tussaud's. In addition Pearson has interests in oil and investment banking through the Lazard houses.

The scale and diversity of the organization means that conditions of employment vary. There is large-scale distinction between, say, Royal Doulton and Penguin. Pearson is a holding company which takes an exacting interest in its offspring but which also gives them freedom to manoeuvre. Financial controller Anthony del Tufo spells out the Pearson message: 'The group has become more centrally directed. Before, there was a much more passive approach.' The parent has created a series of profitable, well-run and stimulating companies, using guidance rather than heavy-handedness. Senior executives point to the current period of consolidation which has reinforced the position of this highly attractive coterie.

Its recent corporate history started with a fully listed float on the UK stock market in 1969. It bought Tussaud's, an apparently unusual choice, in the late 1970s, and has since concentrated on spreading its wings in the publishing and oil businesses. Penguin hit a bad patch in the early 1980s, when it was forced to lay off one-sixth of its 600-strong work force, but the tables have now turned, and with its 1985 and 1986 acquisitions of publishers Michael Joseph, Sphere and Hamish Hamilton in the UK, and New American Library in the States, Penguin employs a total of 2500 people worldwide, including 1100 in the UK. In 1976 Pearson bought into Camco, a US oil services company, and is working on the further expansion of its oil division. Group turnover leapt from £730 million in 1983 to £952 million four years later, with a commensurate rise in pre-tax profits from £77 million to £152 million.

All Penguin employees receive five to six weeks' paid leave a year, depending on length of service, and have private medical insurance, 50 per cent of which is paid for by Pearsons. Penguin women have 25 weeks' maternity leave at full pay, and their jobs are held open for a year.

Elizabeth Buchan, covers editor, who is in her early forties, says she is generally very pleased with the benefits structure. 'I am devoted to Penguin, though I think I am underpaid compared to some people here.' One of her colleagues, Susan Piquemal, who is a secretary in her fifties, comments: 'I think the benefits compare favourably here to other companies. The pension fund and maternity leave are particularly good.'

Sally Floyer, aged forty-two, publisher of a children's list, who at Christmas 1987 was earning £20,000, comments: 'I think Penguin is right at the top of the scale as far as salaries are concerned. I have nothing to complain about. This is a unionized house and things are equitable.'

Penguin is a generally happy ship. It is a dynamically managed enterprise – largely due to the skills of Peter Mayer, a powerful young American who has transformed the legendary book publisher. Rumour has it that Pearson bought the company that he was running, not to get its lists or authors but to bring Mayer on board as MD for Penguin.

Mayer injected Penguin with commercial zeal, empowering it to issue both Shirley Conran's *Lace* and the latest edition in its classics range. But he has not undermined the traditional strengths of the company; rather, reinvigorated them and brought greater scope to its range of titles. According to del Tufo, Mayer is typical of the person that Pearsons seek in managerial positions. 'We want people with a mix of financial and creative talents,' he says. 'We also want excellence and discipline in our labour force. But we use persuasion and tact and are non-confrontational. We ask rather than demand and only rarely use the big guns.'

This analysis of the group's management style is true of all the key companies in the group. There is also something endearingly British

241

about the central management of the company – largely a throwback to earlier, less active days. Christopher Penn, director of management resources, says, 'We are looking for people with ability and drive. We continually want to upgrade the quality of our employees.' Pearson likes lean management. Only two floors of Millbank Tower are maintained as a central base to run its worldwide operations. Only seventy people are employed there.

The group is exceptionally good for women. While only 35 per cent of its employees are female, Penguin boasts 60 per cent women and Longman 70 per cent. Two women are on the UK board at Penguin and both book publishers employ many senior editors who are women. Westminster Press, the local newspapers division, employs many women journalists, and the *FT* has a fair number as well. Racial minorities are rather more rare. Penn says, 'We require higher than average education in many of our companies.'

Madame Tussaud's is also good for women. The head of the sculpture studio is female. Its culture is slightly more eccentric than the rest of the group and several employees work there to get away from the frenetic pace of high-pressure environments. The business is still one of the top tourist attractions in the country. Helen Tweedy, twenty-seven, an executive secretary, says, 'The pay is not fabulous but it is a relaxed and creative place to work. I worked in the City and I did not like the pressure. Here the deadlines are more flexible, and people are friendlier.'

Judith Craig, head of the portrait studio, thinks she has one of the best jobs in the company. She loves the work. 'There is an enormous amount of job satisfaction,' she comments. Management is generally receptive to requests for an improvement in conditions. Craig earns £22,000 after starting ten years ago on £8500. Pay in the group is negotiated locally, with many unions represented in the bargaining process. Though Penn suggests, 'The trend is away from labour unions bargaining, especially in national negotiations – for example, regional newspapers.'

At Royal Doulton, many employees are skilled and can expect to earn the going rate for the job. At Penguin a board member is on £35,000, a senior manager £26,000, a department head between £18,000 and £20,000, a production controller £12,000–£15,000, a PA £10,500 and a secretary £7600–£9000. These salaries are slightly above average for the publishing industry and in 1988 compare favourably with Tussaud's where senior management are on £17,000–£25,000. Junior management grades take home £11,000–£15,000, an executive secretary up to £12,000 and a junior secretary about £9000. Creative jobs earn anything between £9000 and £24,000, depending on experience and length of stay.

There no groupwide training, but the operating companies are net providers to staff in terms of the quality of their courses. Westminster Press run a highly respected journalists' training school. Often the graduates subsequently find work on national newspapers or in broadcasting. Penguin arrange for employees to take outside courses in copy editing, computer usage, management development and production skills.

The reputation of Pearson's businesses means that staff tend to enjoy their work and are proud of their companies. Generally they do not think of themselves as Pearson employees; more Penguin staff or *FT* journalists, Madame Tussaud's sculptors or Doulton finishers. In the early 1980s there was some slimming down of the Doulton work force due to the introduction of new technology, but this has largely been completed and employees are relatively secure in their positions. The *FT*, for instance, has been growing in reputation and influence since the mid-1960s. The calibre of its people and its contribution to business and political life in the UK are renowned. One staffer says, 'The salary and benefits at the *FT* are unequalled in British print journalism. It's a terrific place to work and the team here is first class. I can't imagine working for another newspaper.'

PETROFINA UK

Petrofina UK is the British arm of the Petrofina SA company of Belgium, the fourteenth largest oil company in the world. The UK company is a wholly-owned subsidiary of its Belgian parent and employs 1500 people. Its 1986 turnover figure was £824 million and its pre-tax profit £12.6 million.

pay	☐	ambience	☐
benefits	☐	environment	☐
promotion	☐	equal opportunities	☐
training	☐	communications	☐

Eddie Margison is a stocky trade union activist who joined the company in 1952 and has not looked back. He was one of Petrofina UK's earliest recruits – the company was sixty-one years old in 1988 – when he was taken on as a delivery man. Today he can sit back and smile. Margison is chairman of the lay members of the national negotiating committee which hammers out pay and conditions for the blue-collar workers of Britain's sixth largest oil company.

Some problems pass across his desk every day, but his stance as a tough negotiator does not diminish his commitment to Petrofina. 'If we can get some of these current problems sorted out then it will be the best job in the country,' he says. Margison moans about the centralization of the company, but in the main he is obviously extremely proud of it. All his union colleagues are. Petrofina is like a family. Everyone knows everyone else. Many of the staff have been around for twenty-five or thirty years and they show no inclination to move.

The company's operations are spread around the country in filling stations, depots, offices and a refinery, but the heart of it is in corporate headquarters in the Surrey race-course town of Epsom. The three Petrofina buildings are adjacent to the Ashley Centre – the town's main shopping complex. These buildings are relatively modern and were occupied by Petrofina after the 1983 move from Waterloo.

The visitor is struck immediately by the geniune and spontaneous friendliness of the staff; people appear to really enjoy working here. There is, most definitely, a Petrofina company man. 'I've learned to spot them when I have been recruiting. They are people who fit into the organization. I've met some people who are extremely talented, but would not adapt well to Petrofina,' says the company's personnel manager. The necessary attributes are a sense of endeavour, the capacity for purposeful teamwork and committed hard work. The typical Petrofina employee is a warm, good-hearted individual who enjoys the company of his colleagues in the same tolerant way he would accept the personalities of brothers and sisters.

The commercial persona of the business is tough. Petrofina SA is Belgium's largest industrial company. It was described recently by a broking analyst as one of the country's best-kept state secrets. Its drive and direction have not been hindered by the huge holding-company power blocs which war for shares in the company and seats on the board. Jean-Pierre Amory, president of Petrofina SA, says that the company has been leaner and fitter than many oil companies since the mid-1970s. The UK company is no exception. Its figures show vastly improved profitability, despite increased distribution costs and a significant drop in the oil price.

Much of the current credit goes to the energetic managing director Dr Pierre Jungels who is revered throughout the company. A main board member in Brussels, he has re-energized Petrofina UK. Jungels pioneered the company's vast communications system. This includes a regular team briefing held every four months throughout the company, alternating with an information brief in the form of a four-monthly newsletter detailing company performance.There are also staff consultative councils. All this was launched in 1983 with a great deal of verve, but both management and work force now appear to have lost enthusiasm for them. Alan Haffenden, applications development manager, comments: 'The councils were fine for the first couple of years but they deteriorated into gripe sessions. People would bring up petty things which they should have thrashed out with their managers.'

There are few substantive grumbles at Petrofina. People are relatively happy about the pay and benefits package, and a review was due immediately after we had completed our interviews. Jeff Wrangle, who works in the finance department at Epsom, compares Petrofina with the other major oil companies. 'As payers we are probably not quite as good, but in terms of the overall benefit package we are as good or probably better than most.'

The normal working week is 37½ hours. Managers receive Western Provident medical insurance and they can bring their families into the scheme with a small additional payment. Petrofina was the first company in Europe and probably the first in the UK to introduce share ownership schemes for its work force. The Petrofina Investment Savings Plan operates after eighteen months' service. For every £1 an employee contributes, Petrofina matches it with £1.40, but to retain the savings provided by the company each employee must stay with the scheme for five years, and the savings must be used to buy Petrofina shares. This unusually generous scheme is taken up by many of the staff, and at present between 65 and 70 per cent of all staff hold shares in the company. 'The share scheme is very popular,' says Terry Reid, who liaises with the press and edits *Fina Focus*. 'But when we introduced it, Brussels wanted us to call it the Petrofina Investment Savings Scheme or PISS . . .'

So a five-year saver could reap considerable sums of money. Employees are also favoured when the company has a new rights issue. Discounts will vary according to the extent of existing share-holdings and the length of service. All employees benefit from life insurance which is provided free of charge. The company boasts a valuable and proficient pension scheme. Relocation expenses are also generous.

The canteen at headquarters serves a wide variety of hot meals. The food is traditional and appetizing and minimally priced at 25p for three courses.

The company recruits ten graduates each year. Human resources executives recruit on the milk round, visiting eight universities and two polytechnics. Within Fina Exploration, for example, 75 per cent of all staff are graduates, and 20 per cent of these have doctorates. Richard Hanson, formerly training manager, says, 'After milk-round interviews, second interviews are held at Epsom. There are psychometric tests in the morning and interviews in the afternoon.' The graduate training programme was revived in 1981. By Christmas last year 49 graduates had passed through the scheme and the company retained 33.

Andrew Hockey, a geologist working on appraisals, says: 'I chose Petrofina because the graduate programme allowed you scope for developing your career the way you wanted to. I spent twelve months working in industrial sales. You're dealing with chief buyers at very senior levels who do not appreciate the foot-in-the-door approach.'

Traditionally Petrofina has been a male-dominated company. But things are changing. There are four women in top jobs within the company and one of the subsidiaries has been run by a woman.

One group of people who have a particularly warm regard for the company are its 800 pensioners. The company is keen that they should enjoy special benefits. At Christmas last year each one received a £25 Marks & Spencer voucher, and some pensioners who experienced hardship during the winter had their heating bill taken care of by the company. The pensioners meet twice a year and the company pays for a dinner.

Petrofina was well ahead of the oil business when it slimmed down ten years ago to its present manning levels. In 1984 it took a step forward by agreeing with the unions to limit overtime wherever possible and bring in new people. It is the first oil company which has implemented such a policy. Flexibility is a keystone in the company's approach, and this was mentioned repeatedly by the staff. But what sets the enterprise apart from the other operators in the market is a commitment to human values rarely seen in the oil industry.

PEUGEOT TALBOT

Peugeot Talbot UK, wholly owned by its French parent, is a major car manufacturer. It is the successor to Rootes and the Chrysler-inspired Talbot motor company. Most of its work force are based in Coventry and Birmingham.

pay	☐	ambience	☐
benefits	☐	environment	☐
promotion	☐	equal opportunities	☐
training	☐	communications	☐

The description of Britain in the 1970s as the sick man of Europe was never more pertinent than when it was applied to the motorcar industry. British car manufacture was dogged by hard-nosed antagonism. Unions hated bosses and bosses hated unions. Strike after strike, often about no more than the most trivial incidents, created an atmosphere of mutual distrust. Production capacity was lost and soon the reputation of our carmakers across the world was shot to pieces.

In the last ten years this unenviable position has improved, and a clutch of companies has emerged as proof that harmonious employer–employee relations are a spur to meeting targets and filling order books. Jaguar, Nissan and Peugeot Talbot are among them. The latter has a distinguished history, despite the industrial relations hiccoughs it experienced in the 1950s and 1960s.

Hillman, Humber, Sunbeam and so on – great car names of the postwar years – were created by the Rootes Group, a formidable presence in the industrial motor matrix of the West Midlands. In 1967 Rootes ran out of money and sought backers. Finally Chrysler – one of the trio of great US motor companies – stepped into the breach. But, in the days before the charismatic Lee Iacocca, the men of Highland Park, Michigan, were experiencing their own severe problems. The UK plant became a benchmark for poor industrial relations and low-quality, uninspired products.

Chrysler had renamed the British subsidiary Talbot. In 1979, after lurching from crisis to crisis, the UK group was taken over by Peugeot, the French motor giant, and christened Peugeot Talbot. Although the company had reached rock bottom, the speed with which it recovered was staggering. Today the company has been dramatically pared and is now producing a series of highly popular models which have captured the public's imagination. The success of the Peugeot 309 and 409 as spritely medium-range cars has transformed the company's image. The revival of fortunes has not been solely due to imaginative marketing but also to a highly committed work force.

The attitude on the shop floor has been turned on its head. Replacing the belligerent uncooperative band of workers is a warm, enthusiastic and harmonious team dedicated to the production of successful motorcars. Nearly 80 per cent of shop-floor staff lost their jobs in the early 1980s but a return to profitability meant that the company could soon expand its payroll as well as its market share.

Finance director Terry Neasham says that the company will make 'substantial profits' this year eclipsing the painful years of sustained loss. Ten years ago Chrysler industrial relations were lamentable. Mike Judge, personnel director, puts it neatly: 'The joke went . . . the *Coventry Evening Telegraph* would headline "Situation Normal at Chrysler", but no one was very sure whether that meant working or striking.' Judge is at pains to point out that there has not been a major strike at Chrysler since 1979.

Several factors have combined to cause the radical shift in company fortunes, and Neasham is not slow to give some of the credit to external forces. He specifically cites the appalling state of the UK car industry, the worldwide recession, and government's impact on trade unionism as major influences which have tended to concentrate the minds of both employer and employed. But the success story is not only due to these factors. Peugeot had their own innovations. Perhaps the most significant was a complete rethink of the company's employment policy.

The first task of the new owners was to settle industrial relations. In doing so the aim was to create a more democratic enterprise. Conditions of employment were standardized to introduce the same holiday entitlement, sick pay and pension scheme across the company. Manual workers were no longer penalized for being late. Management have attempted to deal fairly throughout the plant during their tenure of control; an especially difficult task given the backlog of resentment which festered under previous stewardships.

The greatest visible change, however, has been the introduction of new communications media which disseminate fast and accurately the position of the company and its competitors. Unusually the company's radio station survives. It was launched during the heyday of industrial radio in the 1970s. Almost all the others have passed into oblivion – one of the first company extras to face the axe when the recession bit hard. But managers were shrewd enough to realize that as well as providing a diet of pop music which could be tapped from BBC national radio or Mercia Sound, Coventry's independent station, it was also creating a valuable sense of unity among workers. Company newspapers and videos are widely and frequently distributed and Peugeot has made an art form of briefing meetings. The production line regularly comes to a standstill to bring staff up to date about changes in company policy, employment conditions, production schedules and competitive advantage.

Another important aspect in the change of fortunes at Peugeot was the decision to build the 309 at the Ryton plant in Coventry. This decision gave the staff something to aim for; a goal which had been missing for years. The new challenge provided just the stimulus and confidence that they needed, and the team responded by raising productivity and quality to the same level as the French.

Structurally, the French owners have given their line managers much greater local decision-making power. The traditional and highly complicated system of foremen was replaced by teams of supervisors. Far more responsibility was immediately delegated to them and their staff. This represented a move not only to democracy but also to greater efficiency. Foremen are now seen as mini-managers on the shop floor. The system has worked well in other manufacturing companies but the speed with which it was adopted at Peugeot is a remarkable testimony to the performance of both staff and management.

One advocate of the change is Bob Nicholls, a paint shop supervisor who has been with the company since 1967. He has seen managements come and go but is really taken with the Peugeot team. 'The switcharound was a large task and the company has done it in a professional manner. They now let me do my job as supervisor and the whole atmosphere in the company has improved.'

Nicholls emphasizes the new pride which motivates his people and the work force in general. They are great fans of the car which they are making. They see it as a world-beater. Soon after its launch, teams of workers could be seen all over the Midlands on Saturdays to show off their new car to crowds of admiring shoppers. They are so keen to see the product succeed that they are willing to give of their own time. Should the *Evening Telegraph* dare to criticize the 309, then a flood of letters from Peugeot employees follows to put them straight. Coventry is proud of the plant as well. When Coventry City football club won the FA Cup last year, the team was invited up to Ryton so that one success story could meet another.

250

Workers talk openly of the collapse of the 'them and us' attitude which disappeared soon after the present management introduced the changes. But pay is still below the industry average – a relic of years of loss-making. Nicholls is phlegmatic. 'It is understandable. The quality of the cars in the past was poor. But I hope pay will improve with increased profitability.' It would be a bad mistake for the current management not to regularize pay when the predicted profits bear fruit.

PHILIPS

The Philips businesses in the UK are wholly-owned subsidiaries of the Dutch parent company. Philips employs around 20,000 people in the UK at various sites around the country. The corporate headquarters are in central London.

pay ☐		ambience ☐
benefits ☐		environment ☐
promotion ☐		equal opportunities ☐
training ☐		communications ☐

The growth of this paternalistic, bureaucratic giant is legend in the Netherlands, and almost everyone in the world has come into contact with a Philips electronic product. Whether it is a transistor radio, a video, television, a Phonogram record or compact disc, Philips has produced them all and has often been first in the marketplace.

Philips is a Dutch multinational, with interests in most countries across the world. It is a complex organization, combining brilliance in electronic innovation, a typically Dutch mercantile internationalism, and a resolutely long-term perspective. In the Netherlands Philips is a major part of the national economy, with the town of Philipswijk solely devoted to the company. From its headquarters in Eindhoven, in the province of Brabant, Philips controls subsidiaries, product groups and representatives worldwide.

Philips has a matrix organizational structure; a cross-referencing 'grid', with the operating board and the supervisory board at the top, is interwoven with the product groups and territories.

The UK organization is composed of eight product divisions which report to the British management and also to the product groups in the Netherlands. In previous years the Philips companies have numbered upwards of 200. But in order to rationalize and to tidy up UK operations, the companies are now classified into product divisions.

Chris Crook, personnel director, explains that devolution is now extending to his area as well. 'Previously all personnel policy was decided centrally. All negotiations with the unions were done on a national level.' But now Philips is moving away to a more decentralized approach. He adds that each of the operating divisions will have their own personnel function.

252

While the group will be less coherent in its approach, each company will have more opportunity to keep its own people in its sights. Crook says that basic guidelines will continue to exist, but beyond that each company will be able to respond to the needs of its own people. Certain aspects will remain centralized, such as the contributory pension scheme and management training, some of which is done in Eindhoven. Philips offers a fair set of benefits, although nothing out of the ordinary. The staff shops offer Philips products at considerably less than sale price.

One of the Philips installations is at Washington, Tyne and Wear, where the company produces high-definition deflection units for television sets. Plant director Ian Willock explains that it is the only factory in Philips Europe making these devices. Some 30 per cent goes to a Mullards television assembly plant in Durham and the rest is bound for Europe. 'We were very competitive against the Japanese but were losing ground against the Koreans,' he says.

This increasing market pressure caused some internal restructuring which was regarded as uncomfortable by more junior members of the staff. But we found all the more senior people we spoke to extremely enthusiastic, and part of the reason for this has been Philips' unrelenting commitment to quality.

In 1983 the then president Wisse Dekker introduced a corporate quality policy which Philips Washington has wholeheartedly embraced. It is called CWQI – or company-wide quality improvement – and Philips people are meant to carry around a card on which the details are printed.

John Garside, who is the local official responsible for making sure that CWQI is successfully integrated, says that in response to the campaign Washington plant developed an entirely new flexible manufacturing system. Some members of the work force must spend some of their time devising ways of improving the quality of work carried out in the plant. There are currently 10 teams of 45 people at Washington, but management hope that this will grow to 20 teams involving 100 people each.

Philips, by nature, will not be too worried if the process takes some time. It has a long-term view. Profits go up and down year by year, but Philips always has long-term commercial ambition in its sight.

The paternalism of the company is slowly being eroded and a greater freedom to create is taking its place. Philips has never had any problem attracting the science graduates it is looking for, although keeping them proves more difficult. Pay and benefits are fair, but nothing more. Crook says that in the main they are competitive.

253

Philips is an exciting company to join. Its inability to market itself well has been somewhat assuaged by its most recent campaigns, and the bureaucracy is fading away. Most importantly, its commitment to quality remains as solid as ever.

PHILLIPS & DREW

P&D is a stockbroker which is in the process of merging with the Union Bank of Switzerland. It is based in Broadgate in the City. The firm is highly profitable and employs around 1500 people.

pay	▭	ambience	▭
benefits	▭	environment	▭
promotion	▭	equal opportunities	▭
training	▭	communications	▭

There are few firms in the City which enjoy such a good reputation as Phillips & Drew. P&D is among a handful of stockbrokers which enjoy the confidence, respect and even admiration of competitors, industry and government.

For more than a hundred years P&D has developed a growing expertise and professionalism, and professionalism is the key word. This, combined with integrity, is the pre-eminent aspect of the P&D way of doing things. P&D makes major demands on its people but the esteem which they enjoy, and being able to add the firm's name on their CVs, help to make up for the effort. Then there is the money – like most City firms P&D is a high payer and offers competitive benefits.

Shortly before Big Bang, P&D announced that it would be merging with the Union Bank of Switzerland. 'It is one of the leading players in the world banking community, and the largest worldwide after the Japanese,' says Geoffrey Redman-Brown, a senior director at P&D.

The merger will give P&D greater access to world markets and ally it to a bank with a similar standing in its sector to that of P&D in the broking community. It will give P&D staff access to jobs within the new company on a global basis, and to UBS's excellent training facility on the edge of Lake Geneva.

Lesley Watkins, an assistant director in corporate finance, says, 'It was a very good move to link up with UBS. UBS is prepared to offer a lot of resources and to offer job security. It is well established in many of the areas in which it operates.'

There is enthusiasm for the merger and the move to Broadgate from the traditional P&D home of Moorgate is welcomed throughout the firm. Operating from one base will greatly enhance the quality of service P&D provides.

'We are a professional firm, providing highly technical information to our client base which is largely institutional. So our recruitment policy is directed at meeting that need,' says Redman-Brown, who has overall responsibility for personnel matters and has been active in the merger planning.

Andrew Mackenzie, a gilts salesman, says that there are three types of people who join P&D: specialists like arbitrageurs, whose main function is to spot opportunities in the market; salesmen, who tend to be more extrovert and enjoy presenting ideas; and analysts, who in Mackenzie's view tend to be more introverted.

'For years we had the image of the cloth-capped professional,' he says. 'After the war we were one of the firms to specialize in numerical analysis and we had a northern chief economist who appeared regularly on television. It was an image the firm liked to portray.'

Redman-Brown says that it is meritocracy. Watkins says that she went to P&D from accountants Price Waterhouse because it was one of the few places in the City where there are no barriers to women rising. 'It was one of the first things that appealed to me about Phillips & Drew. There is no policy of recruiting specifically either men or women, merely someone who is good for the job.'

It is also good for people from all backgrounds. Many of the people on the trading floor are school-leavers rather than graduates. Michael Abbott, who runs two trading departments, says, 'I don't think I have got one graduate working for me. The average age in options is twenty-three and in market-making twenty-eight. Most of them have worked their way up.' Abbott says he is looking for someone who is quick on his feet, with an agile brain and a resilient personality. 'We want people who can spot the anomaly. It's detective work really, piecing the information together, which leads a client to make an investment decision. It's an instinct for the market. We need someone who is not content to stick on the tramlines.'

It is undoubtedly a high-pressure environment. 'All our assets leave the building at 6 p.m.,' says Redman-Brown. P&D encourages people to come in as early as 6.30 or 7.00 a.m. They get a free full English breakfast in the directors' dining room and they are at their desks at 8 a.m. Tokyo closes as trading in London starts, so people need to be fully briefed on overnight dealing before trading starts in the UK.

Stress is an important factor and Redman-Brown produced a video outlining what the work was like for employees to take home to their families. He is keen to have the support of the families and when

Broadgate opens he will be taking them around for tours on an open day.

The pressure is so high that traders are reputed to burn out at twenty-nine. 'I've heard of some going off to set up market gardens but in reality most of them slip quietly into management,' says Mackenzie. P&D likes to grow its own and is very keen on upward movement within the group.

The pay is an incentive to stay. Graduates start at £13,500, with an annual bonus of perhaps £1000, and after two years they might be on £25,000. But the annual bonus would then be as much as 50 per cent or even 100 per cent of salary. Assistant directors would be on £40,000 before bonus, and usually with a car.

Everyone gets BUPA, there is a mortgage assistance scheme, permanent health insurance, a season ticket loan, and the directors have a dining room. 'We also give LVs but they are not worth very much,' says Redman-Brown. Broadgate has a swimming pool and other sports facilities are planned. Communications are a high priority. 'The dealing rooms are wired for sound so that a meeting can be held without anyone leaving his desk.'

P&D is a superb employer with a justifiably high reputation. Few broking firms in the City combine such widespread respect with the facility for people to rise rapidly and achieve individual responsibility. The merger with UBS can only improve P&D's standing and maximize employee opportunities there.

PILKINGTON

Pilkington Brothers manufactures glass-related products. Based in St Helens on Merseyside, where it employs 6000 people, its total UK work force is 14,000 and it employs a further 40,400 overseas. Its turnover is £2.1 billion.

pay ▭		ambience ▭	
benefits ▭		environment ▭	
promotion ▭		equal opportunities ▭	
training ▭		communications ▭	

The biggest shake-up in the history of Pilkington Brothers came when the acquisitive conglomerate BTR made a widely-publicized bid for it in 1986. Until then progress towards building a leaner, fitter company had been slow. So slow that had the bid happened twelve months earlier it might well have been successful. But Pilkington had already turned the corner. It pulled all the strings at its disposal.

It successfully argued to business, government, the public at large, and, most importantly, its shareholders, that it had earned the right to remain independent. The bid by BTR was even more important for Pilkington than fending off a takeover attempt. It galvanized the whole enterprise. Both management and work force realized that they had a precious possession which had the potential to become a world-beater.

Today the world's largest maker of flat glass is a changed animal. It has lost none of its conspicuous accord with its staff and its community, but it has emerged as a healthier business. It is the largest employer in St Helens and its management fiercely champions the right of its employees to be heard. It is a mutual love affair. Through the trials of the last few years managers and managed have developed a devoted affection for one another.

It is true that Pilkington is a good payer and has provided consistent, valuable employment in the northwest. The company is synonymous with St Helens. Not only the principal employer in town, it influences every area of life in St Helens. 'We believe strongly that we cannot operate behind wire fences. What happens in the community affects us all, and we can continue to develop a successful business in a successful community.' The words of new opportunities manager Peter

Shepherdson reflect the core belief at Pilkington. Without involvement at every level there is nothing.

Staff are kept up to date with the company's progress through a diversity of meetings and printed media. They are encouraged to input their own ideas on everything from their rewards structure to the progress of certain new products. Pilkington managers work on the principle that the well-informed employee is an active one.

The company has needed to work hard to keep the loyalty it has built up. In 1960 it employed 14,300 people, whereas in 1987 it was down to 6000. It has cut its staff sharply by a process of natural wastage, voluntary redundancy and incentives. The programme was all the more painful since the management have cherished the staff since the business was started more than 150 years ago.

Cutbacks started in 1975 and have continued ever since. But, in order to re-establish the business and turn it into a global player, its structure was changed in 1984. It established several autonomous groups accountable to HQ in St Helens. The diversification of the product range meant that the company left the traditional business sector of flat glass and entered new areas. It became a frontrunner in defence with its night vision system, in science with solar cell developments, and in medicine with dietary capsules and contact lenses.

Throughout the 1980s the company has become more international in its thinking, and its overseas persona resembles a dynamic multinational. It made a series of purchases including the West German Flächglas and the American Libbey-Owens-Ford. In 1981 the number of employees abroad exceeded the UK total for the first time. Some 30 per cent of Pilkington income derives from high-tech work, and these two major acquisitions make a significant part of this figure.

As the company started to recover – and indeed for some years before – it put increased efforts into helping the northwest cope with its appalling blight of industrial dereliction and joblessness. The company is active in countless groups which provide extra stimulus for both industry and individuals to prosper commercially.

To alleviate some of the distress caused to former employees, it established in 1977 the Community of St Helens Trust. This is an enterprise agency and as such was one of the first in the UK. To date it has helped more than six hundred companies in starting up, 90 per cent of which are still in existence. It has helped more than two hundred companies to expand, and has recorded more than two thousand consultancies. In 1988 the trust was estimated to have created over six thousand jobs, equalling the number of jobs lost since the first redundancies.

The original concept – typical of Pilkington's care and concern for the town and the area which nurtured their original business – was to make use of their in-house knowledge and equipment outside the company. This proved so successful, however, that 300 similar agencies sprang up in its wake. Now an average of 75 businesses a year open up with advice from the trust.

Another community scheme is the Pilkington Industrial Experience Project. Supported by the EC Social Fund, this provides industrial training for school-leavers under the age of eighteen. Combined with the government's YTS scheme, there are now nearly six hundred people benefiting from it. Of these some 65 per cent have found full-time employment or have embarked on some form of further education. As a spin-off, an adult training agency has emerged. Earlier this year it was on target for 200 full-time jobs in industry. The agencies with which Pilkington is associated seem almost limitless; the most important of them is perhaps Nimtech NW, whose aim is to help other businesses by promoting an awareness of the potential for improvement provided by better technology.

If these achievements were not impressive enough, Pilkington's board of directors sit on a wide range of committees, institutes and corporations which promote good industrial practice. Anthony Pilkington was chairman of Business in the Community, until it merged with the CBI.

Pilkington's approach to the community reflects its attitude to its people. This is a business which cares passionately about its performance in its markets and about its reponsibilities as an employer. The loyalty displayed by staff is indicative of the company's genuine dedication to them.

POLAROID

Polaroid UK is the wholly-owned subsidiary of the Polaroid Corporation, Cambridge, Massachusetts. It was responsible for the invention of the instant camera. Worldwide turnover is $1.6 billion. It employs 1500 people in the UK at its plant in Dumbarton, Scotland.

pay	▭	ambience	▭
benefits	▭	environment	▭
promotion	▭	equal opportunities	▭
training	▭	communications	▭

When Edwin Land started Polaroid he wanted it to be different. He wanted a company where, under his almost feudal control, invention and individuality could prosper. He established a creative tension which, despite his departure from the business, still lives on in both the parent company in America and its subsidiary in Scotland.

The company made a name for itself by designing and marketing the first instant camera. In doing so it also made history. Together with its other principal product – sunglass lenses – these unique cameras bring in a global turnover of more than $1.6 billion. It is a staggering achievement. Land was determined to make his mark. He did so in manufacturing but also in the evolution of a corporate culture which is still regarded as a trail-blazer. Polaroid was an early participant in equal-opportunity programmes, it established an employee committee which represented workers to management, and staff were able to vote for one paid holiday a year. It also introduced daytime child care for working mothers in 1971.

The American experience has been repeated in a different format at Polaroid's base in Scotland. The company came to the UK in 1962. It set up a marketing organization in St Albans, which still exists, but the main thrust came with the opening three years later of its manufacturing plant in Dumbarton. This is now the largest private employer in the region. It produces a wide range of products in addition to cameras and lenses, among them instant film and keyboards for IBM.

Alistair Liddle, Polaroid's personnel manager at Dumbarton, maintains that Land's belief in employee opportunity is deeply respected at its UK subsidiary. 'We have held a number of employee-attitude surveys to discover views on stress at work, shift-working and a variety of other matters,' he says. While there is some suspicion that the results of such surveys are soon forgotten, Liddle argues that action is taken. 'The personnel department does react to these surveys and it quietly gets on with its job,' he adds.

There is a lot to do. Following on Land's commitment to continuing education, training is taken very seriously. Several courses are on offer to every member of staff. These range from management development, run in conjunction with Strathclyde Business School, to problem-solving for supervisors and employee representatives. Training time is split. Half is taken in the company's time and the remainder in the employee's. This is designed to elicit commitment from the staff to the training programme. Many take up their right to further education, and eight were on MBA courses when we visited. This is supplementary to on-the-job training, which everyone receives. The company has ten full-time trainers in the assembly division.

Polaroid does not confine itself to work-related topics. Strathclyde region has a poor health record, and the company has created the Vale of Leven Health Project as a result. This is centred on the factory but also extends into the community. It encourages healthy eating and cleaner living and embraces fitness programmes. The company organized its own fun-run recently and a large number of the staff entered. It has been teaching workers about the dangers of a high-cholesterol diet and Liddle claims that his colleagues at every level can now talk knowledgeably about the subject.

Polaroid is also aware of its responsibilities as the largest employer in the region. The area suffers 22 per cent unemployment, so the company sponsors local activities. The most visible is the adoption of the local football team, but Polaroid also backs school competitions and funds an enterprise trust, to help create small businesses, and an information technology course to encourage people to learn computing skills.

'We are looking ahead and giving people the skills to cope with challenges in the future,' says Liddle. More training is scheduled, and groups of people are looking at everyday working conditions in an effort to improve them. A model production line has recently been opened which tries to make camera construction more efficient and less tedious for the line worker. The company is also working on a job redesign programme, which involves ten people from every sector of the factory meeting regularly for a year to find new ways to improve the job.

This is combined with a generous level of pay, and conditions of employment which are standardized throughout the factory. However, an underlying air of discontent can be detected among some workers. Liddle puts it down to machoism. But people on the shop floor suggested different reasons. Hugh Gillespie, chairman of the employee representation committee, faults the company on poor communication. 'The personnel department are almost never on the shop floor,' he remarks. He recalls an incident where a manager, genuinely impressed by the speed of work, happened to mention it as he was showing guests around. 'He meant well,' says Gillespie, 'but he upset the workers.' To many staffers this illustrated a lack of knowledge on behalf of the management of the standards being upheld. Some shop-floor workers were also unimpressed by the number of training opportunities on offer. Either they did not know about them, or did not feel that they were open to them. All the supervisors we spoke to, however, were supportive of and enthusiastic about management training programmes.

On balance it seems that real opportunities are perceived by the workers to exist only above the shop floor. In spite of this all workers are happy about pay and conditions.

Apathy on the shop floor is a by-product of the lean years between 1979 and 1985 when management were seen to have been 'railroaded through' with little consultation. Gillespie says, 'There is an untapped source of talent on the shop floor.' Liddle's response is that his team are looking at job descriptions and that they want to delegate more responsibility to individuals.

As a part of the worldwide group, Polaroid UK is the most efficient subsidiary. Quality and efficiency are regarded as paramount objectives. Joe Hector, central accounting manager, explains that as an employer dedicated to meeting staff needs, 'We are a cost centre as well as a profit centre.' Gillespie suggests that the staff could do with being told more often the painful facts of economic life as well as that they are the best-performing arm of the Polaroid body corporate.

The essence of Polaroid's success in the role of employer lies in its status as a company which truly and unreservedly cares about its people. The UK business has remained loyal to Land's policy. Its training, pay and benefits are worth shouting about. Where it lacks strength is in its communications. In some areas management can feel justly proud of their efforts. The company won the British Safety Council Award in 1980, 1982, 1984, 1986 and 1987, and threw a huge party for every member of the staff. In 1987 a Gala Day was held to celebrate twenty-five years of the UK enterprise. They took over a local park and laid on free food, free beer, bands and a fun fair. More

263

than 6000 people came. One employee says, 'They would never have done that unless the Yanks had thought about it first.'

So, although there has never been a strike, and Gillespie is able to say, 'There's nothing left to fight for', and despite a staggering array of benefits, employees do not seem to appreciate their lot. A slight revision of communications would surely do the trick.

PROCTER & GAMBLE

Procter & Gamble is the UK arm of a major American multinational. It employs 2700 people in the UK and reported sales in 1986 of £443.3 million, with a gross profit of £42.3 million. It is based in Newcastle-upon-Tyne.

pay	▭	ambience	▭
benefits	▭	environment	▭
promotion	▭	equal opportunities	▭
training	▭	communications	▭

It is remarkable that a company like Procter & Gamble has so little published information on its UK arm. The company is also publicity-shy, preferring to keep a low corporate profile and let its products speak on its behalf. These are an impressive array, including Pampers disposable nappies, Vortex detergent cleaner, Tide washing powder, Crest toothpaste and Head and Shoulders shampoo.

Since P&G did not want to talk to us, we talked around the industry about them. We discovered a company which has high ethical standards, spends time, effort and money testing a product, and is committed to research and creating a sound foundation for its people. It is also highly conservative – or prudent as its protagonists would say. Its main competitors – Unilever, Colgate-Palmolive and Kimberley Clark – have a considerable amount of time for P&G.

It is regarded as a company which trains its people solidly and gives them demanding work to do. There is a strong sense of P&G as a traditional marketeer driven by values which have been cured in oak over the last century. In America the company is regarded as one of the great all-time business ventures and is the nation's largest advertiser. In 1985 it owned six of the top ten best-selling products in the US consumer market.

Observers say that the UK company, although autonomous, is guided by the States. The American identity is a powerful one which builds in strong loyalties. People who have trained at P&G, which makes extensive use of on-the-job schooling, tend to stay.

A home-grown culture is very much in evidence, drawing in a high number of graduates into positions like assistant brand manager and encouraging people to stay for bigger bites of the cherry. As many as three-quarters of the current senior management of the company were recruited as young graduates in the UK, and they have captured positions as high as vice-president in the international organization.

'P&G looks for men and women with excellent academic records who have also shown leadership and achieved success in extra-curricular activities,' according to the company. It recruits on average between 60 and 80 such individuals each year. Some are technically qualified, others can be drawn from any discipline.

P&G is fastidious when it comes to the personal qualities of the people it takes on. Essentially it wants good or potentially good leaders: people who are adept at visualizing the parameters of specific projects, and are capable of delivering them. There is a heavy emphasis on communication skills since much of the work is done in a team environment. P&G is one of the companies where meetings and arriving at a consensus – if apparently expert – are important parts of the process.

Critics in the market suggest that P&G is solid, even too narrow in its general attitude, but there is some evidence that the group is stretching itself to allow some flexibility. The company is right to be proud of the success of its products and the continued headway which they make in the market.

P&G people have strong characters, but individual presence is tempered by the influence of the corporation. They are propelled by a deep satisfaction and belief in their products, and argue that excellence should drive industry.

'We like self-starters,' says one person who breached the wall of silence to comment on the business, 'people who respond to a challenge, who like to dig deeply to find a solution to a given problem and find an answer which will get the job done.'

As you might expect with an organization that breeds its own leaders and is heavily into research, the personal assessment process is a detailed one. Each member of staff is assessed, checked and pushed as far up the ladder as he or she can go.

P&G has a great reputation as a company with a long-term devotion to the welfare of its staff. Its benefits package is one of the best in British industry, as you might expect for the business which was ahead of its age when it introduced profit-sharing in 1887, sickness, disability and life insurance in 1915, and a stock option plan ahead of almost everyone else. All this innovation took place in the United States, but the company has been active on the welfare front in Britain too.

The company has factories in Newcastle upon Tyne, Manchester and West Thurrock in Essex, and sales offices throughout the country. In 1985 it announced the building of a new nappy production plant for its Pampers product.

The most exciting publicity the company received in recent years was over its man and thirteen stars symbol. In 1985 it was forced to drop the logo after three years of fighting anonymous suggestions that the badge was a satanic symbol.

That did not put P&G – never anxious to court unfavourable publicity – on friendly terms with the media. Nevertheless, the company has been roundly praised in various media for its intelligent, considered, well-thought-out, caring and energetic approach to its markets and its staff.

P&G enjoys a well-earned reputation as a dedicated employer. It is evidently good to its people, and former employees speak highly of its benefits package. While its approach may seem somewhat earnest, at times austere, internally it is a friendly company, and its staff have a common purpose which extends beyond selling the brands. P&G people tend to be as similarly self-contained as the company they work for.

PRUDENTIAL CORPORATION

The Pru is the largest insurance company in the country. It is based in central London but has many offices and outlets throughout the UK. Its pre-tax profit in 1986 was £178.1 million. The corporation employs more than 35,000 staff.

pay ☐		ambience ☐	
benefits ☐		environment ☐	
promotion ☐		equal opportunities ☐	
training ☐		communications ☐	

For years the Prudential was symbolized by the man in a trench coat and trilby hat. A 1950s figure, friendly and almost avuncular, but decidedly out of touch with a multinational corporation in the 1980s, he was pensioned off in 1986, and was replaced with a great deal of ballyhoo by Prudence. She is now the emblem of the young, vigorous but worldly-wise corporation. The question which remained was: is the new image merely window dressing or does it represent a deeper change? The Pru has always majored on expertise. Its fund managers are some of the shrewdest in the City. It has commanded a growing range of product with deft intelligence. But it has also appeared bureaucratic, an image which is only reinforced by the forbidding presence of its gothic headquarters in Holborn Bars. This Victorian monstrosity houses a company which had never been known for its speed of movement.

The change in identity mirrored a growing awareness within the Pru that it must become tighter and more efficient. 'The underlying purpose of the new corporate identity is to draw together the diverse strands which make up the Prudential Corporation and present them under a common banner with a common purpose. Prudential's new identity underlines our determination to play a major role in the financial services markets,' says the 1986 annual report.

Arthur Watson in personnel consolidates the message: 'We are shaping the corporation to meet the needs of the twenty-first century.' His vision is confirmed by Bill Mills, a Pru accountant. 'We embrace the virtues of the old Prudential, but bring it up to the twenty-first century.'

The Pru started life 140 years ago selling life assurance to individuals, and subsequently graduated to property insurance and financial advice. The Man from the Pru developed as a comforting image in the more solid times of the early 1950s. 'The customer base was narrowing – we were losing touch with the younger generation, so we started new services for young people,' says Mills.

The corporation has also entered the property market in a big way, and has the largest chain of estate agencies in the country. The aim, says Watson, is to create a more total financial image.

There are Pru subsidiaries and branches in Canada and Australia, and the organization is expanding in Europe. The Irish Insurance Company was recently acquired, and in late 1986 it bought Jackson Life of America – a major coup say the Pru.

The business is divided into six main operating groups: life and general insurance, investment management, unit trust managers, mercantile and general (reinsurance), pension fund services and property services.

Liz Church, a PA at Holborn Bars, says, 'The corporation is much more progressive, much more open to market forces than it was. There's a distinct shift in age – downwards – particularly in the management area. We're getting more of the non-Pru-bred people – the organization needs these. We are still a family though, and we remain very friendly.'

Church is on secondment before moving to a new position in the market-planning division. She says that she has been in a good position to see how the organization works from all angles. She believes that the rewards offered by the Pru are particularly good.

Shirley Boyt, who was on a two-year secondment from the Reading office to work on the corporate identity, is happy with the £15,000 which she currently receives. 'At my level salaries are very good and the graduate level is highly competitive,' she says. 'I created a niche for myself. If you have a bit more ability and ambition you can get on. I have been the one who has been driving my career. I like the emphasis on training,' she adds. Boyt has been sent on several external management courses, such as Women In Management and Leadership.

The corporation has a straightforward and well-defined training policy. There is a high emphasis on providing the right training scheme for people to advance within the organization. Among the different schemes offered is the option for graduate recruits to do their MBA with the Pru.

The benefits package is extensive, and one which is particularly attractive for many staffers is a mortgage assistance plan. Almost everyone we spoke to in the corporation was enthusiastic about this, and many had taken up the option. There are Christmas bonuses and bi-annual, salary-related bonuses, share option schemes, a fair pension scheme, and good sports and recreation facilities. Management grades receive profit-related pay and BUPA is also available.

Promotion is reasonably quick. 'We like to grow our own timber,' says Watson. This is particularly the case in the field sales force where there is a structured line of promotion. Otherwise promotion is there if people seek it and are up to the mark. 'When we take someone on it is because they should in the future be able to be promoted and there are increasing chances for that. The company's so big that there will always be room at the top for those with ability,' he adds.

Ginnie Willis, an advertising executive, says, 'It's up to you at the Pru.' She agreed that this might be a fair summary of the overall staffing philosophy. She says that the training scheme is excellent. 'I have taken advantage of day-release courses and I am going to be sent to an advertising agency for a two-month personal development programme.'

Willis's experience is typical of the new Pru – positive, relevant and commercial. It takes on both graduates and school-leavers and is keen for both groups to prove themselves. Training is very good but the corporation wants its people to be self-starters. If anything is symbolic of the change in direction in the corporation, it is the encouragement given to individual initiative.

The cultural transition has progressed sufficiently for the Pru to be included in the top 100. Whether this proves to be long-lasting or not, only time will tell.

RANK XEROX

The wholly-owned subsidiary of an American parent, Rank Xerox UK employs 4500 people. It is famous for the photocopier, but it also makes a wide range of business systems. The company is based in Uxbridge.

pay	☐	ambience	☐
benefits	☐	environment	☐
promotion	☐	equal opportunities	☐
training	☐	communications	☐

In the early part of 1988 Rank Xerox engaged popular psychologist Edward de Bono to present its new advertisements on television. While de Bono talked about office systems designed to suit the way in which people think, he also did something else. Rank Xerox had slipped behind the field in its prowess for marketing. A perception had been created that Xerox was stuffy and out of date. The de Bono ads attempted to redress the balance.

Another misconception had also developed, but the roots of this were probably much deeper. The popular impression of Rank Xerox was of aggressive hire-and-fire merchants who had little interest in their staff. It is an image which the company has actively tried to dispel, and it is one which is difficult to equate with the current state of the business.

It is true that Rank Xerox has changed enormously in the last ten years alone. It is also true that Xerox demands hard work from its staff, but the commitment to staff is now pronounced. Today Rank Xerox is among those fifteen or so benchmark industrial companies which offer the best pay and benefits packages in the country.

The company had fashioned a culture which is hard nosed, fast paced and committed. Les Jones, personnel manager for the company, says that Xerox is market- rather than product-driven. 'We are looking for people who are happy to change fast and who find change stimulating,' he says. 'This is an environment which is constantly changing.' There is no doubt that senior management at Xerox believe change to be a catalytic force which brings out the best in people and keeps them on their mettle.

'We want people who can think on their feet and who will enjoy taking an opportunity to input into the business,' adds Jones. His view is reinforced by Ian Morris, of public relations, who says that a typical Rank Xerox employee is 'hard-hitting, someone who doesn't suffer fools easily'.

To match the profile of the ideal Xerox high-achiever, the company has come up with an extensive benefits package to keep the best on board. The company boasts a most extensive and up-to-date sports complex at the top of its building in Uxbridge. What appears to be Europe's largest Jacuzzi is linked with a computerized gym, where everyone's personal fitness programme is stored on disc. The restaurant in the building is gourmet standard and a bar next door serves a wide range of drinks at rock-bottom prices.

Rank Xerox finally acknowledged that the copier market had become static. It was faced with the choice of staying with copiers and trying to chisel away the odd percentage point from the competition, or embarking on a wider market. Xerox chose to broaden its base and created a foundation for the company as it is today. The enterprise became fitter, more clear-sighted and more intelligent.

David Oliver, finance director, says that the company operates three-year business plans which are annually refined and updated. The three-year plans set the overall goals and targets, while the specific budgets needed to achieve them are outlined annually.

'In five to ten years we have come a long way,' he says. 'The company has come through a very tough period. It did not conduct itself as well as it might. It displayed the less favourable aspects of a monopoly organization. It has coped with its changing situation, with increasing competition – partly from Japan – and it has been quite successful, especially in the UK.'

This resilience in the face of dramatic and dynamic transformation lies behind one of the key facets of the Xerox personality. Wherever you go in any of the company's buildings, across the company one concept is now repeated with mantra-like devotion. To work at Xerox you must worship on the altar of change.

Flexibility is all-important. Sales people are moved rapidly from patch to patch, and it has become a source of complaint. Someone told us that sales people fear the annual review because this inevitably means that, having worked hard to develop personal relationships with clients and prospective clients, they are then moved to another district.

The company believes that it is creating flexible people with the experience and initiative to go anywhere and sell the Xerox product.

Certainly, the training given to them to do so is superb; among the best in UK industry.

The company's extensive training courses for all levels of personnel, especially sales and management grades, are based at its excellent training centre in Newport Pagnall, Bedfordshire. This 130-bed residential base is busy for most of the year. Account managers, for example, are trained in two blocks of three weeks. They come to the centre for the first period, go back to their offices for a three-week period of work experience, and then return to Newport Pagnall for a further three weeks.

Among the other attractions for prospective recruits are BUPA for all staff and their families from the first day of employment, 25 days' holiday, a reasonable contributory pension scheme (5 per cent employee contribution), and staff discounts on many products, including holidays.

Rank Xerox is archetypical of a company transformed. As its product base has broadened, so too has its attitude towards its personnel. Xerox is a much more aware and responsive organization today than ever before. Although among the most demanding employers in the UK, it does more than most to look after its employees.

RAYCHEM

Raychem is an American-owned business. It makes plastic products using radiation chemistry. The company is based in Swindon where it employs 1300 people. In 1987 the UK company did £100 million worth of sales.

pay	☐	ambience	☐
benefits	☐	environment	☐
promotion	☐	equal opportunities	☐
training	☐	communications	☐

Swindon must be a strong contender for the title of top town outside London with good employment practices. Allied Dunbar, W H Smith, Reader's Digest and Dana are all based there. Another of the key employers in the town is Raychem, a company which makes products with corrosion-proof insulators made from plastics which have been bombarded with electrons.

Four years after Raychem was born in Menlo Park, California, it started out in the UK in Manningtree, Essex, in 1961, and later moved to Swindon. Headquarters also includes Raychem's European research and development base, and the UK manufacturing, selling, marketing and distribution functions.

The company is organized on a matrix structure with small profit centres and autonomous product divisions. These 'cells' appear to create the most appropriate working environment in which to breed innovation. In 1972 Raychem collected the Queen's Award for Industry, and its latest venture is in domestic appliances.

The UK company has the same set of corporate values as the US parent, even if they are sometimes voiced differently. There is enough room in the group for everyone to adapt a little to suit local demand. Its central values are responsibility, informality, getting the job done, freedom and flexibility. There appears to be little structure for putting these core beliefs into practice, but, in a Californian kind of way, these qualities create a framework of their own.

Communication – between individuals, groups and departments – is an important function of life at Raychem. Every six weeks each department holds briefing meetings, which are presented either by the divisional manager or by a member of the personnel team. They are designed to be consultative as well as providing the opportunity to pass on items of news and information.

'Raychem is a way of life,' says John Simons, a senior production manager. 'It's sometimes very intrusive because you can get hooked. But it's worthwhile and you can get a lot of satisfaction. We like smaller groupings because they enable better communication. There are fortnightly meetings between leaders and their groups. It's very competitive in my division – more often than not work is changing – and problems are discussed on the spot.'

This intense communication breeds a mutual understanding and supportive effort. Several people told us that there is a true sense of being a family. 'In fact a lot of families work here as well,' says Bob Lodge, a manager who has been with Raychem since 1978. 'There's pride here. It's not Utopia, but it's better than most.'

In the Swindon area Raychem is reputed to be one of the better employers, and pay rates among the best half dozen companies. The staff work 38 hours a week, which allows them to have every other Friday afternoon off. Everyone gets five weeks' holiday and a non-contributory pension scheme. This includes life insurance and a disability pension.

In addition there is a profit share bonus scheme which is paid quarterly in cash. There is also an option to buy Raychem shares at 15 per cent below the market price. Some 70 per cent of the work force has taken a slice of the company cake. Everyone is paid fortnightly in advance. Almost everyone gets either a car or is paid overtime. A private health scheme was introduced in 1983.

At Christmas everyone gets a free turkey, a ham or a veggy pack – for vegetarians. There is a party for pensioners and for children of the staff.

With all the R&D going on at the Swindon plant, technology is sometimes developed which does not fit into the corporate plan. One of the more unusual benefits of working at Raychem is that employees are encouraged to spin-out the technology into a separate company with the backing of Raychem. This has already been done with Rayfast, which detached itself from the mother company to service small customers.

The company did make redundancies in 1974 and 1985 but on both occasions they were handled with sensitivity and compassion. Information was given on alternative opportunities and early retirees were offered an enhanced package. Everything was done with full consultation and the minimum of disturbance.

Turnover on the shop floor is tiny, says group personnel manager

Ian Gray. 'For seven years we didn't lose one graduate, but we did lose out from the 1985 intake.' Gray says the atmosphere is happy and loosely structured. 'One might say that controlled chaos is tacitly encouraged – it is an exciting environment.'

Staff assessment has been introduced and people are trained to understand what this involves and how to handle it. 'Training is meant to make people more effective in the job they do,' says Gray, who presides over a department which addresses the provision of core skills in a pragmatic fashion.

'Raychem is about finding a technological solution to replace a conventional one to a particular problem,' says site manager Nicholas Godden. 'Much of what we do here in Swindon goes abroad – about 60 to 70 per cent is exported, generally to Europe but also to Canada. We enjoy a fair degree of autonomy from the States, but each part of Raychem is competing for resources so there has to be a cutting edge.'

This is an exciting and enthusiastic company. Godden says that the buzz comes from the president downwards. It is a lively and open-minded environment. People are paid well, and benefits are excellent and the atmosphere is fun. When staff come to Raychem they tend to stay. One comment we repeatedly heard was: 'It's never occurred to me to leave.'

276

READER'S DIGEST

Reader's Digest Association is the British vehicle of the US-owned corporation. It publishes *Reader's Digest* magazine and a wide range of books and musical products. It employs 800 people in the UK. Worldwide turnover in 1987 was more than £1 billion and the UK's portion was £90 million.

pay ☐	ambience ☐
benefits ☐	environment ☐
promotion ☐	equal opportunities ☐
training ☐	communications ☐

The current Reader's Digest Association corporate video explains that its popular magazine is designed for 'those little moments', when the carefully researched and written articles will both inform and entertain the gentle reader. But this image is illusory. Put aside the notion of the magazine as the friendly companion which assuages fear at the dentist. Circulation of the magazine in 1988 – the company's fiftieth year of publication – is one and a half million copies a month, with a projected readership of seven million. There just aren't that many dentists.

In fact Reader's Digest is one of the world's largest publishing ventures. UK finance director Brian Gray says that turnover in the UK rose from £59 million in 1983 to £90 million in 1987. Profits have proportionally risen much higher, but as a private company RD keeps the figures close to its chest. About 20 per cent of UK profit comes from the magazine. Other activities include condensed books, a division with titles covering nature, gardening, DIY and motoring, and RD musical products such as compilation LPs.

All these products depend on direct marketing for their success – and the Reader's Digest organization is recognized as one of the finest direct-marketing organizations in the world. Communications with clients buying the magazine, books and records is effected by post. Some books and magazines are sold through retail outlets, including six shops in Britain and one in Dublin. The company used to market through many more UK retail outlets, but downsizing at the end of the 1970s – when the whole country was going through an economically tough time – led to the closure of retail units and numbers on the payroll dropping from 1200 to 800.

Staff turnover rate is low, with most employees clocking up a respectable long-term service record with the Digest. The main area of staff turnover seems to be in the secretarial and administrative roles.

The Digest recognizes that talented creative staff like to follow a career path which does not always move across into management roles. Of course, for those wishing to shape their career in the more traditional way, the opportunities are there, but the Digest has also established a dual career path within the creative areas to make sure that the careers of writers or designers can run alongside those of managers.

'We like to see some assertiveness in our staff, but we are always looking for team players,' says senior associate and director of personnel and training, Frank Ross. 'Staff have got to work very closely with other people on projects to put all the integral parts of a package together. Initiative and creativity are important, but you must be able to work as part of a team.' Individual staff performance is monitored, with an annual review performed by line managers.

Sheila Smith, project manager in systems development, says of the annual review, 'If you have got any problems, the environment here is such that you can say exactly how you feel, and if you have a problem it is sorted out. The standard of training is very good. Any area that you need training in will be seen to. I think I'll go to Swindon in 1990. I'd like to live in the country, and I am happy in my job. I've got ambitions, and if you don't take the initiative, you don't get anywhere. At the performance appraisal they will ask you what you want to do, and then push for you.'

According to Ross, promotion within the Reader's Digest really does depend upon the individual, and the contribution that they are making to the company. 'In our creative areas we are always looking out for talent, and we give individuals the opportunity for advancement, moving them through the business, if they display the ability.'

Promotion selection within Reader's Digest Association is by choosing the best person for the job. All vacancies are posted on noticeboards for all staff to see, and sometimes individuals are encouraged to apply for a particular position. Ross says that the company prefers where possible to fill up the more senior positions internally, topping up the bottom of the promotion ladder with external recruitment. However, 'We do consider external applicants,' he says. 'When we do recruit from outside the company, we look for someone with the commitment to stay and move up. We don't want someone that will block a job.'

Chris Tribe, promotion print buyer, said, 'The management style is very sound, and the company seems to be very orderly in the way it promotes people.'

Despite there being no positive discrimination in favour of appointing women within Reader's Digest, the split between the sexes at the moment is roughly equal, and 90 per cent of the magazine's editorial team is female. This is encouraging, but there is as yet no female representation on the board, although about 30 per cent of managers reporting to board members are women.

Job applications from disabled people are considered purely on applicable skills for the job. If any employee needs special equipment because of a disability, this is provided. Access for the disabled to and around the company's offices is good.

'I love my job,' says customer relations training officer, Belinda Baulf. 'If I have an idea, I will be listened to, and my suggestion taken into account. All the managers are approachable. If I wanted to I could go and see anyone, I wouldn't feel inhibited at all. The company expects you to do your job. It won't stand for you doing nothing all day, but it will reward people who are working hard and contributing.'

Training is recognized as an important aspect of individual performance. Following their initial induction week, all staff are involved in a company familiarization programme which is designed to give an overall view of the Digest's business activities, and their department's contribution to it. Graduate management trainees, of whom there are just a few each year, follow a detailed programme of their own. Other management and professional courses are run in-house and at all levels from junior manager workshops through to pre-retirement seminars.

'I joined six and a half years ago as a graduate trainee, and I am somewhat surprised to find I am still here,' said Mark Dugdale, who is now marketing manager for a new business area within the company. 'I've been lucky, because whenever I have begun to feel a bit frustrated, the company has allowed me to move around. At the moment I am progressing at the right speed to fulfil my own ambitions. Quality is a company objective. We take it for granted that our products are excellent value, but that is very difficult to achieve. One of our corporate statements is to sell products that don't come back to customers that do.'

'I enjoy my job because it is varied. I'm busy in my own office. I should be earning more, but that is up to me. The salary for the job that I am doing is about right,' said Sandra Louis, who is secretary to an associate director. 'The company is very traditional in its ways, and everything that it does reflects the prestige of the company. Everything has a Reader's Digest standard. It's nice to know that you are working for a company that has achieved a lot, but wants to achieve more.'

The Digest has a clearly-defined salary policy aligned to market levels as identified by the Hay salary evaluation scheme, recently implemented. Salary policy has been set in the upper quartile of the Hay scheme for all levels of the company, with the aim of making the Digest a very competitive employer in the open marketplace. 'We are a quality company producing quality products and with high expectations of our staff, and this should be reflected in the way we reward them,' says Ross. 'Our view is to pay for performance. Someone who is not performing well would tend to fall down to the bottom of their salary scale.' Interestingly, the company does not recognize any official unions, although some staff are members of an industrial body or professional association if it is appropriate to their work.

As the Reader's Digest is a privately-owned company, there is no share option programme for staff. However, there is a generous profit share arrangement, initiated in 1974, with a maximum annual payment of 25 per cent of an individual's basic annual salary. This 25 per cent commitment has actually been met in recent years, and the profit share percentage payments at the end of the financial year are normally high.

The company pension scheme is contributory, with staff paying 2½ per cent of their salary up to the upper earnings limit, and 5 per cent above that. Standard maternity-leave obligations are met, complemented by a gift of six weeks' full pay to any woman who leaves the company to have a baby. There is no official arrangement for paternity leave. At the time of visiting free membership of BUPA had just been introduced to all permanent members of staff. No length of service qualification criteria will apply.

The Reader's Digest offices at 14 and 25 Berkeley Square in London's West End do not provide staff with any restaurant facility, although the comfortable and well-designed offices do include a number of drinks machines, of a higher than usual quality, which are set on free vend. Pictures and photographs on the walls encourage the generally relaxed atmosphere. There is an active sports and social club, based on their buildings at the Old Bailey.

Each member of staff receives a free issue of the *Reader's Digest* magazine, and can award two free gift subscriptions of the magazine to friends or relatives. On joining the company, a new member of staff is eligible for 21 days' annual leave, rising to 26 days after two years' service, and it continues to escalate with length of service. After five

280

years' service, staff are given a free copy of every special book that the company publishes. All of the company's products are available to all staff at a 33 per cent discount.

Staff writer David Moller joined the editorial team on the *Reader's Digest* magazine in 1966. 'I still find the job a challenge,' he said. 'There is a lot of variety in the subjects I cover. I feel I can work at full stretch.' Moller feels that people within the company work hard through self-motivation rather than fear, a reflection of the open-door management style that is promoted. 'The style is paternalistic in the best sense – that is, if you treat people decently, you get a decent day's work out of them. People stay a long time here because they think it is worthwhile. I came here, and have just gone on liking being here.'

REUTERS

Reuters is world famous as a news agency but the company also provides business data to clients around the globe. It employs nearly 10,000 people worldwide. Pre-tax profits in 1987 were £178.8 million. The company's headquarters are in Fleet Street, London.

pay ☐		ambience ☐	
benefits ☐		environment ☐	
promotion ☐		equal opportunities ☐	
training ☐		communications ☐	

Reuters is the world's largest news organization, providing accurate communication of hard-core news and current affairs information to the media in more than 158 countries. Equally as important, although not so widely realized outside the business sector, is that the company also leads world markets in the provision of computerized information services, providing data to business clients in more than 124 countries.

Reuters' headquarters are in London, where a small corporate staff of about 300 people handle corporate finance, accounts taxation and administration. The rest of the operation is divided into four worldwide operational areas: Reuters Europe, Reuters North America, Reuters Asia and Reuters Overseas – the division which includes Africa, Latin America and Israel. Each division is accountable for its contribution to the corporate results. Yet Reuters is an annual business in that the divisions are all highly interactive, and thus no part of the worldwide operation could really be regarded as standalone.

Services to business clients now represent a major part of Reuters' worldwide operations, and include constantly updated price information news and data supplied by clients, databases of historical information, facilities for computerized trading, and the supply of advanced communications and interface equipment for dealing rooms.

Reuters' service for media clients, such as newspapers and radio and television stations, includes general and economic news and news pictures. The company has journalists in more than 100 bureaus in more than 70 countries, gathering and editing news for both business and media clients for delivery over the world's largest private news and business information network.

As a public company with some 19,000 shareholders, the share structure has been designed to guarantee Reuters' independence and integrity; two of the main principles to which the organization has firmly adhered since Paul Julius Reuter first began telegraphic transmission of stock market information between London and Paris in 1851.

Between 1980 and 1984, Reuters enjoyed a dramatic increase in profitability leading to the flotation of the company in 1984. Flotation raised £52,000,000 of new capital, after payment of costs, which was then available to finance future growth. Profit before tax for the 1987 financial year was £178.8 million, giving earnings per ordinary share of 26p, and dividends of 7.3p. This was a dramatic comparison to the 1982 pre-tax profit of £36.7 million, with share earnings of 5.6p and dividends of 1.6p.

The company intends to consolidate its leading position within global communications markets through four main areas of strategy: maintaining the best communications network available; improving services and introducing new products at a pace which will outstrip competitors' efforts; and investing heavily in databases in order to maintain and offer a better range of information than any other information organization. Subscribers will also be offered facilities for computerized training.

Around the world, and including staff working in subsidiary companys, Reuters employs nearly 10,000 people. This figure has swollen from 3205 in 1982, reflecting the enormous growth that the company has experienced. Within the UK, 35 per cent of the total work force fall into a management category, according to European staff manager, Ken Jones. 'Today, there are more employed in London alone than there were ten years ago worldwide,' he says, 'and there are more staff within Europe now than there were worldwide ten years ago.'

Jones identifies the cause of this rapid expansion rate as a direct result of the development of Reuters' business operations, which has in recent years included the introduction of new services, as well as the acquisition of a few companies. Placed against headcount growth, and the fact that by the end of 1987 about half the staff had been with the company less than two years, Jones indicates that attrition within Reuters is generally low, with a turnover in the UK of about 6 per cent a year. 'Reuters has always looked for people who feel that they would be long-term employees,' he says.

'One feature of Reuters that keeps people here is that it is a friendly place to work,' says the Europe technical development and planning manager, Martin Davids. 'Reliability and loyalty helps to steer you through turbulent times. I feel the company has dealt with me fairly.' Davids has enjoyed promotion during his time with Reuters, as well as job satisfaction within a 'dynamic environment'.

The company embraces distinct groups of employees, ranging from journalists and photographers to those with considerable experience in computers, electronic databases and international communications, as well as financial and marketplace experts. It has always been tough to get a job as a trainee journalist with Reuters. There are usually 500 applications for 10 trainee places from candidates who all have a good academic degree and fluency in at least two languages. Those applying to management-trainee, marketing and accountancy positions are also expected to be fluent in at least one language apart from English, and to hold a good degree. Some 44 per cent of the company's staff are employed in the technical departments.

Project manager Camilla Sugden, who has recently been posted to Hong Kong, joined Reuters as a graduate management trainee. 'Some of the formal expectations offered are not always fulfilled to the letter,' she says. 'But the variety of the work gives you responsibility, and opportunity, so my own expectations have been fulfilled. This is a slightly chaotic but very dynamic company, with a lot of enthusiasm. The people are great. They tend to be younger than average, especially on the commercial side. People socialize a lot.'

'We are looking for people who have determination, and a considerable ability to cope with stressful situations in a flexible and ever-changing environment, who can use their own initiative and yet be able to cope with ambiguity,' says Ken Jones. 'We look for individuals who can push boundaries and take reponsibility for their own development, with guidance. We expect a lot of them.' Growth has led to excellent opportunities for promotion both for managerial and administrative staff, who can frequently take up opportunities to develop their careers in new areas.

Correspondent Ralph Bolton, who joined as a graduate trainee in journalism, has held posts in Reuters' Berlin and Moscow bureaus, and now works in the London newsroom. 'Speed is important, as we are in competition with other companies,' he says. 'The organization has become more aggressive, yet without losing all its human qualities. Chances for promotion are good, and my salary compares favourably with other news agencies. The company does expect, when the chips are down, that you work twenty-four hours a day without getting tired. You are expected to accept disruptions and situations where a correspondent has to sacrifice his private life. The reward is the nature of the work, which I don't think I could have had with any other job.'

Reuters is actively pursuing a policy of developing career opportunities for women. The most senior woman within the organization is the corporate personnel manager, who first joined Reuters as a secretary. Even before the official company equal opportunities policy was established, Reuters had, by the very nature of its international organization, encouraged the employment of nationals of all countries.

Major accounts manager Susan Wade has been promoted four times during her seven years with Reuters. She has a company car, and a competitive commission-based salary package. 'Speed, initiative and accuracy are key things,' Wade says. 'I enjoy my job because it enables me to do what I am good at – selling. Careers for women in Reuters are looking good. There are a lot of women in good positions, but very few in senior management. The company has brought a lot of women on quite quickly. There is an enormously strong sense of loyalty to the company. If you stick it for two years, you are a lifer. People don't leave.'

There is no defined 'mission statement' regarding Reuters employees, but the company has always had great respect for individuals. According to Jones, 'We believe in being as fair as can be, and in being genuinely supportive on a personal level. Financially, salary policy is to offer remuneration somewhere in the upper quartile of the going market rates for the job.' Jones comments that this policy is to attract, and then keep, good people. By and large it works. 'We believe that as the company is profitable and successful, although we do not have a profit share, salary is one of the ways in which people benefit. We try and ensure that everyone worldwide gets at least inflation increases every year. We are not in the habit of reducing the standard of living of our employees.'

The company is aware that on the technical front salaries do not compete too favourably with those offered by the banking institutions within the City. Some staff qualify for a profit-related bonus scheme, but this is not regarded as an official profit share arrangement. Sales people work to a commission-based remuneration package. Employment packages for the many staff posted overseas compare favourably with UK rates, but they vary according to the local economy.

Employees also participate in a pension scheme, now voluntary. Membership of BUPA is offered to all UK employees at the provincial rate, and has been taken up by about two-thirds of the staff. London staff enjoy six weeks of annual leave across the board.

Reuters expects to extract the most from its staff. The working week of a non-executive member, without meal breaks, will average about 35 hours, and more time is expected from executives. Staff can, if they want, work a nine-day fortnight by arrangement with their department. Some departments, such as field maintenance and technical operations, require split-shift and twenty-four-hour maintenance. Twenty-four-hour coverage in the newsroom involves only a handful of journalists, as the responsibility for the main news 'world file' is handed on around the world, following the sun from London to New York and then to Hong Kong, back to London again, and so on.

Women employees who have been with Reuters for more than fifteen months benefit from an excellent maternity-leave package including full salary for thirty weeks.

'Management attitudes are both traditional and forward-looking,' says John Wright, an installation manager who was just about to move, with his family, to take up an assignment in Norway. 'Tremendous growth in the past three years has created a lot of interest. We have unique products, and projects that we work on can be anything from small to large, but there is always a timescale and a lot of pressure. Rarely is one job the same as the last. If you let it get to you, you could be stressed, but most of us cope with stress very well. Reuters recognizes skills, and goes out of its way to identify people's abilities and to improve them, to get people working to the best of their capabilities.'

ROBERTSON RESEARCH

Robertson Research Group is based at Llandudno, North Wales. It employs 900 people. The company is engaged in mineral research. Its turnover in 1987 year was £21 million and it reported pre-tax profits of £4.8 million.

pay	☐	ambience	☐
benefits	☐	environment	☐
promotion	☐	equal opportunities	☐
training	☐	communications	☐

Robertson Research is hidden in a mansion just behind the seaside resort of Llandudno. Hundreds of scientists are working here on secret projects, and flying all over the world to advise governments and giant corporations. The locals are not quite sure exactly what happens at Ty'n-y-Coed (the house in the woods), but they say that one word from Robertsons can make a nation rich or poor overnight.

Robertsons call themselves natural-resource consultants. They have found gold in Australia, oil in the Sudan and mineral water in Buxton. The staff come from all over Britain and from a dozen other countries. Many could earn more by moving to a big city but a surprising number prefer to stay in North Wales. It is pure chance that Robertsons ended up there but the company now sees the location as a major asset.

Local people, who make up 200 of the 530 staff employed on the site, mainly work in administration or as technicians. They join because Robertson has a good name and because most alternative employment in the town is seasonal. One of them describes Robertson as '*the* company to work for in North Wales'. Geologists and specialists come to work here because of the reputation of the company, foreign travel, adequate pay and the life style.

Ty'n-y-Coed is five minutes from the beach and ten minutes from the mountains. 'I go climbing in Snowdonia at the weekend,' says lithostratigrapher Liz Dyke, 'or even after work in the summer.' If you like clean air and water sports you cannot beat it, but if you want the 'big city lights', as Liz points out, it's not the place to live. When they have finished the new road, Liverpool will be just over an hour away and Manchester and its airport a little further.

Robertsons was a shipping and quarrying firm. In 1961 it hired geologist R. H. Cummings to advise them on limestone extraction. He turned out to be an empire-builder who took on increasing amounts of outside consultancy work as companies started to prospect in the North Sea. By the end of the decade he had a team of 150 researchers bursting out of a collection of temporary buildings in an abandoned quarry.

Robertson Research moved a few miles along the coast to the Ty'n-y-Coed convalescent home, now a mixture of Victorian pile and modern laboratory blocks. Quarrying and shipping soon diminished in importance, and Robertsons evolved into a limited company specializing in earth sciences. Agencies such as the World Bank have commissioned Robertsons to evaluate the Sudan, Morocco, Ethiopia, Zaire and India as oil producers. The company is also carrying out studies in the rest of East Africa, the USA, Canada and Colombia.

When the oil price slumped from nearly $30 to $10 a barrel in 1986 exploration was hit hard. Robertsons shed 50 mainly administrative staff. Around 100 employees are members of ASTMS, which is the only recognized union, and it seems that union members were given better redundancy terms than the rest. Robertsons is trying to protect itself from such fluctuations by diversifying. It has recently bought Hydrotechnica – which specializes in water resources, advising Perrier, for instance, on how to develop Buxton Spring Water – and Gould, which specializes in agriculture and fisheries research.

Robertson's costs reduction programme saved £500,000. The bonus scheme – which shared 15 per cent of pre-tax profits among the staff and could amount to as much as an extra month's wages – was also cancelled. This was unpopular. Staff felt that the company no longer appreciated that its profits depended directly on their performance. In a bad year there would be less to share out, but they felt the principle was important.

The company realized this was a problem and at Christmas 1987 gave a small across-the-board cash payment with a view to reintroducing the bonus in future. This has done wonders for morale. When times are hard the subsidized canteen is often regarded as expendable, but at Robertsons it is still a place where all grades of staff can sit down together in a good atmosphere. In 1988 it won an award from Heartbeat Wales for healthy but tasty eating.

There are now 30 staff at Hydrotechnica in Shrewsbury, 170 at Robertson Gould in Warwick and 50 at the Aberdeen base, which provides rapid analysis to the North Sea oil industry, but everyone has a foreign-travel clause written into their contract. The clause is necessary because 150 employees are in Robertson subsidiaries around the world and hundreds of others find themselves in remote locations in Colombia, the Sahara or Indonesia. This can be a mixed blessing, as the staff who found themselves on the last plane out of Teheran will tell you, but it certainly makes life more exciting.

Wages are not high by oil industry standards but house prices and the local cost of living are relatively cheap. At Llandudno 180 employees earn less than £10,000, 300 between £10,000 and £20,000 and 50 over £20,000. There are 130 in admin, 150 technicians, 170 scientists and geologists and 50 managers. Laboratory assistants start on just over £4000, or less if they are on a YTS scheme. After training, including block or day release, they can double that figure, and eventually as a supervisor earn between £7000 and £11,000. The company will put promising technicians through a degree course to enable them to progress on to the scientific side. Most senior staff, however, are recruited straight from university, with the company perhaps sponsoring them through a Ph.D. and offering practical as well as financial support. Specialists are usually recruited to fill specific vacancies, and people with five or ten years' experience in a relevant field may be employed even if they have no formal qualifications. But finding recruits is not difficult – except perhaps accountants. 'This is not their natural habitat,' says Richard Joplin, the finance chief, waving a hand out of the window. 'Accountants are city creatures.'

After seven or eight years a geologist could earn £17,000–£18,000. A big city oil company would pay more, but allowing for house prices it would need to offer £30,000 to compete. One manager on £25,000 claimed he would not move to London for less than £100,000. Robertsons staff work hard for their money. As Kevin Tooby, a palynologist, points out, 'We may be at the seaside but it's no holiday resort.' He says, 'If you put a lot in you'll get the rewards. If you work strictly nine to five you'll be treated in a nine-to-five way.' Managers tend to work 50 or so hours a week but few take work home, preferring to put in extra hours at Ty'n-y-Coed – especially since most of them live within ten minutes' drive away.

The atmosphere is a strange mix of academic and ultra-commercial. 'Everything has to be sold,' as Richard Joplin says. The structure has been tightened up with 37 profit centres, even if these are threatening to drown the company in paper. For every 1000 external invoices, 700 are now generated internally. Traditionally managers are home-grown – the MD is a chemist and the chief executive a geologist – but marketing specialists are now being brought in. People are more aware of the finished product. 'What we sell is a piece of paper.' There is an awareness of the need for professional management. 'Just because they're a good geologist doesn't mean they're a good manager.'

Robertson Research has regularly been cited regionally as an excellent employer. Except among scientists, it is less well-known nationally. For research specialists who would appreciate superb facilities and the calm of the North Wales countryside, this company offers great opportunities.

ROLLS-ROYCE

Rolls-Royce are world-famous engine makers. Turnover in 1986 exceeded £1.8 billion, with a pre-tax profit of £120 million. The company employs 42,000 people worldwide, some 37,000 of them in the UK. Headquarters are in London, and there are manufacturing plants in Derby and Bristol.

pay	☐	ambience	☐
benefits	☐	environment	☐
promotion	☐	equal opportunities	☐
training	☐	communications	☐

Many people dream of owning a Rolls-Royce motorcar. They visualize themselves elegantly reclining in comfort in the back of a Silver Cloud. Rolls-Royce is the last word in excellence, but the company does not make its real money from making motorcars.

The company provides engines for an enormous range of aircraft, including the Boeing 747 and 757, Airbus A320, Lockheed TriStar, Concorde, Jaguar, Harrier and Phantom F-4. It also builds power plants for electricity generation, gas and oil pumping, oil platforms, hovercraft, ships and nuclear submarines.

In 1986 Rolls showed a 12.5 per cent increase in turnover. This was largely due to a decline in oil prices, a resurgence of the airline business and increases in military spending in the USA and the UK. The business was privatized in 1987.

'We search for excellence and must maintain and improve a very positive worldwide image,' says group personnel director D'Arcy Payne. 'We must continue to be associated with excellence.' This is the core belief of Rolls-Royce – that excellence will triumph. Payne adds: 'We want to increase both market share and profitability, and we have expanded our product range, especially in the jet engine division. Our prime mission is to remain an independent concern.' RR enjoys high self-esteem after the lean years in the early part of the decade.

When the recession bit hardest Rolls cut back a 60,000 work force to 40,000 and some of the company's smaller plants were cut back altogether. But the employee tally is stable today. 'We do not foresee any further involuntary leavings,' says Payne.

The style of Rolls as an employer has not changed radically, however. 'We are rather paternalistic in that we look after our employees well. Things are changing though, and we see the need for more employee involvement. This does not necessarily mean more union involvement,' comments Payne.

Among the moves initiated by management for greater employee participation is the instigation of quality circles. Groups are appointed to assess how production can be improved, and staff and management sit down together to discuss changes to the product and its process. Staff are now also consulted on any changes to the organization of their plant. Workshop layouts and the introduction of new computer systems are typical examples of where discussion takes place to make things work properly for everyone concerned.

The kudos of working for Rolls-Royce is immeasurable in the engineering industry. 'We are looking above all for people with a desire to succeed,' says Payne. 'Working in a team is essential here and we want people who plan a career at Rolls-Royce. Loners tend to fall out here.' Salaries are above average for the engineering sector, though somewhat behind chemical engineering. Payne says it may take longer to get big salary increases for technical/engineering positions because it can take years to learn specific jobs. 'The reward,' he argues, 'is that RR-trained engineers can always find work.'

Average salary scales at Rolls-Royce include £9000 for a graduate recruit; £15,000 for a graduate after five years; £7000–£10,000 for a technician; a secretary would be on £8500, and an engineer anything between £12,000 and £20,000. Department heads earn between £30,000 and £35,000; general managers £40,000 and £45,000, senior engineers between £40,000 and £50,000 and senior directors £50,000–£60,000.

Benefits include a pension scheme which compares favourably with many other sectors of industry, some 13 weeks' paid maternity leave, some 26 weeks' paid sick leave and subsidized canteens at most of the company's plants and facilities. There is also a broad range of sporting and social activities at many of the company's installations.

Around 95 per cent of employees have shares in the company. When RR was privatized some 10 per cent of shares were retained for employees, and there were a number of highly popular share schemes which were available to staff.

Despite occasional strikes, industrial relations in the Rolls plant is not a problem. 'We have a very good industrial relations record,' suggests Payne, 'and we lose very few days of production time.' The last major stoppage was in 1985 when clerical workers walked out for twelve weeks over pay. All bargaining is done at site level. RR never negotiates at a national level except with pilots and nurses.

The company displays a dedication to training, and has built a centre solely for the purpose in Mickleover, Derbyshire. 'Most people enter the company on a training scheme. We train heavily and retrain because of the specialized nature of the work we do,' says Payne. One per cent of turnover annually is spent on training. Rolls-Royce has acquired a name for the quality of its management training courses. The natural progression from training is promotion. 'There are very good opportunities for promotion. But people are expected to show initiative and to do work on their own. Most of our senior board started as apprentices,' Payne says. RR claims that anyone showing initiative should spend no more than two years in one job.

Having recovered from the doldrums of the early 1980s, RR has fashioned itself into a major civil and military defence contractor. It has established itself as a quality manufacturer with original and flexible ideas. It has also retained its dedication to its work force and as such has proved itself to be an enlightened employer.

293

ROWNTREE

Rowntree are confectioners based in York. The company employs 32,000 people around the world, half of whom are in the UK. Pre-tax profits in 1987 were £112 million on sales of £1.4 billion.

pay	☐		ambience	☐	
benefits	☐		environment	☐	
promotion	☐		equal opportunities	☐	
training	☐		communications	☐	

Rowntree encompasses household names like Kit Kat and Rolo, Aero, and Polo. This giant concern makes one-fifth of all the sweets and chocolates eaten in Britain, yet manages to keep a homely image.

While rivals Cadbury and – in particular – Mars are seen as dynamic, Rowntree still has the reputation of yokels from York growing steadily but slowly. More Quality Street than Black Magic. Rowntree points to change, and has restyled its corporate logo to prove it: A lower case 'r' with a roughly sketched halo resembling a round tree.

Since 1987 Rowntree has had more workers abroad than in the UK. It sells more boxes of After Eights in Germany than in Britain, more Lion bars to the French than to the British. For the last five years most of its sales and profits have been made abroad, and Rowntree believes it has made the breakthrough into the American market and now into Europe. Rowntree is ready for the Single European Market in 1992.

Rowntree is now a multinational branded-goods marketing company with all the opportunities and uncertainties which that implies, but it is still not a place for high-rolling gamblers. Gung-ho new recruits are told the cautionary tale of how in 1973 Rowntree unsuccessfully bet a substantial part of the company's assets in an attempt to corner the cocoa market. Take another look at that new Rowntree symbol and you can see that it is also a 'Q' – a clue to the firm's Quaker history.

Quaker Mary Tuke opened a grocer shop in York in 1725, and later married into the Rowntree family. By 1862 the Rowntrees were running the chocolate side of what was about to become a big business. The Rowntrees realized that the newly-prosperous working classes could not only produce chocolate, but could also afford to buy it.

294

Along with the other Quaker confectioners Rowntree took chocolate out of the hands of the wealthy and made it a highly profitable product for the mass market.

Like Cadbury, Rowntree pioneered many benefits for employees as well as trying to create a good impression in the community. In the early years of the century the company was one of the first to appoint a works doctor and dentist, to set up a canteen, school rooms and a gymnasium in the factory, and institute an annual paid week's holiday as well as company pensions and unemployment schemes. The City of York was given swimming baths and a park by Rowntree, and a library and theatre were also opened. Wages and conditions were negotiated with a unionized work force. Today's chairman Kenneth Dixon echoes traditional Rowntree beliefs when he says, 'If we succeed, all will benefit: employees, shareholders and the communities we live in.'

Rowntree took over smaller confectioners as it grew, perhaps the most important being the merger with Mackintosh in 1969. In the last few years the company has sought to rationalize production facilities. The British work force has been cut by about 1000 a year, while overseas operations are still expanding their staff. Over the last five years productivity has increased by 7 per cent per annum. Although most of the reduction has been through natural wastage and voluntary redundancy, job security is no longer a good enough reason to work for Rowntree.

York has the largest factory in the company, where 5500 workers churn out Kit Kats, Aeros, Smarties, Polos and Black Magic. The old Mackintosh base in Halifax employs 2500, turning out Quality Street and Walnut Whips. In Norwich 1100 produce Yorkies, Caramacs, Munchies and Rolos, while Castleford's 700 concentrate on making After Eights. The Newcastle plant employs 1000 Lion bar, pastille- and gum-makers, and the 300 in Leicester produce boiled sugar sweets, such as Fox's glacier mints.

Rowntree has had mixed success with its attempts to diversify. It has found it easiest to do well with Sun Pat peanut butter and Gale's honey, for example. The attempt to break into the snack foods market with crisps in Britain and peanuts in the USA has been a failure, and there must be considerable doubt whether Rowntree could ever grow into a general food company.

Rowntree's attitude to graduates is best summed up in the title of their brochure – 'Our Future in Your Hands'. It has taken the sticky-food industry a long time to convince college-leavers that they can offer an interesting, varied and exciting career. On its annual milk round Rowntree is looking for problem-solvers – people who can kick out the log jams quickly.

It recruits around 50 graduates a year and puts them through a common training programme, usually in York, which starts with business games and ends with the new recruits expected to solve real problems. In the meantime they are carrying out full-time jobs in the departments. York is not a place for city-slickers, although Leeds and Bradford are less than an hour away. London is only two hours on a fast train. York itself sends the Americans swooning – and you do not have to go far beyond the city walls to find yourself in wild country.

Most departments recruit generalists, but they expect a high level of numeracy. Languages are increasingly important and obviously specialist skills are needed in the technical and engineering areas. Staff must be prepared to travel and move within the UK, and increasingly managers are expected to serve a term in one of the European or American locations. Pay is good but not the best. At all levels Rowntree pay is supposed to be equivalent to other major employers – upper quartile rather than 'We'll top any offer'. Early starts and long hours are essential rungs on the management ladder. Outside sales and marketing promotion is not particularly fast, but there is plenty of opportunity to move within the company and potential managers are expected to have varied experience.

Joining Rowntree is not as safe, or perhaps as dull, an option as it once was. The company is still not as aggressive as some of its competitors, although that is changing. Critics say it is not very innovative. They point out that the last 'superbrands' to be launched successfully were Yorkie twelve years ago and After Eight twenty-five years ago.

On 23 June 1988 the chocolate wars for Rowntree came to an end when an agreement was signed with the Swiss manufacturer Nestlé. Rowntree had made a lusty, if not sufficiently well-thought-out, defence against Nestlé and its other aggressive suitor, Suchard.

The impact on the strong employee relations has been slow to emerge. Observers believe that one or more of the Rowntree plants could be closed. Certainly a policy of voluntary redundancy was in place in August 1988. Union officials in York remain remarkably balanced about the possibilities for ultimate prosperity of the plant. One official said, 'Nestlé and Rowntree are remarkably similar companies in some ways. In two years time some of the Nestlé economics could build this into a very profitable company indeed. But how much the workforce will share is open to debate.'

296

SAATCHI & SAATCHI

Saatchi & Saatchi is the world's largest advertising agency. It employs more than 15,000 people. Group turnover stands at £4 billion with pre-tax profits of £124 million. Headquarters are in London.

pay	▭	ambience	▭
benefits	▭	environment	▭
promotion	▭	equal opportunities	▭
training	▭	communications	▭

Terry Bannister, joint chief executive of Saatchi & Saatchi Advertising International, breezed into his office and put his feet up on the table. 'We've tried to push things to the edge here. The highest accolade you can give in this company is to describe someone as a Saatchi person, or a solution as a Saatchi solution. That means inspiration, a constant process of refinement, and a supportive environment – if you fail you haven't let the side down. The personnel department is everyone who works in the company.'

Saatchi & Saatchi is the only advertising agency that everyone has heard of, mainly due to their handling of the Tory Party account during the 1979 election. But there is a lot more to it than that. In the last seventeen years they have come from nowhere to being the world's largest advertising agency, with a stock market capitalization of £650 million and more than 15,000 employees. They have achieved this through a series of startling acquisitions, upsetting the advertising establishment first in the UK and then in the US. Saatchi's is not popular with the competition, and it is a little bit proud of that fact. Richard Myers, a copywriter who has been with the company for thirteen years, claims that he is a Saatchi man: 'I rather like the roguish connotation.'

The company face that looks out to the world is fierce, competitive and uncompromising, but its internal complexion is caring, supportive and surprisingly shy. This is a reflection of the characters of Charles and Maurice, brothers of Jewish Iraqi stock who have built up the company. According to one famous story, a newly-employed executive sacked a manager soon after his arrival, only to be rung up by Maurice as he was waiting to board a plane. 'We don't do that here,' he was told. 'We'll transfer you to another department.' Everywhere you go in Saatchi's people are nervous of talking to the press. Even though everyone we spoke to had been told – contrary to usual practice – that it was all right to speak their mind to us, they were all very careful about what they said.

The company has the atmosphere of a tight-knit family; there are plenty of internal rows, but to the outside world they present a united face. One reason for this *esprit de corps* is simply the success of Saatchi advertising. Its ads are based on the idea of the 'single-minded proposition'. Bannister says, 'There is a desire to produce something away from the norm. When looking at an idea we ask ourselves, "Could someone else do it?" and if the answer is yes, we rethink it.' This has generated some of the most striking advertising campaigns of recent years. Perhaps its biggest success at the moment is the Castle-maine XXXX campaign, which has been so popular in the UK that Saatchi's has now displaced the agency which was promoting the lager in Australia.

This is not the only reward for working at Saatchi's. When Richard Myers's wife broke her leg he faced a serious problem with the combination of his work and looking after the home, so his creative director hired someone to do the housework for a few months. There is also a feeling that if you do good work it will be recognized. Tristan Layton joined Saatchi's as a post-boy after leaving school. 'It's very tough to get in if you're not a graduate and I was told I'd have to spend at least eighteen months in despatch. To get on I knew I had to outshine my competitors, so I wore a shirt and tie every day and made it my business to talk to people in every department. I went to see the head of TV Production every week until he gave me a job.'

Saatchi's is now so big that only 16 per cent of its profits come from the UK. The major profit centre is the US, but the company uses its Charlotte Street agency as a role model for its newly-acquired businesses. John Sharkey, joint managing director of the London agency, described his office as 'an academy for Saatchi'. Bannister calls it 'the beating heart of the network'. There are about fifteen account groups in Charlotte Street. Each one combines all functions of finance, creative, planning and production – with a team spirit all of its own.

If you look for any formal organization beyond this you'll be hard put to find it. There is an emaciated personnel department, which is mainly responsible for recruiting graduates, but there is barely any system of group communications, and salaries are a matter of negotiation between the individual and his or her manager. John Sharkey said, with disarming frankness, 'We resist making an intellectual construction out of big business. I don't know what is going on, within the account groups, but whatever it is, it is done in good faith.'

Pay and benefits, like elsewhere in the advertising industry, are pretty good, but will vary a lot between individuals. A graduate starts on around £9000 and a non-graduate on about £7000. After that, it's up to you! There's a company pension scheme when you've been with the company two years, a bonus of around 10 per cent of salary based on trading results, and a SAYE share option scheme. There is a staff BUPA scheme (contributory), and about 200 of the 900 staff in Charlotte Street have company cars. Most training is carried out on the job, although the company does run a variety of management training schemes.

Saatchi & Saatchi has grown very quickly on the basis of a loose and freewheeling management system, which allows people to get on with their job while the brothers get on with expanding the company. The formula has been successful both internally and externally; evident both from the volume of new business that the agency creates and the enthusiasm of the staff. Many people, particularly in the City, are cynical about the ability of the brothers to hold the company together now that it is so big, but they have been proved wrong every time so far. According to John Sharkey, 'We have a belief that the company can do anything at all.'

It takes a lot of faith to run an organization this large and then sit back and let the employees get on with it, but, as Maurice Saatchi says, 'As a company we believe it is good to be big, and it is better to be good, but it is best to be both.'

SAFEWAY

The Argyll group, which includes Safeway, operates 155 foodstores across the UK. Its turnover in 1988 was £3.6 billion with pre-tax profits of £175.6 million. It employs 60,000 people in various locations around the country. Argyll's head office is in Hayes, Middlesex.

pay ☐	ambience ☐
benefits ☐	environment ☐
promotion ☐	equal opportunities ☐
training ☐	communications ☐

In 1986 the food and drinks business Argyll lost its bid for Distillers. This cathartic experience eventually led to a transfer of power within the group. As chairman of Argyll Jimmy Gulliver had seen the capture of Distillers as an important move in his strategy to build his company into a major force within the drinks industry. But the mercurial chairman lost to Ernest Saunders's Guinness – and the rest is history. The failure led to a change in emphasis in the Argyll power structure. While Gulliver remained in the chair, his able and long-serving lieutenant Alistair Grant asserted real authority as chief executive.

Grant is a quietly spoken Scot whose calm authority commands impressive loyalty from his people. 'When we came to the end of that big battle I thought that we should come away from our ambitions to be big in drink. I saw it as a market which had become crowded with the Australians and other major players,' says Grant. 'I thought we should concentrate on developing a quality food business.'

In August 1986 discussions with the American owners of Safeway led to the sale of the British end of the business to Argyll. 'The management of the American business sold the UK business to us for $1 billion,' said Grant. It was a shrewd move. Safeway opened in Britain in 1962 and had gained a strong reputation as an ethical, imaginative and vital retailer.

In February 1987 the sale was completed and within forty-eight hours Grant was able to address all members of the new combined work force by video. He spelled out the elements of Safeway 1990. Grant has always had a passion for campaigning. 'I was able to tell them that we had evolved a plan to take all the Argyll stores which currently trade as Presto and convert them to Safeway. And secondly we would add to the Safeway development programme. Instead of ten new Safeway stores a year we would throw our whole weight behind the programme and open twenty-five a year.'

The decision has meant a move into the first division of food retailing, and Grant aims to go up among Sainsbury and Tesco leaving Asda and Gateway with the scraps. Safeway and Argyll have different cultures and moulding them is quite a task.

Within ten weeks of the takeover, two Presto stores, Morden and Farnham, were converted into Safeways. They were seen as test cases to establish how much the programme would cost and how difficult it would prove logistically. The Presto stores are somewhat smaller than their Safeway counterparts, and attitude to the job varies remarkably. Grant cites a typical example. 'In Safeway if a member of staff sees a bruised apple on display he will put it in the waste bin. Whereas at Presto an employee might think he is reducing the gross profit by removing the bruised apple from the shelf.'

Safeway lays great emphasis on the customer being the number one consideration of staff. To that end Safeway is a bright, cheery environment where staff appear genuinely pleased to see the customer and anxious to help. Each store sells items in addition to food and drink and some include a post office, pharmacy and bakery.

Training is structured with a heavy priority on customer relations, hygiene and an extensive knowledge of the product available. Malcolm Parris, a freezer warehouseman who is a comparative freshman with five years' service, is in no doubts about why Argyll was interested in Safeway. 'The reason Argyll took us over is because we are better. We're a team here – lots of blokes have been here a long time.'

Safeway evinces a remarkable team spirit, something difficult to engender in a high staff-turnover business. Sally Gunning, a part-time cashier at the Maidstone branch of the chain, says, 'I notice that when I go into other shops they are not nearly as friendly.' Gunning says that the training is exceptional though some of it is common sense.

Recruitment patterns will be radically altered by the new company. Above all, the recruitment base will be extended. It will include graduates, YTS people, people who currently work for other supermarket chains, catering groups and hotels. Safeway derives a large proportion of its staff from local advertising, scrupulously identifying the sort of people who will get on well within the company. Tony Coombs, public relations manager, says, 'We look for people who are

301

presentable, but not necessarily experienced since we train everybody in our own way. They must be able to relate to the customer.'

Safeway is not especially good for women. There are only two women store managers in 155 shops. 'On the whole they don't want the time commitment involved in being a manager,' says one personnel officer. There are a few women department managers in the delicatessens and in dairy products. The company argues that lack of physical strength prevents women from working in other areas where heavy lifting is involved.

Extra emphasis will go into training. Every store has a room set aside for training, equipped with posters and leaflets setting out company objectives, all job descriptions, training manuals and videos. Every member of the shop staff will go through an induction programme and will be assessed at regular intervals. Each store also has an officer whose responsibilities include training.

Training, retraining and assessment are keystones for those people seeking promotion within the company. With the widening base of stores Safeway offers exceptional chances for promotion. The company encourages movement between stores and departments. Grant says that by 1991 the operational structure will be reformed. 'We'll have a managing director for the store business and he'll have seven regional managers each responsible for about sixty stores and they will each have five to six district managers.'

Safeway's unique character, resolute commitment to training and quality and re-energized management could make it an unstoppable force in the high-pressure world of food retailing.

J. SAINSBURY

The largest supermarket chain in Britain, Sainsbury's employs 69,000 people in the UK. In 1987 group sales amounted to £4 billion with pre-tax profits of £268.1 million. Head office is in southeast London.

pay ☐	ambience ☐
benefits ☐	environment ☐
promotion ☐	equal opportunities ☐
training ☐	communications ☐

No other company caused us such a bitter exchange of views as Sainsbury's. During the course of our research we spoke to more than 500 key professionals who work with companies on a daily basis. Our team of researchers on the book reported divided opinion. There were those who argued that Sainsbury's evinced everything that a good employer should be. Equally, there were those who cast the supermarket company as autocratic, narrow-minded and publicity-seeking. When we spoke to ex-Sainsbury employees there were those who were fulsome and those who were less enthusiastic.

Sainsbury's is arguably a strong culture. The stores are a byword in the retail sector for high-quality products, cleanliness and good service. The stores are spacious, well lit and well designed. It has a phenomenal name among the public generally as a byword for quality. Yet it has its detractors. Our doubts were settled by talking not so much to people in middle management, but to workers on the shop floor.

The stores we visited displayed a warmth and friendliness which would be difficult to manufacture. The people we talked to displayed a sense of belonging to the Sainsbury culture and a real appreciation of Sainsbury's position in the marketplace.

The culture is personified by the initials JS. Sainsbury people speak of JS as the identification of the business and its culture. The original JS was the founder John James Sainsbury, who married the daughter of a dairyman from north London and set up his own dairy at the tail end of the 1860s. By 1891 he had fourteen branches and two depots. By 1914 there were 115. While other chains had accumulated more, Sainsbury decided to concentrate on quality rather than quantity.

The development of the suburbs and the suburban railway brought further growth during the 1920s and 1930s. After the Second World War food was rationed, imposing constraints on the business, but in 1950 the first American-style superstore was opened and in 1955 the largest foodstore in Europe was introduced.

Sainsbury became a public company in 1973 and it now has around 58,000 shareholders – a third of whom are employees. Today Sainsbury has 270 stores carrying 10,000 lines, including 4000 own-label. It also has interests in the DIY and gardening sectors, in the form of Homebase, and is in partnership with British Home Stores in the hypermarket area as SavaCentre.

Sainsbury's places great emphasis on training, recruiting the right people and providing a high-quality service to customers. A Department of Education and Science investigation into Sainsbury's education and training policies confirmed the company's high reputation in this field. 'Sainsbury's provides its employees at all levels with high-quality in-company training. Its well-designed training programmes make extensive use of audiovisual aids and carefully-prepared training manuals to free trainees from the burden of extensive note-taking. Trainees are encouraged to manage and direct their own learning,' says the report.

Everyone we spoke to saw training as directly related to promotion opportunities – not only within the store but also within the group. Tony Rooney, a supervisor in the frozen foods department at the Finchley branch, says, 'If you're in the position to do the job, the opportunities are there but it is up to you to go for it.'

Stewart Mitchell, a senior buyer at head office, says, 'If you work hard and do things out of the ordinary, the promotional opportunities are there. People who are hungry get on.'

Graduate recruit Susan Winser, who is now assistant buyer in fresh poultry, joined Sainsbury's because she saw it as a fast-moving business. 'I liked the training opportunities as well. They always find courses to send you on, for example Negotiation Skills. It's very comprehensive and you can't miss a course – they are very strict about participation.'

Heavy emphasis is placed on the quality of training and opportunity. Staff say, however, that the nature of both varies from store to store. In fact the atmosphere is different in each outlet. Many of the staff we spoke to at Finchley had worked at Islington and had not enjoyed their time there.

Observations on pay were interesting, since Sainsbury is above average for the retail sector. Staff both at head office and in the stores grumbled about pay and said that it did not compare well with other major retailers.

Rosalind Abrahams, a sales assistant, says, 'The pay's not wonderful but they are good to work for.' Jenny Card, a store instructor, thinks the pay is OK but not brilliant. Marc Tavernier, a meat supervisor, comments that 'It could be a bit better.'

Middle management people think that the salaries are fairer. Mitchell says, 'I think the general feeling is that the salaries are pretty fair.' Bill Love, a chargehand in the head-office engineering department, confirms this view.

Love was a steward representing the Union of Construction, Allied Trades and Technicians (UCATT) for eight years. 'I believe staff–management relations are good. It works – if there are problems we always feel we can go to personnel and they will sort it out. In general the company does everything to help you.'

Communications are good. The company publishes a monthly magazine, *J S Journal*, which has won the award for the best house journal in the country. Sainsbury's also produce an annual employee report to keep staff up to date on company performance and its implications for stores and staff.

Sainsbury is equally good on benefits. There is an acceptable pension scheme, free health insurance for middle management upwards, 10 per cent staff discount across the board, a profit share after two years' employment, SAYE scheme for all, and share options – 25 per cent of staff are shareholders. The company has a vigorous staff association which organizes dinner dances, charity fund-raising and sports days at the Sainsbury's field at Dulwich.

There is a vibrant, intensely commercial personality at Sainsbury, which the potential recruit may react to warmly or positively dislike. There is no doubt that the company does a lot for its people and those with ambition can rise. Some may find the company autocratic, others merely well disciplined. It has nevertheless been remarkably consistent in its success.

CHRISTIAN SALVESEN

Employing 5865 people around the UK Christian Salvesen is a diversified company operating in the food distribution, refrigerating, marine and industrial services sectors. The group headquarters are in Scotland.

pay	☐	ambience	☐
benefits	☐	environment	☐
promotion	☐	equal opportunities	☐
training	☐	communications	☐

By far their most significant area of operation is the food-related transport business. From thirteen locations in the UK and others in continental Europe, Christian Salvesen services Marks & Spencer and J. Sainsbury, Delhaize and GB-Inno-BM in Belgium, and Carrefour in France. The Rugby depot of Christian Salvesen is a jewel in the corporate crown. One of six bases which supply the prestige Marks & Spencer contract, Rugby claims some of the highest efficiency quotients in the company. It supplies 32 stores with 1600 lines derived from 400 suppliers. Goods worth £750,000 pass through the depot every day.

The pride and enthusiasm of the CS team at Rugby is immediately apparent. Chris Hudgton, a traffic supervisor for the last four years, sums up the atmosphere. 'We're a well-knit group of people with a good team spirit. Everyone is accepted into the fold. Newcomers fit in quickly and there are no odd men out. We're the best paid in the area and staff turnover is surprisingly low.'

The company's lorries roll across the UK landscape bearing their distinctive livery modelled on the Norwegian flag. The design is no aberration – the original Christian Salvesen was Norwegian. He created his company in 1872 in Leith. The founding company dealt in shipowning, timber and coal-broking, paraffin-refining and agency work. Except for shipowning, all these businesses have disappeared with the passage of time.

Although the nature of the business today would probably be unfamiliar to Salvesen, the entrepreneurial spirit with which it is conducted is identical to his own.

CS has around 100 locations in the UK and staff concentrated in these sites form tightly grouped communities. Hours at the depots are dictated by one requirement alone – what the customer wants. The bulk of the deliveries are made at 6 a.m., making the busiest time from midnight to 5 a.m. Staff work on a 16-week cycle which includes seven Sundays and two Saturdays. Five out of every eight hours are worked at night. The only day everyone takes off is Christmas Day.

So dedicated are the drivers that in the heavy snows of early 1987 CS staff were the only people on the roads delivering food. 'We couldn't keep them in,' says one manager. All CS lorries have sleeper cabs and any driver who gets stranded is put up in a local hotel.

Emphasis is placed on initiative and individual enterprise. Paul Wood, a traffic manager, says: 'It's a friendly and informal company, with everyone on first-name terms. There is a structure but you don't feel trapped. There's a lot of flexibility with no set limits, so you can develop your job as you want to – even as a driver. Fewer restrictions bring out better performances, with nudges to keep people on the straight and narrow.'

Wood was rapidly promoted from driver, and the company maintains that promotion is fast. It is not unusual for someone to be promoted after only six months in the company. 'There is a lot of democratic discussion and generally the guidance from management is happily accepted. It's a meritocracy. And, to a certain extent, you choose where you go,' he told us.

John Bell, a driver who has been with CS for seven years, is irked that he did not make the decision to join up sooner. 'I rue not coming here ten years ago. I'm on the job appreciation scheme at the moment and it's a marvellous experience.' The idea of the scheme is to give employees a wide-ranging view of how the company operates and where the individual slots into the complete picture. Bell says that it has been an eye-opener. 'I now appreciate the problems of the boys in the office. I've seen the other side of the lads. They're friends not bastards.'

Communications is a keynote and an intelligently used vehicle for keeping the team together. Weekly briefing meetings handle operational issues. These are augmented by bi-monthly injections of scene-setting material which places the company in the context of its markets and performance.

Robin Nye, a shift manager, comments: 'Communication is good – the information is fed through very effectively. The head of personnel walks round the shop floor each day before going up to her office. It's a family atmosphere really. Good ideas are regularly passed up from below.'

The company runs a quarterly newspaper called *Salvo*, and a video is prepared every year to explain the annual results. Family involvement is encouraged with open days when spouses and children can visit depots.

CS likes its people to be active in the local community. It helps with work experience for local schools and promotes teacher secondments. Employees regularly talk to local organizations such as Women's Institutes, rotary clubs, round tables and young farmers groups. It also provides financial help to the Enterprise Trust. The Scottish National Orchestra and Scottish Chamber Orchestra are direct beneficiaries of the company's largesse. The style is to support local causes rather than donate on a national scale.

Pay compares favourably with the sector and benefits are remarkably good. The CS share option scheme is open to anyone with three years' service. Around the UK 48 per cent of employees are members – many of these buy up to their maximum. Since 1 January 1988 a new pension scheme has operated. This now includes anyone working 18 hours a week and beyond. It is a 6 per cent contributory plan and is compulsory for all monthly-paid workers over the age of twenty-five. A nest-egg scheme also operates for hourly-paid staff and is non-contributory.

Drivers are insured against losing their HGV1 licences, other than for illegalities. Salaried staff also benefit from BUPA membership which covers both employees and their families. One driver says that the company provides them with their uniform. 'You get boots and overalls, six shirts, a tie, a top coat, three sets of gloves and goggles. Warehouse workers also get a pullover, socks and a body warmer. There's also two Christmas meals and you get a free meal when visitors come.'

The company's caring image is acknowledged unanimously by its staff. Wood says: 'The response to sickness and injury is always good. When my wife had our first child the company sent round a bouquet of flowers which arrived even before I did.' Bell recalls a colleague who had a heart attack. 'We put up a collection and we raised £1000. Here people help first and ask questions afterwards.'

Hudgton remembers the bad winter of 1977 and the assistance CS provided to its drivers. 'Lorries were breaking down all over the country due to frozen diesel. The company sent cars and Sherpa vans out to pick up stranded drivers with flasks and sandwiches. There's no false feeling.' CS also keeps to its word about keeping employees on the payroll during bouts of sickness. One employee recently had two years off with a knee injury. True to its commitment, the management kept his job open and he was now back at work. CS can afford to be generous. It's a young company and absenteeism is low.

All jobs are advertised internally. In practice the company draws almost evenly from inside and outside. A small management training scheme exists for the handful of graduates taken on each year. All staff are performance-assessed and training is monitored to ensure that promising recruits rise quickly. Once in management, training – which is considerable – is overseen by local managers. The CS approach is to combine the formal and the informal, tutorial and on-the-job.

Redundancies are few. When they do occur, as at the Atherstone depot recently, they are handled with sensitivity. Every attempt was made to help employees find alternative work. Some volunteered for early retirement and others for redundancy with a sizeable cash handshake.

All staff canteens are subsidized so that food is charged at cost and everyone eats in the same canteen.

Alan Sturrock, regional manager, points towards growth in the company. 'We need to build up our food services division, possibly by acquisition and not necessarily connected with our current operation. However, we will probably maintain our service status rather than dealing with the public direct. We plan healthy growth for the next three years. We are expanding our food service business in France and we have a foothold in Germany – we are really making an effort on the continent.'

He explains that two of the food division's sectors, Salserve and Salstream, are doing particularly well. 'They are model depots. They account for 20 per cent of divisional and 10 per cent of group profits. The processing plants tend to be older, run on somewhat more traditional lines, but modern methods and concepts are spreading.'

Sturrock says that depots are almost autonomous but that a strong company culture pervades them all. 'A CS type will succeed anywhere. The management are very committed – they don't just work nine to five – and that commitment spreads to the work force.

'Working for CS is exciting and good fun,' he comments. It is this feeling which underlies many of the expressions of goodwill and team spirit which we found in the company. There is no denying that people work hard. The secret of CS's success is in keeping its operations small scale and recognizing its people as individuals and human beings. It is one of the few places which we visited where a genuine fraternal spirit exists among staff *and* between staff and management.

Bell says, 'The job is done professionally, you're constantly checked on to keep you out of bad habits. You know that you would be reported for not wearing a tie but I'm proud of this company.'

SCOTTISH & NEWCASTLE BREWERIES

One of the UK's major breweries, Scottish & Newcastle is based in Edinburgh. Its turnover in 1987 was £827.5 million and its pre-tax profit £90.3 million. The company employs 20,000 people, mainly in pubs and hotels.

pay ☐		ambience ☐	
benefits ☐		environment ☐	
promotion ☐		equal opportunities ☐	
training ☐		communications ☐	

Dedicated staff do not just demonstrate their loyalty by working flat out. There are other subtler ways of showing the company you work for is *your* company. Senior staff at Scottish & Newcastle Breweries not only love the products they brew but show their affection for the business with personalized car registration plates – paid for out of their own pockets. That's the sort of dedication to duty the brewery achieves from its willing work force.

Wherever you live you will know S&N products: McEwan's Export (top-selling canned beer in the UK); Newcastle Brown and Amber; Kestrel lager; Scotch Bitter; Harp; Tartan and Exhibition. They are some of the top names in the average drinker's dictionary. One in five carryouts bought from an off-licence comes from one of S&N's breweries. This thriving market, which necessitated the start of a new company, S&NB (SALES) in 1984, balances out the slight decline in pub sales. Unemployment, violence in town-centre pubs, drink-drive laws – whatever causes a slump, S&N is ready to cope.

The present company was formed in 1960 by a merger between Scottish Brewers Ltd and the Newcastle Breweries Ltd. The former came into being as a result of a merger between Wm Younger (founded 1749) and Wm McEwan (founded 1856). The latter resulted from a number of mergers of companies operating in and around Newcastle.

Head office is in Edinburgh, although brewing is now done elsewhere. All of the Scottish beers bearing the Father William and Cavalier trademarks are produced at the New Fountain Brewery in the city.

Other breweries operate in Manchester, Newcastle and Nottingham – a recent addition to the group being Home Brewery. The group also has franchises to brew and sell Harp lager brands and to sell Becks Bier. S&N also includes Thistle Hotels – mainly four-star hotels on prime tourist and commercial sites. There are eight in London for example, including the prestigious Selfridges in the heart of the West End. A massive £30 million refurbishment programme on hotels has just been completed, and money spent on acquiring properties for development under the Country House Hotel Programme.

Turnover and pre-tax profits have shown a healthy increase since 1983 when the figures were £641.8m (41.1m). Comparable figures are: 1984, £692.5m (£55.2m); 1985, £707.2m (£65.2m); 1986, £773.6m (£75.1m); 1987, £827.5m (£90.3m). Brokers predict a turnover of around £110m for the 1988 financial year.

The company employs around 20,000 people, the bulk of whom work in pubs and hotels, with 4000 full time, 2000 management and 7000 part-timers. Henry Fairweather, group personnel director, said staff turnover was naturally high in the pub trade, but low among T & G craftsmen and core management. Policy over the last five years has been to reduce numbers by natural wastage.

Bar staff, uniquely among brewers, have their own committee set up by management, but the floating nature of the bar population means only a few take advantage of the opportunity for discussion and negotiation. Bar-staff wages are comparable with competitors, and usually higher, with the recommended £2.16 being used as a base rate.

Two types of university graduates are hunted: the best of the crop who can expect to be boardmen by the age of thirty, and degree-holders who will specialize in areas such as distribution, production and marketing. They can expect to be middle managers within three years and senior managers within seven years. Fairweather says: 'We would rather take on someone with a second-class degree if he shows personal qualities we are looking for. He might have been active in the Students Union, run a college newspaper or organized charity functions.'

Most training is at business schools, but S&N think highly of outward-bound-type activities. They aim to make 80 per cent of appointments from within, but this is rarely achieved. 'We do need an injection of fresh blood and skills sometimes,' Fairweather commented. S&N was one of the first companies to be granted training status by the Manpower Services Commission and had some 160 youngsters on various schemes in Edinburgh, Newcastle and Manchester. 'It is good for us, good for the kids, and good for the managers.'

Women are welcome and there is a good chance that senior management will be welcoming some female colleagues within the next couple of years.

John McColl, full-time officer with the T and G, seemed to regard S&N as a model company. He has responsibility for the whole of the food and drink industry in Scotland. He says: 'It is unusual for us to have a headquarters in Edinburgh but good that we have a first-class involvement with a national company.' He told us S&N had made great strides in union involvement, introducing a chairman's forum which involved representatives from all of the bargaining units. 'This has been very successful. It lasts all day and gives people at shop-floor level the chance to find out things that had been behind closed doors. We can ask any questions we like and the entire board of directors is there to answer.'

McColl is particularly appreciative of S&N's approach to redundancies. The company does not announce closures out of the blue but gives at least 18 months' notice, giving time for alternative jobs to be found. There is a three-year agreement – vital for a company spread so wide afield. More than 100 shop stewards came together to elect 18 representatives to sit down for a week and thrash out the deal. Ballots are an accepted part of that deal.

McColl says, 'This company wants to wipe out suspicion. If it has a problem they say to us: "Let's sit down and talk about it." I wish all companies viewed us in the same way. There has never been a national strike, only local disturbances when a manager has made an unpopular decision. I am on first-name terms with senior management.'

Safety has never been a problem and cash is available if safety is at stake.

Brian Stewart, corporate development director, cautiously revealed plans for development outside the UK, probably in the hotel business, but eradicated rumours that S&N was interested in new lines of business. 'We will be looking at areas consistent with our experience and have no intention of becoming a conglomerate.' Looking back over the last few years he can see many changes. 'Things are very different. It is a lot more demanding, but I think that is a reflection of the industry in general. We have learned not to get in a position where painful and awkward decisions have to be made. Now we face up to things and plan ahead.

'There is a lot of pressure but much of it is self-induced. The bulk of us enjoy it. We have been given our heads and told to get on with it.

We are well geared up to deal with a changing market situation. Our business is structured to cope.'

Gordon Ball, a supervisor in the central engineering workshop, who has worked for S&N for twenty-three years, starting as a fifteen-year-old apprentice, was a little dubious about the flow of information from management to shop floor. But he says the company is a good one to work for, has always been fair, and has provided plenty of opportunities. Staff appreciated the perks of the job, particularly a drinks voucher and the chance to take a Highlife Break at a Thistle Hotel at half price.

More critical of the company is Bobby Jameson, an internal worker, looking after beer in its final stages before delivery. He believes there was too much secrecy and dismissed the success of the chairman's forum as mythical. 'The majority of people have little knowledge or even interest in the new ideas, mainly because middle managers don't hand down information. How can the workers go to this forum? The work force has been cut to the bone and there are no spare people. A few people on winter holidays and a couple of cases of flu would mean you literally have to close a place down. We have one of the best union–management agreements going but a lot of middle management don't study it and don't know it.'

Jameson was approving, however, of the wages, pension scheme, beer issue, regular safety meetings and the chance to attend courses on subjects outside his normal range of experience. Lorraine Gunn, secretary to the operations director for S&N beer production, says that the company prefers to look outside to fill jobs rather than recruit from within. She feels a little in the cold, having progressed well in her ten years with the company but seeing little prospect of being chosen for higher things. But she enjoyed her job and said, 'Basically, it is a good company to work for.'

SHELL

Shell is one of the largest companies in the world. Its primary interest is in oil exploration and development. Shell UK produced sales of £6.6 billion in 1986 with pre-tax profits of £1.1 billion. It employs 22,000 people in the UK.

pay	☐	ambience	☐
benefits	☐	environment	☐
promotion	☐	equal opportunities	☐
training	☐	communications	☐

Potential is a big word in Shell. If you show it you can go anywhere within the company – and what a company it is. Shell is principally an oil exploration business, but has interests in chemicals, metals, natural gas and coal. It is not only one of the largest oil companies in the world but one of the biggest global businesses.

The group is involved in many countries and is fiercely internationalist in approach. In fact, Shell's presence in so many countries leads people to wonder who actually owns it. The British think Shell is British, Dutch people believe it to be Dutch, and Americans assume that it is a US company. It is in fact an Anglo-Dutch company. Some 60 per cent of Shell is owned by Royal Dutch in the Netherlands and the remaining 40 per cent by Shell Transport and Trading in London.

It originated in the East End of London in 1833 when shopkeeper Marcus Samuel started selling bric-à-brac. Among his lines were oriental shells which proved so profitable that he arranged regular shipments from the Far East. His son Marcus took over the London end of the business and moved into kerosene. He ordered a fleet of eight tankers under the banner of Shell Transport.

At the same time petroleum was being produced in the East Indies, and the Koninklijke Nederlandsche Maatschappij tot Exploitatie van Petroleum-bronnen, later Royal Dutch, was formed to develop an oilfield in Sumatra. Samuel and Royal Dutch were then in direct competition. Their successes and their failures forced them into a working arrangement. In 1903 they formed the Asiatic Petroleum Company. This was the foretaste of their eventual union in 1907. With motor vehicles in their earlier stages of development, widescale expansion followed, and Shell has enjoyed unremitting growth.

Its status as one of the great companies of oil production and exploration has made it an attractive company to work for. The company encourages its people to travel widely and to experience work in the field – at drilling sites in Venezuela, Oman or the North Sea. They also move around product areas with ease. Shell people are expected to demonstrate great flexibility and bags of energy – both intellectual and physical.

Ross Johnson, personnel director of Shell UK Oil, says that for its fast-track people the company is looking for the top ½ a per cent of graduates in Europe. To win them over the company faces tough competition from other international companies. 'We have no difficulty in recruiting from the top 20 per cent of graduates,' he says. But he does concede that the top ½ to 1 per cent are not presenting themselves to any companies. The major international employers need to go looking for them.

Shell has a lot to offer the most able of graduates. It has a powerful training establishment which offers a broad selection of courses particularly tailored towards moving people with potential up through the company. 'Some graduates want to get experience of a merchant bank, a multinational company and then perhaps management consultancy,' says Johnson. 'What we attempt to show is that they can get all those different qualities of experience here at Shell.' Shell is one of the biggest traders in the world market. Graduates can then move into running small departments in marketing, for example, where they will be involved in the promotion of the Shell brands at the pumps. The organization also engages internal management consultancy.

Shell has a definite personality which may suit some and not others. It has moved away from the highly paternalistic venture which it was ten years ago. It is emphatically democratic. There is a committee to discuss almost anything, but decision-making has become much tighter in recent years. People with ideas that are good, well thought out and accurately costed, can get a decision from the people who matter in some of the fastest times in the commercial world.

The Shell image is smooth, technically astute and accomplished, aggressive in the marketplace and highly cultured. Shell appears to be urbane, but is rather more reminiscent of the iron fist in the velvet glove. As one manager told us, 'Don't be fooled by the exterior. We are assessing people all the time.'

The key factor of potential is there all the time. If you've got the magic ingredient, and manage to keep it, Shell will support you. The company is committed to planning heavily for the future. They see this year's topnotch graduates as their managing directors twenty-five or thirty years hence. 'Everybody who joins at the graduate level will have expectations of working within perhaps two to three companies and probably working overseas several times during their career. So there's a degree of discontinuity if you like, compared to working in the one company in one environment,' says Johnson.

Shell in London is divided between the international organization, which is housed in its architecturally renowned building on the South Bank of the Thames, and the UK business, based in Shell Mex House on the Strand. The international company has two headquarters – London and The Hague. The board meets alternately in the UK and the Netherlands. This could give rise to some dichotomy of thought, but it seems to suit the gentlemen of Shell well enough.

Gentlemen is the operative word. Women have yet to secure the highest positions in the group. However, progress is being made within the operating companies and barriers are slowly being removed. Pay and conditions are the best in the industry, and among the best in the country. Shell also has a heavy commitment to sports and social activities.

There is no doubt that Shell is one of the finest companies in the country. It needs to make greater efforts on behalf of its women and its non-graduate talent, but anyone who manages to get in and can take the pace will get a good deal in return.

W H SMITH

W H Smith is one of the largest newsagents, booksellers and distribution companies in the UK, with outlets in almost every town and city. It employs more than 25,000 people in the UK. Turnover in 1987 was £1.5 billion and pre-tax profits £63.8 million.

pay	☐	ambience	☐
benefits	☐	environment	☐
promotion	☐	equal opportunities	☐
training	☐	communications	☐

'Progressive, not aggressive' is how one employee summed it up. W H Smith has changed rapidly in the last few years. Whereas its image had faded a little in the early 1980s, the company has since had a new lease of life which enabled it to prepare for the 1990s with a high degree of vigour and vim. Sir Simon Hornby, the recently knighted chairman, says that the move to change had been in train throughout the 1980s but that the impact of the hard work behind the scenes has materialized only recently.

The history of Smiths is a fascinating one. The family were the orginators of London's first newspaper delivery round in 1792. But the real milestone of development was the coming of the railways. W H Smith and Son became an operator of bookstalls on station concourses and platforms. But by 1906 the Great Western and London and North Western railways rents became so prohibitively expensive that the company secured sites immediately next to stations. Within three months, 90 shops had been opened. The company also moved into lending books.

By 1960 the lending side was disposed of, but Smiths was now the leading bookseller and stationer in the UK with 368 stores. Since then the company's base has broadened. It has moved into an acquisitive phase. Malcolm Field, managing director of the group, explains that this has given the group a new role. 'We saw a change in the channel of distribution of products,' he says. This means that Smiths rapidly saw themselves as a distribution company rather than as simply a newsagent or bookseller. It also meant that the group might venture into any area which could be labelled distribution. Certainly, the group had built up a large wholesale business which contributed significantly to group profits.

The company then became involved in television – it is a 20 per cent shareholder in Yorkshire Television. Satellite beckoned and the group took holdings in Screen Sport and Lifestyle. It also bought the upmarket bookseller Sherratt & Hughes. Through a process of acquisition and expansion, it now owns 260 stores in Canada and 270 stores in the United States.

Since 1979 the group has been active in the DIY market with the Do It All chain, and more recently W H Smith acquired Our Price records. This collection of record shops generally stocked a different selection of products from the record departments of the W H Smith stores, so the purchase was complementary.

Today W H Smith is the biggest stationer, the biggest bookseller, the biggest distributor of magazines and newspapers and the biggest retailer of recorded music in the UK. Field puts part of the success down to the culture of the organization. 'Style is a major factor,' he says. 'We care about design, about how the stores look, and we give strong guidelines from the top in what is sold.

'We give people responsibility and authority and they get on and do it. We have respect for the individual. On the whole we believe that people will not find a better job elsewhere.' Great stress is placed on individual contribution at Smiths and there is a transparent honesty about what has been achieved and what is left to be achieved. There is an eagerness to deliver from both employee and employer.

Tricia Ryan, a secretary in Strand House, off Sloane Square, says, 'Smiths has the competitive edge. The High Street has changed, the customer wants more and I see Smiths as progressive.'

The same sentiments are echoed in Do It All – one of the autonomous subsidiaries. John Hancock, deputy managing director for Do It All nationally, says, 'Smiths were historically a bit bureaucratic – paternalistic and rigid – but they now have a conscious policy to create a transitional period. They have thought quite carefully about retaining old values with new market values and their blend of strengths comes from parentage and the new commercialism.' Hancock believes that Smiths were quick to listen to what the customer wanted. 'The company discovered fairly early on that customer awareness pays off in the long term. We need strategic principles to keep the customers.'

The fusion of the traditional concepts of good service and high-quality merchandise with modern virtues of clever marketing and good design has made the W H Smith group stand out among retailers.

But its attitude towards its staff is also extremely positive. One of the greatest manifestations of this is in training.

The company is one of the best industrial trainers in the country. Rodney Buse, managing director of Do It All, is fulsome. 'The training has been sharpened immensely in the last few years – our internal course is now recognized by external educational institutes as contributing to external qualifications. Smiths recognizes that the education world and the business world should work together.'

Peter Bagnall, staff and services managing director, outlines the idea behind the training. 'Smiths structures training to supplement deficiencies. We aim to make courses work for the individual.' Personal strengths and weaknesses are tested by self-measurement and assessment. Then weaknesses are addressed by personal involvement in training schemes.

The quality of the courses is such that they are highly regarded by industry as a whole, and by academic authorities which recognize the standards reached as credits, for example, towards the national diploma in management. Much of the training for shop-floor staff is on site, but management training schemes are held at the W H Smith staff training college – an old mansion in the Oxfordshire countryside. Around 1800 staff training courses are held here every year. Younger recruits are offered an outward-bound-type course.

Pay and benefits are average to good. The company maintains that salaries are very competitive, and certainly for the retail sector they are not bad. Benefits include at least four weeks' holiday a year, staff discount after three months' service, a good non-contributory pension scheme and share ownership and share option schemes. BUPA membership is extended to all managers.

Judith Cowens, manager of the Leadenhall branch of Sherratt & Hughes, argues that the salary is above average for the book trade. In December 1987 she was on £17,000. She rates the training highly and is also impressed by the incentive bonus scheme where employees earn a prearranged percentage of salary if they hit sales target.

The W H Smith group is a powerful and broad-based organization, but it is also friendly and supportive of its staff. Its training is testimony to its commitment. Sir Simon Hornby has repeatedly said that it is key to the success of his businesses. The opportunities presented by the high growth levels within each of the divisions of the group means that the company is able to offer 500 new positions a year.

SONY

Sony UK is the wholly-owned subsidary of the Sony Corporation of Japan. It manufactures electronic and electrical goods at its plant in Bridgend, South Wales. It employs 1650 people in this country. Its turnover in 1987 was £350 million.

pay ☐	ambience ☐
benefits ☐	environment ☐
promotion ☐	equal opportunities ☐
training ☐	communications ☐

In 1973 Sony became a household name as the first company from Japan to set up in the UK. Fears of xenophobia were unwarranted even when Sony built its factory on top of a Second World War ammunition dump.

The company has plenty to be proud of at its Bridgend plant. In fifteen years it has grown from a unit with 300 staff to a complex employing 1200. It now produces as many TV sets in a month as it used to in a year, and it is on the point of doubling production again. By mid-1989 some 800,000 sets a year should be coming out of the factory. No one has ever been made redundant, even during some short-lived upheavals. In fact, the success of Sony has drawn other companies to the area.

There are 250 staff at Sony UK's Staines HQ dealing with sales, marketing and finance, and 200 others scattered in sales and distribution offices around the country, but Bridgend is where you see the Sony ethic at its strongest. A further 300 are being recruited to work in the latest extension to the clean and relatively quiet factory. Bridgend is not just an assembly plant. It is the most integrated Sony factory in the world, already responsible for more than 10 per cent of Sony's worldwide TV production – and still growing. It manufactures and tests key components from tubes to printed circuit boards, then puts them together.

After fifteen years the plant still exudes energy and youth – the Japanese who came to set it up were all under thirty – but over the years Sony has responded to local culture. You do see workers doing exercises at 7 a.m. but it turns out to be the night shift warming up for a game of football in the sports hall after finishing their work.

If you think success has been achieved by slavishly following techniques from Tokyo you would be wrong. Single status is the first sign. There is one canteen and all the office staff – even senior management – have to wear company uniform. Accountants and cleaners alike are expected to stick to rigidly timed tea breaks. Only the top 100 managers get private health care, and there are no company cars except for the Japanese and the top dozen Britons at the plant. Alun Jones, Bridgend personnel chief, does not think that uniforms suppress individuality: 'Look at the Welsh rugby team. We're group conscious – like Liverpool FC.'

Sony starts from the principle that the customer comes first. 'Many British companies have lost sight of this,' says Jones, 'and sometimes customers don't know what is possible. The Japanese customer is very tough.' This determines employment policy and the shape of the factory, because 'to produce first-class product you need first-class people in a first-class environment. Of course, if we pay employees too much then the customers will buy other goods.'

If a newly produced TV works that is not good enough. Sony tries to make every employee aware the 'a scratch on a knob is not acceptable'. Production operators have video screens which feed back information about any problems down the line. It improves quality and makes the job more interesting. Once a week a quarter of the staff stay behind for a couple of hours on overtime to discuss how to improve production. These are the Quality Activity Groups – not 'Circles', because Sony believes Quality Circle is about to become a dirty word as more and more companies introduce QCs but still produce junk. The groups have also helped adapt systems so that handicapped workers, such as the twelve deaf and dumb operators, can work on the production line. Each year the teams which have come up with the best ideas get the chance of a trip to Japan or Germany to explain their ideas. Others are rewarded with portable stereos or other Sony products.

At times the company's drive for improvement can be demoralizing. 'Whenever you do something here someone is saying "next time we will do it better – what went wrong?" It would be nice if someone said "you can relax now" but if mankind had adopted that attitude we would still be living in caves.'

Sony makes no guarantees of a job for life, but the work force knows that 'We've had situations where we've had more people than we need', yet the company has taken the firm decision to keep people on in the belief that they can generate more business in the future.

321

Sony founder Akio Morita approves: 'I cannot understand why there is anything good about laying off people.'

Morita helped to set up Tokyo Tsushin Kogyo after the Second World War but it was only in 1958 that TTK became Sony Corporation. It is hard to believe that this company, which turns over $7 billion a year, is so young or that Morita started out cooking ferric oxide in a frying pan before painting it on to paper strips in the hope of producing usable recording tape. He played an important part in the establishment of the British factory in 1973. Prince Charles allegedly met Morita at the Expo '70 exhibition in Japan and suggested he open a plant in Wales, but Akio already knew the area. In the 1960s he sent his son Masao to school at Atlantic College in an old castle just ten miles from Bridgend.

It is easy to see why the site was attractive to Sony: a potentially large local work force – half a million people – living within 30 minutes of the plant. There are good communications by motorway and high-speed rail links to London and the rest of Britain.

Japanese companies tend to treat women badly but Sony makes more of an effort than most, both in Japan and in Britain. The first female supervisors felt they had been appointed by local management in the face of Japanese opposition, but now 25 per cent of supervisors and managers are women and the number is increasing. Changes in legislation have opened up higher paid shift jobs and the increased use of robots to transport components means that strength is no longer a prerequisite, even in the TV tube plant. Three of the graduate trainee engineers are female.

Bridgend recruits a dozen graduates off the milk round each year and many more go to the Staines HQ. But Sony often finds that polytechnic students are more effective, and the company has an excellent record for promoting and training managers from the factory floor. Sony can point to the head of research and development who started as a warehouseman ten years ago, and to youngsters taken on as apprentices who have reached all levels in the organization.

Sony is not a soft option. The company is strict on time-keeping and some staff complain about petty restrictions – such as a ban on hanging cards over the production line at Christmas. There is a single union agreement with the AEU which works well. Wages are fair by local standards. Most workers are paid £120–£160 for a 7.30 a.m.–4 p.m. day rising up to £200 with overtime. Supervisors earn around £11,000, and the top 100 managers earn between £13,000 and £25,000. The canteen is subsidized and staff get one-third off Sony products. The surgery 'deals with everything from broken legs to broken marriages'. The sales and marketing operation in Staines pays much higher salaries, is freer with company cars and is more conventionally organized,

Sony insists on commitment from its staff during working hours, but it is not after your soul. The rigid work structures would not suit everyone but it is a responsible employer and, provided you have a reliable alarm clock, it must be one of the most secure jobs in South Wales. It is also a unique opportunity to learn the best of Japanese techniques in an atmosphere which still supports experimentation and encourages you to think for yourself.

THAMES TELEVISION

Thames Television is the largest programme contractor in the IBA commercial TV network. It covers the London area on weekdays. In 1987 its turnover was £222 million and its pre-tax profit £24.7 million. The company employs 2500 people, the majority of whom work at Euston and Teddington.

pay ▭	ambience ▭
benefits ▭	environment ▭
promotion ▭	equal opportunities ▭
training ▭	communications ▭

Thames Television is the flagship of the commercial television network. While it shares the London franchise area with LWT, and breakfast time with the national contractor TV-AM, Thames is the senior programmer. The company, which celebrates its twenty-first birthday in 1988, was the product of a powerful shake-up among programme contractors in 1967. It was born out of Associated Rediffusion, which originally provided weekday transmission to London.

The company's largest shareholders are BET and Thorn-EMI, but the composition of the holding in the company was broadened by a rights issue in 1985. Personnel manager Peter Fiske is clear about Thames's perception of itself. 'We see ourselves as professionals. We have high expectations, but reward quality work,' he says. In many ways Thames is a traditional company with a long-standing work force. Attrition rates are low even for the industry. It has a committed team who recognize that Thames represents a pinnacle of achievement in the television industry.

It is an organization with a reputation for high political drama, which would appear to be largely unjustified. Fred Steed, who is a supervisor at master control, has been with the company since the early days of Rediffusion. 'It is a good company to work for but I would like to see more management involvement with the staff. Thames used to be way ahead on salaries although the independents are beginning to catch up.'

Paul Greene, a reporter, joined in 1985. 'Thames salaries are well above the industry average. I feel very lucky to be here.' He started on

£23,000 and by the end of 1987 year was earning £30,000. In fact, although Thames compares well with industry at large, in the television sector it is generous in all-round packages.

Everyone gets five weeks' holiday. Women are entitled to thirteen weeks' maternity leave with full pay and have the right to return to their original posts up to six months after birth. Private medical insurance is available for senior managers, and there is an annual bonus scheme which averages 10 per cent of salary. Perks for reporters and researchers include free TV sets and videos, and occasional theatre tickets. There are also company tennis courts, a subsidized canteen, restaurant and bar.

Thames has suffered little history of industrial malaise. A strike at the end of the 1970s was fuelled by long-standing discontent felt by certain members of staff wanting a larger slice of an extremely rich cake. There is little sympathy to be found today among Thames staff who regard that eleven-week stoppage as appalling self-indulgence. The company has made no redundancies in the last ten years. Profitability is good and people are queuing at the door to join.

However, the low turnover of staff – especially in management grades – means that opportunities for promotion are limited. Nevertheless, secretaries can move up to become researchers and there are former sub-editors among the reporters and presenters. Cameramen and video editors move from local news output to networked programmes and magazines. Greene says, 'There are a lot of opportunities to move around, with new programmes opening up and things improving all the time.' Greene maintains that the company has a wide range of activities open to committed members of the team.

Victoria Morgan-Bellemy, a picture editor, has been with Thames for nine years. 'I started out as a secretary and it took me a long time to reach my job. Too long.' But despite the company's cautious approach to her promotion, she is enthusiastic about the atmosphere and conditions at Thames. 'It is probably much better than any other television company.' Thames paid for her to go on a three-day self-assertiveness course to help her cope with newsroom tensions and aggression.

The low turnover rate also leads to some sluggishness in taking up new ideas. But since 1982 matters have improved radically. Until then BET and Thorn-EMI, as principal parents of Thames, had acted in a fairly paternalistic fashion. There is now a more arms' length approach.

This was appreciated in particular by Andy Crossley, the financial controller, as it has meant that Thames can afford to be more adventurous. The company now has a 5 per cent holding in Astra, the

Luxembourg satellite station, and is sharpening the quality of its domestic output. Crossley says that 10 per cent of all Thames income now comes from Thames International, which sells comedy shows like 'Benny Hill' and sitcoms such as 'George & Mildred' and 'Three's Company'.

Thames has been a significant provider of programmes to Channel 4 and hires out its studio space to independent producers. Crossley is dubious about any short-term gain from satellite television but sees Thames as a net winner in the medium term. Nonetheless, staff are enthusiastic about the chance of expansion into fresh areas. Adrian Lesley, a news cameraman, comments: 'Thames is not a particularly innovative or forward-looking company.' But he applauds the Astra venture and adds that Thames is attempting to come to terms with the threat of multi-channel, satellite and cable broadcasting. 'Thames is the richest of the programme companies, but I wonder what will happen to the existing contractors if the government's plan to stipulate that 25 per cent of material is provided by outsiders is enforced.'

Lesley is typical of Thames employees. Most are proud to work there, and are pleased with the array of benefits. They like the opportunity to move around the company, but there is some criticism of the apparently slow reaction to changes in the industry.

J. WALTER THOMPSON

JWT is an advertising agency which employs 1000 people in the UK. Set up in 1925 as a subsidiary office of the American company, the UK practice of JWT is based on Berkeley Square, central London. Figures for the company, which is part of the WPP group, are not available separately but turnover is probably £250 million.

pay	☐	ambience	☐
benefits	☐	environment	☐
promotion	☐	equal opportunities	☐
training	☐	communications	☐

Among the mêlée of takeover bids and contested acquisitions in 1987 there was one in particular which surprised the City and shocked the advertising business. A small UK company called WPP, headed up by its ingenious boss Martin Sorrell, mounted a successful reverse takeover of one of the advertising sector's most distinguished names. J. Walter Thompson spans the globe. Its roster of clients includes the corporate great and good, but large parts of its empire do not, and are not expected to make money. Sorrell was able to put together an audacious bid for the American giant. The UK business of JWT is somewhat different to the rest of the company, and, while the other parts of the enterprise can expect a shake-out, it continues to ride high.

'It's business as usual,' says Miles Colebrook, JWT's UK managing director. Colebrook has 550 people working for him in London, plus another 450 in the rest of the country.

The company has an enviable position in the UK advertising industry and their greatest strength has always been in packaged goods. It has an impressive list of accounts, including Nestlé, British Telecom and Philips, and many dating back to before the war (Rowntree, Lever Brothers, Kelloggs). As Richard Barrick, a copywriter in the creative department, says: 'One of the attractive things about working here is that you get to work on big accounts.'

The most distinctive feature of JWT has been the pioneering of a strategic approach to advertising. In the past the bulk of advertising was simply a search for USP – the unique selling proposition – which would be reiterated over and over again until everyone knew what the product stood for. JWT developed the concept of the planning cycle: Where are we? How did we get there? Where could we be? How could we get there? Are we getting there? A series of studies is initiated around this, 'to produce,' in the words of the mission statement, 'the most distinctive and effective advertising in the marketplace'. This is achieved through the planners, the creative team, the media team, market-modellers, and the account reps. The planners research the market both qualitatively – interviews – and quantitatively – with the market-modellers. Market-modelling involves the use of complex statistical techniques to analyse the factors influencing demand for the client's brand. The creative team produce the advertising ideas to a brief, the media people turn them into an ad and the account reps coordinate relations with the client. JWT claim both planning and market-modelling as being their inventions. Barbara Wingate, an assistant director in planning with a wide experience in the ad industry, comments: 'The planning function is well established here but most agencies didn't do it ten years ago. Planning works like a dream here, but can cause a lot of friction in other companies.'

As a long-time market leader JWT built up an image of a paternalistic, rather stuffy company. It is still known in some circles as 'the university of advertising' – the training school for the industry – a term which is not appreciated inside the company. It used to have a reputation as a centre for Oxbridge graduates, but this is less so nowadays. Its commitment to quality advertising did not always include making a profit. Colebrook says, 'If we'd gone bankrupt producing good advertising no one would have cared in the past – that's not true now.' The catalyst came with the emergence in the late 1970s of rivals such as Saatchi & Saatchi, and the realization that JWT was losing its market leadership. The company now employs half the number of staff it did twenty years ago and has fifteen times the turnover, but the company still has an excellent reputation as an employer. Barbara Wingate says, 'When you come to JWT the headhunters say, "We'll never get you out of there."'

One of the explanations for this comes down to the dynamic culture in the company. It is not one of the best payers in what is a high-paying business. A graduate account rep might start on around £10,000, rising to between £20,000 and £30,000 with ten years' experience. At this point you get a company car and private health insurance, but up until then the fringe benefits are scarce. A PA with a few years in the company will get £11,000 with no other benefits.

The company does not seem terribly good at communicating with their staff. Apart from an annual briefing by the chairman and MD to the whole company in a local cinema, there are few channels of communication (though this is compensated somewhat by a well-established grapevine). The paternalistic attitude is going, and the company admits that in the past it used to carry a lot of people out of sentimentality. Colebrook says, 'Now it's more of a meritocracy. Everyone has to pull their weight, everyone has business responsibility.' But the fact is that staff tend to stay a long time with the company, and many that leave end up returning to the flock. Tim Priestley, an account manager who has been with JWT for twelve years, says, 'People here have the slightly arrogant view that it's the best agency in town.'

Each time a new account is won paper medallions are handed out to stick on the walls, plus a few free vouchers for the staff canteen, the Commodore. Training, mainly for the professional staff, is another positive aspect of the company, and covers performance appraisal, negotiation skills and so-called Thompson Way Workshops. One of the more exotic courses included two weeks in Portugal developing ideas for the twenty-first century.

Not unsurprisingly, JWT is difficult to get into. In the milk-round process ten places exist for around 800 applicants. But those who do get in enjoy early responsibility. Steve Carter, a law graduate who started as an account rep, moved up to working on two of his own accounts within six months. The workload varies radically from day to day but there is very little routine and quite a bit of pressure. There is a strong sense of unity within the business. Colebrook sums up the attitude within JWT: 'We are a bit old-fashioned – we think enjoying working for the company is important.'

THOMSON HOLIDAYS

The largest marketeer of package holidays in the UK, Thomson is based in north London. It employs 900 people full time in the UK, with a further 2000 at resorts overseas during the summer. In 1987 Thomson reported sales of £1.03 billion with pre-tax profits of £42.9 million.

pay ☐	ambience ☐	
benefits ☐	environment ☐	
promotion ☐	equal opportunities ☐	
training ☐	communications ☐	

One in four of all UK holiday-makers flies out for their annual trip to the sea, mountains or lakes with Thomson Holidays and Skytours, who together form the largest holiday tour operation in the world. During 1989, nearly four million people will travel on holidays bought from the Thomson Group.

Thomson Holidays, Skytours and Portland Holidays, a direct sell company, are part of Thomson Travel, which operates its own airline, Britannia, a travel agency chain, Lunn Poly, and Thomson Vacations, a North American tour operator based in Chicago. The group is part of the International Thomson organization, based in Canada. Thomson Travel announced sales during 1987 of £1034m, compared to £793m in 1986, achieving in effect a 30 per cent growth, as well as clocking up sales of £1 billion for the first time ever. Pre-tax profits at £42.9m were the second best ever recorded by the group, 15 per cent lower than the £50.2m (before capital profits of £10.1m) achieved in 1986.

The majority of Thomson clients head for the popular, well-established Mediterranean sun spots, but over the past few years the company has responded to changes in the package-holiday market by moving into the specialist field. Thomson now offers a wide range of self-catering holidays, wintersports, city breaks, holidays for the over fifty-fives, and an air-fare programme for independent travellers.

Reflecting the strong nature of the holiday industry at the moment, Thomson currently creates over one hundred new jobs within the UK each year. Thomson's business has doubled in the past three years, and as a result there has been an increase in staff of 10 per cent. Of the 900-odd UK staff currently on the payroll, one quarter occupy management positions within the company.

As the holiday industry is itself fairly young, it is not surprising that most of Thomson's employees belong to the younger age groups, even those commanding senior management positions. The managing director, for example, who joined as a graduate trainee, is a youthful forty-three. At the moment, the ratio of employees runs at just 30 per cent male, compared to 70 per cent female staff. However, this balance is not carried through to the management levels, where the men to women ratio pans out at about 50:50. On the board, only the marketing director is female. The international nature of the industry means that people from many nationalities and ethnic groups are employed both within the UK and overseas. 'All we are concerned with is their ability to do the job,' says personnel manager Peter King.

'Opportunities for promotion are quite good,' says marketing executive Helen Anderson. 'This is a female-orientated business. There is no discrimination. We work hard, long hours under pressure. Tight deadlines mean you don't have time to sit down and think about something, you just get on with it.'

Turnover of staff tends to be high, at around 200 a year. This is due mainly to natural wastage as well as maternity-leavers, says King. A young company means that anyone who has been with Thomson for more than five years is regarded as having put in a long period of service. Nevertheless, the company does create a strong sense of loyalty among its staff. King says that around 17 per cent of his staff have been with the organization for more than ten years.

'Our policy is to promote our managers from within wherever possible. To grow our own,' says King. 'Many of our managers have come through the ranks, or are ex-graduate trainees. We advertise as many jobs internally as we can, and promote from within where possible. An exception would be when recruiting for a specialist area, such as a legal specialist or a software expert for the systems department.' Proof of the tough competition to join the company lies in the fact that there were over one thousand applicants to join the company's graduate training scheme in 1988. Thomson also participates in the government YTS scheme, and about 70 per cent of the young people who come to the company in this way are offered permanent jobs at the end of their trainee programme.

As a market leader, with a rapid growth in the holidays on offer and services to clients and travel agents, Thomson is highly committed to the development and use of new technology. In 1976 the most advanced systems-technology within the holiday industry was introduced. The service was implemented to save travel agents' telephone bills and to improve service, as well as to control the sales of holidays

331

with greater accuracy and enable the general public to make a quicker and more informed choice.

An important management philosophy is that each member of staff is well informed about what is happening within the company. Departmental meetings and briefings are supported by staff newsletters and information communications when an important announcement is to be made. Staff get their own product briefings and launches before the press and the marketplace are alerted. 'Staff need to be kept in touch because Thomson is operating in a very competitive market,' says Alison Sungupta, internal communications manager. 'One of my jobs is to make sure that the management style is carried through. By being open with communications, information cannot be used as power.'

When it comes to salaries, the policy is clear cut. 'Within the tour operator areas, we will pay within the best part of the marketplace when compared to our competitors,' says King. 'We are one of the best, but not *the* best.' British Airways is widely considered to be the best in terms of salaries within the travel industry.

The salary package is supported for every employee by a generous holiday concession scheme, allowing significant discounts on pre-booked holidays as well as the facility to take up to six heavily discounted flights a year, booked forty-eight hours before take-off. There is an across-the-board holiday allowance of five weeks a year, supplemented by statutory bank holidays. Since most of the staff are in their twenties, there is not a lot of interest in the voluntary pension scheme which the company has established. Some management levels entitle staff to a company car.

Each member of staff receives an annual performance appraisal from their line manager. Salary increases every year are arrived at from a combination of cost-of-living increases and individual performance. The company does not operate either a profit share or bonus scheme.

Staff working at the company's headquarters in Camden Town, about 75 per cent of the total UK work force, are able to enjoy the subsidized facilities of an excellent in-house canteen, where prices are calculated solely on the cost of the ingredients. Staff can also make use of the local gym and health club. All staff are offered an interest-free loan on season tickets.

Although the company does recognize the TSSA, membership of the union is low. 'Our policies are good enough to remove the need for people to be in a union,' says King, 'but we are not anti-union, and staff are free to join if they wish.'

332

Paramount in the success of the company is training, and the company has brought in specialists to create training courses geared especially to their specific needs. Once written, the courses are run either by external consultants, or by in-house managers.

'We set up the systems graduate-trainee programme because we saw that we needed technological, management and communications skills within the system,' says systems director, Colin Palmer. 'We try to be among the best employers in the data-processing market for like applications. We have a pretty low labour turnover in the systems department, which for this type of installation in central London is very good.'

'We have gone through two years of enormous growth,' says managing director Charles Newbold. 'We now have to consolidate that absolute growth, and sort it out within the company. That will be with us this year, and the next, making sure that the products we have got are of the right quality, and that the operations are efficient. Then we will be looking to return to expansion. The industry that we are in has a good future, with a compound growth of 15 per cent a year.

'I expect the holiday market to double in the next ten years, if not sooner, and I expect Thomson's share of that market to increase. Consequently, we will be double the size that we are now within five to ten years' time, and still be number one.'

333

TNT

TNT is the world's largest transport company. The UK arm is the wholly-owned subsidiary of the Australian parent company. The UK company employs 7000 people and turns over more than £300 million. Head office is in Atherstone, Warwickshire.

pay	☐	ambience	☐
benefits	☐	environment	☐
promotion	☐	equal opportunities	☐
training	☐	communications	☐

'We are a company of 7000 people which means that we have 7000 sales people. When one of our drivers goes out to a delivery and he sees a Federal Express or United Carriers van outside the door, he is concerned to win that business over to us. He will go in and get the name of the transport manager. He takes the contact name back again and our sales people will try to win that company. If we win the business that driver is paid a commission based on the first four weeks' income.' The speaker is Ken MacCall, director of personnel at the company's headquarters in north Warwickshire.

TNT is a remarkable success story, not only around the world but also in the UK where it is a comparatively new venture. In 1978 TNT – the vast Australian transport network – bought Inter County Express, a company employing 500 to 600 people. It had a turnover of about £5 million. MacCall recalls, 'We launched TNT formally on 6 May 1980. It's one of those days which is forever etched on my mind. In the first year we budgeted to make £900,000. In fact we did £11 million. We reasoned that there must be a market out there.' As Inter County the company was doing £6 million a year, in 1988 TNT brings in £6 million a week.

The big difference in the service was that TNT launched an overnight parcels delivery service, which had never been done before. Previously people had offered three to five days' delivery time. With TNT it was guaranteed overnight.

The company's approach is simple and straightforward. It has a disarming Australian clarity about its thought processes. The company pays higher than anyone else in the marketplace and reinforces the basic with overtime and bonuses. MacCall says that the company pays on average between 15 and 40 per cent higher than its leading competitors. Overtime starts on a higher level and it is supplemented by productivity.

The whole business is incentive-orientated. If you bring in more custom you get more money, if you deliver more goods more quickly you get a bonus. The sales people, especially, are driven hard, but are rewarded with free trips to Disney World or Kenya if they make their targets.

What is staggering about the enterprise is the breadth of vision which goes into planning its services, and the creativity it displays in finding solutions to market dilemmas. To Overnight, the company has added Same Day, Skypack and Garment Express. Almost everywhere where TNT operates there is a specially-adapted service to meet customer demand.

The company runs a fleet of lorries for customers in their own logos. The drivers and the fleet management are organized by TNT. The company runs its own fleet of STOL (short take-off and landing planes) based in Windsor, and has a courier on every Concorde flight across the Atlantic delivering packages in North America. The organization runs motorbikes, small vans and large vans. In the UK it has 550 outlets, including 440 parcel collection and pick-up offices which are all franchised. There are 70 Same Day sites, mainly at coach stations around the country.

Innovation is a thread running throughout the company's history. Whenever a market need arises, TNT appears to be there to meet it. The germ of this can probably be traced back to Ken Thomas who founded Thomas Nationwide Transport with one lorry in 1946. One of his more innovative marketing techniques for building customer confidence was to have his drivers run up and down past the offices of new clients. The idea was to create the impression that TNT was a much bigger and busier business than it really was.

'The success of the company is based in the attitude that it can be done, that it can be achieved. People didn't believe we could offer a guaranteed next-day service. But TNT were doing it in Australia. If you can do it in Australia you can fit it into a glove over here,' says MacCall. 'We made the market understand what could be done and what was available. It grew and grew from there.'

MacCall says that the person who joins TNT must have energy. 'Someone who is innovative, positive, has determination and aggression, and requires a certain amount of job satisfaction.' The company

335

is starting to recruit graduates, about four or five a year, who are drawn mainly from Cranfield, the transport college.

'The company is growing at a tremendous rate. By 1990 we may have as many as 10,000 staff. We say to people that your future in the business is entirely in your own hands,' says MacCall. TNT is a rapidly-developing enterprise where academic qualifications do not matter – it is your commitment to the business which really tells.

TNT achieved national publicity when it helped Rupert Murdoch's News International beat the unions in the Wapping dispute. TNT Newsfast was the biggest single operation which the company had mounted, but it succeeded in getting *The Times*, the *Sun*, the *News of the World* and the *Sunday Times* out in record time. What is particularly remarkable about the enterprise is that TNT was fully unionized and none of the drivers was willing to support the printers.

The penalties were unpleasant – smashed car windows and threats to drivers – but the TNT men stuck together. The company gave them its full support and managing director Alan Jones was often with the drivers at 4 a.m. when the papers were going out.

TNT's is a superb story. It is a company with energy and vitality. For people looking for a career in a vibrant and lively company TNT could well be the answer. Sixty per cent of the work force are women, some in senior positions, and the influence of women is growing. TNT is a global network with a developing UK business which is making a powerful contribution to British business.

UNILEVER

Unilever is an Anglo-Dutch concern which employs 53,000 people in the UK. It manufactures detergents, foods, drinks, chemicals and a range of other products. In 1986 worldwide turnover was £17.1 billion. Head office in the UK is in London.

pay	☐	ambience	☐
benefits	☐	environment	☐
promotion	☐	equal opportunities	☐
training	☐	communications	☐

The merger of the Margarine Union with Lever Brothers in 1930 was the foundation of one of the world's great commercial enterprises. Unilever, like Shell, is an Anglo-Dutch business. It operates as a joint holding company with parallel UK and Dutch boards composed of identical memberships.

Unilever Ltd in the UK and Unilever NV in the Netherlands fuse innovation, mercantile skill and global product-marketing in a distinctive approach to business. Combined turnover in 1986 was £11.1 billion and pre-tax profit £1.1 billion.

The company employs more than 300,000 people across the world, with operating companies in more than 75 territories. By any measure Unilever's influence is vast. Even so, the name Unilever could easily be unfamiliar to anyone outside its market sector or the business community. But its products have a much higher profile. Among them Flora and Blue Band margarine, Bird's Eye frozen foods, Wall's ice cream, PG Tips and Lipton's Yellow Label tea, Fray Bentos canned meat, Sunlight, Lux, Persil and Lifebuoy soap, Comfort fabric softener, Jif liquid cleaner, and Signal and Mentadent toothpaste.

Many of these products are familiar to the UK market but Unilever makes these and a whole range of other goods for Western Europe where 60 per cent of its sales lie. Unilever manufactures other products for North America which takes 20 per cent of total group sales. The company also makes speciality starches, adhesives for packaging, so-called oleo chemicals which are derived from natural oils and fats, flavours and fragrances, and medical products such as diagnostic kits based on monoclonal antibodies. Unilever is also a distributor of capital equipment, including earth movers and commercial vehicles, and operates a chain of fish restaurants called Nordsee, which are prominent in Germany and are now opening here.

It would be easy to envisage a sprawling company with interests in a medley of markets, territories and product lines and nothing discernible to link them. But Unilever is a remarkably homogeneous business. It is intensely market-driven. The blood of true Unilever people courses with mercantile fervour. The evangelical belief in the product is matched and tempered by shrewd, objective analysis of the market and what can realistically be achieved. This company culture, while favouring devolved management, is an undercurrent of every activity within Unilever.

'Unilever have got it right,' says one enthusiastic former employee. 'In recent years they have trimmed the business down to three main core operations and it is clear that the company is a very tightly run organization.'

Despite headquarters in both Rotterdam and the extraordinary art-deco building at Blackfriars, London, there is no sense of schism or duplication. The business is run as one concern. At the top sits the special committee composed of the chairman of Unilever Ltd, the chairman of Unilever NV, and one other senior director. This sets out policy guidelines on a broad range of areas. It picks the chairmen of the operating companies, from the 200 top individuals among the 20,000 managers in the company. It discusses objectives with regional managements, functional divisions, such as accounting, engineering and research, and with the product groups which govern the areas of operation.

The product groups coordinate the activities of the highly autonomous companies which have been assembled into the Unilever group. There are eight product groups, and each is supported by central research teams who brief management on market conditions, scientific and technological movements and product development.

Each of the companies reports to its respective product group, regional management and functional management. This matrix approach is a familiar mechanism of corporate organization. The companies exhibit their own personalities underpinned by the Unilever brand. The people who work in the operating companies, although selling Persil soap powder, making Wall's choc ices, auditing the income from Oxo cubes, boxing Cup-a-Soup or planning the market strategy for Bird's Eye frozen peas, are in no doubt that they work for Unilever as much as for the brand name.

Since its inception the group has placed heavy emphasis on recruiting trained personnel into the business and providing the kind of career development programme which will prove useful both to Unilever and the recruit. The company may well be the first corporate organization in Britain to have sent recruiters around the universities, in what is now known as the milk round, to identify and sign up promising graduates. It is a process which continues today. Getting into the company as a graduate trainee is one of the stiffest tests a young graduate can face. The boards which interview candidates can be awe-inspiring, comparable with the BBC, and often include very senior personnel. The potential recruit is put through a series of exercises to test his worth and only the strongest survive.

This is organized centrally through the Unilever Companies' Management Development Scheme which aims to locate and train people with senior management ability. Parallel to this is a similar scheme for engineers and a direct-entry programme for people with good middle-management potential.

Recruits also take part in the Business Education Programme which is run in conjunction with several UK business schools. In Unilever Research some use is made of post-doctoral candidates and there are considerable travel opportunities in UAC International. Learning Dutch is not a prerequisite to success in Unilever, but it is useful for those people dealing with the Netherlands as a daily part of their work.

Pay and benefits vary radically across the group, depending on the market sector and operating company, but the universal minimum is high. Anyone who secures work in the group can expect to be paid reasonably highly. In no way is this a fat American multinational with inflated salaries and a clutch of perks, but the company does take good care of its people and recognizes that they are a valuable asset.

In some senses the Unilever group is traditional in its approach. Status and contribution to overall goals is recognized. Unilever training is rightly praised very highly, and many ex-Unilever staffers speak warmly of the company. Michael Angus, chairman of the UK company, says, 'The qualities which we look for in our future managers are the same as when I joined Unilever thirty-four years ago. Our methods of selection and training have become more sophisticated, but the essence of our management development programme remains the same.

'We give people responsibility very early. You progress rapidly through this business. I went through this whole process. I suppose I am living proof that the system works,' he says.

UNITED BISCUITS

United Biscuits makes biscuits, cakes and snacks. It runs the Wimpy and Pizzaland restaurant chains and it has frozen food businesses. In March 1988 UB acquired Ross-Young, Britain's second largest frozen foods business. This purchase gave coherence to UB Frozen Foods, and represents the largest part of the group. Its 1986 turnover was £1.93 billion with profits of £125.2 million. The group employs 40,000 people worldwide. Headquarters are in Osterley in west London, but the group operates many sites across the UK and abroad.

pay		ambience	
benefits		environment	
promotion		equal opportunities	
training		communications	

More than half of all biscuits sold in the United Kingdom are produced by United Biscuits, who are also the second largest manufacturer of biscuits in the United States, claiming some 17 to 18 per cent of that market. It has good reason to believe that after Nabisco it may be the largest biscuit manufacturer in the world.

Quality distinguishes every facet of the business. UB is dedicated to the excellence of its output. The company is rightly proud of its achievements but it does not sit back on its laurels. It recognizes that there is a hard fight to be won merely to stay on top. Honesty and integrity are co-existent features of the group culture, and the visitor is struck by the openness with which UB people at all levels discuss their successes and their failures.

In many ways the company owes its values to the unique combination of family enterprises which were fused to form the UB group. Each one had a strong, vigorous and readily identifiable persona. The culture which emerged, and to some extent is still emerging, is a commonality of excellence, drive, objectivity, commercial aggression and human understanding. There are few companies in Britain today which match up to UB in sheer dedication to employee welfare and the provision of job opportunities.

Its origins lie in Scotland in the nineteenth century. A generation of master bakers, including William Crawford, James Lang, John

McFarlane and Jonathan Dodgson Carr, laid the foundation of the great biscuit-making companies. Perhaps the greatest of them all was William McVitie, who opened a provisions shop in a converted tenement in Edinburgh. Later joined by his son Robert, the pair moved up-market and sold goods from thir own bakery. Alexander Grant joined the business in 1887 and six years later created Digestive. The pattern of modern biscuit-making had begun.

William Macdonald's company, formed in 1922, introduced individ-ually-marketed products such as Penguin. In 1948 McFarlane Lang and McVitie & Price formed United Biscuits in a financial merger. But operations came together only in the 1960s after the introduction of Crawford and Macdonald into the UB fold. The 1960s saw the start of unprecedented growth and by 1983 Meredith & Drew, KP, Carr, Keebler (USA), Wimpy, Pizzaland, Specialty (USA) and Terry's of York had all been acquired.

The creation of UB has been a formidable exercise, yet the group has retained its family personality. 'When I tell acquired companies that they will fit into the UB group within a year, they don't believe it,' says current chairman Sir Hector Laing. 'But a year later they come back and tell me that I was right.'

UB's approach is infectious. It gives a lead which its people find difficult to better. While the group is not the best payer in the sector, it does offer reasonable pay and adequate benefits. However, its staff do not work with the company for its pay and benefit levels. They enjoy the chance to prove themselves and to be listened to if they have good ideas. They feel part of a team which is producing the best product in the market. Rapid promotion is enjoyed, especially by the 110 graduates taken on each year. The training package is one of the most exceptional in industry.

John Warren, finance director of UB Brands, which makes biscuits and cakes and is the biggest part of the group, joined from accountants Arthur Young. He says it was the most highly regarded client by staff at AY. 'The best thing about United Biscuits is that it is good at trusting people and allowing them their head to produce results. It is bad at bringing them into line when they make a mistake.'

When Wimpy was bought one UB employee, Max Woolfenden, wrote to complain. He was horrified that a company with a reputation for quality like UB should have acquired a chain noted for its bad food, bad service and dirty restaurants. Woolfenden is a typical UB' success story. He joined in 1969 for two years' experience. Today he is managing director of one of its operating companies. After working as a food technologist with Meredith & Drew, which had made its name producing own-label biscuits for supermarket chains and other components of the group, Woolfenden tried marketing and was eventually sent to Japan as vice-president of a UB venture. On his return he was made operations director of Wimpy. 'When we took it over in 1976 it was a disgrace. Today it has a very exciting future.' Woolfenden is now MD of Wimpy. Ian Petrie, who was put in by UB to revolutionize the business, had a difficult task. Petrie was fighting on all sides. The franchisees – Wimpy is mostly franchise outlets – the staff who came over from the old Allied-Lyons management and many people in UB headquarters were unsympathetic. Petrie imposed the UB ethics of good service, fair dealing with suppliers and staff, commitment to the product and a certain amount of personal verve and drive to win through. 'Before I took on Wimpy I had a full head of hair, now look at me,' he says. Despite rumblings among UB board members, the chairman stayed firm and eventually his faith was justified. Wimpy is well on the way to a complete transformation.

As soon as Petrie had rescued Wimpy, the group had another crisis in the form of Pizzaland. Despite improving profits UB management eventually realized that unit sales were in decline. Petrie was made head of UB Restaurants which embraced Wimpy and Pizzaland. It is part of the UB creed that Pizzaland is referred to not as a problem but as an *opportunity*. Pizzaland is now back on the road to recovery. His colleague Brian Waltham, who runs a group of production lines, says, 'UB has a tremendous reputation and I have found it to be justified.'

Bob Clarke, group chief executive, says that the company has moved into a phase of consolidation after twenty years. Biscuits and cakes are a mature market, but growth can be expected in non-grocery outlets such as petrol filling-station shops. The snack market is still wide open, especially since the distinction between organized meals and snacking is blurring. UB's frozen food businesses are growing, as are the restaurants. 'We are always looking for new acquisitions if they willl further the business,' Clarke commented.

The company's intake of graduates may well slow down somewhat if the pattern of high acquisitional growth changes. It may need to find a better blend of graduate and non-graduate talent, though the problems that UB faces in this area are nothing like as pronounced as elsewhere in industry. Clarke acknowledges that the group needs to improve its record on equal opportunities, and there is a genuine desire to make efforts in this direction. Although there are few women in senior management, the management training scheme is now equally attended by men and women.

UB has a formidable reputation in community service activities, and

Sir Hector Laing is chairman of Business In The Community. The group is also a powerful supporter of leisure activities for its people. Almost everyone in UB has a story to tell about how the company has helped a colleague in times of necessity, whether in a professional or personal dilemma. UB is slightly paternalistic, but only in the best sense. It is very British and individualistic. It is a loyal concern, and that loyalty is reciprocated by its people. Above all, it is a caring business while also being hard-hitting in its markets.

VICKERS DEFENCE SYSTEMS

Operating from Tyneside, Vickers Defence Systems is a subsidiary of Vickers plc. It manufactures engineering products for the services.

pay	☐	ambience	☐
benefits	☐	environment	☐
promotion	☐	equal opportunities	☐
training	☐	communications	☐

Vickers Defence is a proud company with a tremendous history behind it. The core of the Tyneside operation was established by Lord Armstrong in the muck and grime of the nineteenth century. The Vickers links were forged in 1927.

Nowadays Vickers supplies the British Army with the Challenger battle tank and its support vehicle derivatives. It is prominent in the export market, and does business particularly with Nigeria, China and Brazil. Stuart Wilson, the company's energetic finance director, emphasizes that since it is an engineering company, turnover can vary dramatically from year to year. It can fluctuate from anywhere between £50 million to £130 million per annum. However, things are going well, he says. So well that the company could sustain a £15 million turnover for four to five years with a low acceptable loss.

Like other key players in the market, the company's normal approach is to tender for all relevant jobs. When these contracts are won, the company has sufficient cash in hand to pay for development work. The same applies to work for private clients: at any one time Vickers is engaged on a number of jobs from private sources.

Industrial relations on Tyneside have not been without their problems. During the interwar years the highest level of unemployment in the UK was on Tyneside – one of the primary reasons why union militancy grew so fiercely after the Second World War. The tension between union and management led to an unhappy saga of lay-offs, strikes and works-to-rule.

Vickers Defence Systems had its share of the trouble and the Elswick plant had some of the worst industrial relations in the region. But its move to a clean, bright building at Scotswood in 1982 proved the watershed. The management have built a new order of industrial

344

relations and succeeded in carrying the unions along with it. Joe Mathews, works convenor at the new plant for the Confederation of Shipbuilding Unions, described the change as dramatic, and, despite a degree of cynicism and wariness, the workers have responded favourably to the turnaround.

George Richardson, TASS representative, describes the effect of the new procedures: 'They make you feel you know what you're aiming for. They make you feel part of the company.' This is a far cry from the suppression of enterprise through insensitive management and bullish unions.

Sue Wilson is the recently appointed director of employee relations. She outlines some of the facets of the new-broom approach which have paid dividends. 'We have regular employee briefing sessions, a successful social club, lively company trips and a raft of policies in the Employee Development Scheme.' This is a long-term policy designed to answer Vickers's previous failure to recruit graduates.

The company has implemented a student sponsorship and graduate recruitment policy which has brought many talented people to Vickers. It has created a certain amount of resentment on the shop floor as older employees see their traditional employment prospects blocked by the arrival of bright young graduates. The EDP aims to avoid this by helping existing employees add to their qualifications, including giving them access to higher education.

Another aspect of the new employee relations has been its retention policy. Previously, when work was in abeyance workers would be laid off until volume increased again. Now the company has a strict no-lay-offs standard. Wilson explains that the members of the work force who are being deployed on current work are retained. They are re-trained for new work or despatched to help on other projects. The atmosphere in the plant readily suggests that this pays off. Instead of mutual suspicion, an air of friendly cooperation is discernible.

Vickers has bought the old Royal Ordnance factory at Barnbow in Leeds, and the company is planning to build a new plant there along similar lines to the Scotswood installation. The same policies which have proved so successful on Tyneside will be applied to the new site.

Since the change in attitudes – on both sides – and the consequent improvement in business, Vickers Defence Systems has become a stimulating and exciting place to work. The great strides forward in industrial relations have transformed it into a company where workers actually enjoy what they are doing.

The new policies are evolving and the atmosphere is positive. The unions are now consulted at each stage in the development of company policy and there is a real sense of partnership. The Vickers Defence Systems story is a case study in the turnaround of a company – to everyone's benefit.

VIRGIN

The Virgin Group is made up of the entertainment and leisure businesses started by Richard Branson. In 1986 the group went public. The group reported pre-tax profits of £31.1 million in 1987. Its growing work force presently numbers 2500.

pay ☐		ambience ☐	
benefits ☐		environment ☐	
promotion ☐		equal opportunities ☐	
training ☐		communications ☐	

Virgin began in 1970 when Richard Branson established a business selling popular records by mail order. The first Virgin shop was opened in Oxford Street, London, in 1971, and by the end of 1973 a record company, music publishing company, recording studios and an export company had been acquired.

The Virgin Group's activities are concentrated in three divisions: Music, which markets the work of songwriters and artistes; Retail, which now boasts 72 stores and 23 concessions within Debenhams; and Vision, which is involved in film and video distribution and television. The less stable companies – Virgin Atlantic, Virgin Holidays and its nightclub interests, which include the Roof Gardens and Heaven – remain in private hands under Richard Branson's chairmanship.

Virgin has expanded enormously in the last year. Sixteen hundred people were employed at the time of its flotation, and the present roll-count is 2500. Pre-tax profits for the year to July 1987 showed a leap of 45 per cent from the previous year, and the company is now concentrating on expansion overseas. It recently set up music and communications activities in Hollywood and Japan as well as expanding operations in Europe and Australia.

Despite its phenomenal growth, Virgin offices remain entrenched in Notting Hill, west London, in properties that are forever being remodelled to squeeze in the expanding work force. Branson believes that working in small units enhances initiative and team spirit, and develops a greater depth of general management. Thus, the group's headquarters are split between a row of terraced houses in Ladbroke

347

Grove and a newly acquired office block in Campden Hill Road. Accounts is in Queensway and the music division in Kensington House, a large Victorian mansion with extra offices tacked on, beside the busy Harrow Road.

In all the offices the atmosphere is distinctly informal. The latest sounds from Capital Radio greet visitors in reception. Ken Berry, managing director of Virgin Music, and one of the founding fathers, has a small office in an attic. 'I'd like to think we provide a good environment to work in. The people who own the company are all very actively involved. We're not sitting in huge offices in ivory towers; Richard's on his boat in Little Venice, I'm in an attic. We're always approachable. That's the Virgin way.

'Our great strength is staff loyalty. Not because we pay more than the competition, but because of the atmosphere. We were all in our early twenties when we started in the 1970s and a lot of people from that time are still around. They're just a bit older, that's all. But we're still interested in similar things to our employees and so there's a lot of social contact.'

Strictly speaking, around 15 per cent of the work force are management, but at Virgin everyone mucks in. Enthusiasm, adaptability and the confidence to speak up with ideas or criticisms are the order of the day. Jonathan Gilbride, managing director of Caroline Exports, the mail order division, clocks in and out just like his staff. 'Management here is strictly hands-off. We are set targets and as long as we meet them we are left to get on with it. It makes you enthusiastic, and when we think up new projects, we don't have to get Richard's permission to put them into practice.

'Flexibility is important. You could be taking an order from a Japanese client one moment and helping pack boxes the next. The environment's relaxed and the staff are encouraged to come to me directly with new ideas. You can't make someone work until 10 p.m. unless they want to do it. They have to feel involved – a part of our success. I try to give as many people a chance to travel as possible: six of my staff have joined me on Japan trips and they are sent to foreign trade fairs on a rota basis.'

It's obvious that one of the great attractions of working for Virgin is this absence of hierarchy. 'I'd say we were relaxed but not casual,' says Don Cruikshank, the group's managing director. 'It's in the nature of this business. Some of the most important people at Virgin are not at the top but on the creative side. We interfere the minimum amount necessary and try to adapt to their way of doing things. It's an

348

approach which has been handed down from Richard Branson almost by a process of osmosis.'

One of the great advantages of this management style is that it gives people their heads. You can move onwards and upwards in Virgin at a faster rate than in more structured organizations. The company has a policy of promoting internally wherever possible, and jobs are advertised in all divisions. Expansion has led to a large number of internal promotions and new job oppportunities in the last few years. If a receptionist shows a desire and an aptitude to work in marketing or computing, he or she can move over and train on the job. New faces in the music division could well have been drafted in from the record stores.

Twenty-three-year-old Paul Bradford, now assistant accounts payable manager, joined Virgin two years ago as an internal auditor. 'I moved from a shipping company in the City which was much more regimented. You simply couldn't leap up two or three scales. But at Virgin the prospects are there – you're paid what you're worth and you can work your way up more rapidly and fulfil your potential. It's a friendly place, everyone's on first-name terms and you don't have to wear suits.'

Around half of Virgin's employees are women, and, although there are no directors on the board yet, according to Lily Lou, head of group personnel, half the top managers in the divisions are women. Lily Lou joined Virgin seven years ago as salary manager when the company employed just 450 people. She has since been responsible for setting up the whole personnel system, one of the few centralized operations in the group. 'I like to think we work as one big family. We are always ready to help with any problems.'

Virgin doesn't have pay scales as such, but generally makes sure that salaries keep up with the market. A sales assistant in a record store would take home a basic salary of around £67 a week; a top manager would earn around £13,000 a year. A seventeen-year-old junior secretary might start on £5000 but, apart from the directors, very few members of staff earn more than £30,000 a year. But that's just basic salary. There are profit-sharing share schemes, profit-sharing schemes, Christmas bonuses (£500 for everyone in December 1987) and an attractive benefits package.

'The profit-sharing share scheme applies to the whole group,' says Cruikshank. 'We buy shares in the company for employees and hold them in trust for two years. If the employees own them for five years there are tax incentives. Essentially it's a scheme dictated first by length of service, so it doesn't discriminate against the lower grades, then by seniority and the success of the particular division. In the shops there are profit-sharing payments every month which relate to the performance of the particular store. They're the hardest to work out.'

Virgin offers private health care through PPP to employees over twenty-five, paying 50 per cent of the premium for the first year and the total premium thereafter. Most unusually it also covers common-law husbands and wives. Pensions at Virgin are fully portable. Everyone has their own personal policy with Sun Alliance, and Virgin matches employees' contributions up to a maximum of 5 per cent of salary.

Other perks include free London Transport passes for lower grades (who also receive overtime payments), valued at around £400 a year; or, if they commute using British Rail, the same amount towards the cost of an annual season ticket. In addition, of course, there is a 30 per cent discount on records, cassettes and compact discs. There are also 12–15 per cent discounts on airline tickets and holidays booked through Virgin Atlantic.

Virgin is keen to create a sense of total involvement among its employees, something which appears to be unaffected by its rapid growth. Encouraging teamwork and creativity is important in the entertainments business. As Cruikshank remarks: 'We have no assets as such. We're a classic twentieth-century business. It's the people working for us that make Virgin a success.'

WADDINGTON

Waddington is a plastics, cartons and games company. Head office is on the outskirts of Leeds, West Yorkshire. In 1987 sales reached £131.7 million with pre-tax profits of £12.2 million. The group employs 3500 people.

pay	☐	ambience	☐
benefits	☐	environment	☐
promotion	☐	equal opportunities	☐
training	☐	communications	☐

Most people have played Monopoly, and may also have tried their hand at Cluedo or Lexicon. The name on the side of the box is Waddington. The company is familiar as the maker of Monopoly, but to assume that producing the world's largest board game is the *raison d'être* of Waddington would be to miss the point.

The company started as a printing outfit but broadened out into a range of activities. 'It started in 1895,' says David Watson, a director. 'John Waddington was the best friend of the manager of Theatre Royal in the days when Leeds had five theatres. One day the manager complained that he could not get tickets and posters. Waddington, who was quite a wealthy man in his own right, bought some printing presses and started his own business.

'In 1913 Waddington resigned after a financial crisis and nobody has heard anything of him or his family since. My grandfather Victor Watson was a lithographic foreman and saved the company from closure.'

The company diversified into printing playing cards and cigarette cards, and ultimately into folding cartons. This opened the door for jigsaw puzzles and Santona, waxed paper.

The company's own card game Lexicon paid dividends, and in 1935 it acquired Monopoly. At the same time the company was developing its reputation in the cardboard and paper sectors. The company moved ahead in the 1950s. 'We were making the waxed paper cartons for orange juice which was sold in cinemas. Unfortunately the drink didn't taste particularly pleasant, so we devised a new plastic container. This became familiar with Kia-ora orange juice, and at the same time it was the beginning of the thermo-forming industry,' says Watson.

'But in the 1970s we made a very bad mistake. We assumed that board games would go into decline and we invested a lot of money in electronic games. Videomaster, the electronic games company, lost us millions. It damn well nearly sunk the company. It was closed with very great losses. And then recession hit the cartons and plastics businesses.'

The impact of this dual assault on Waddington was to kick the company into renewed life. Management woke up. They realized that their business needed to be much more efficiently run. But before they could get their breath Norton-Opax launched an aggressive takeover bid. 'It was a former Leeds bookies printer, and it was like the poor relation, or the local fish and chip shop, mounting a bid,' says personnel manager John Hockenhill.

No sooner had they sent Norton-Opax packing than Robert Maxwell came calling, twice. 'Maxwell was touch and go both times,' says Hockenhill. 'But the loyalty we enjoyed from the staff throughout this period was tremendous. To a man they backed us up.'

If the message had not got through to the company during the 1970s then it was clear in the 1980s. They had to become a tighter, fitter business to succeed. In 1983 during the contested bid stage the company's market capitalization was £7 million. By 1987 it was worth £170 million.

The final Maxwell bid further spurred the company into life. The company set out on an acquisitional path, acquiring Vickers Business Forms, House of Questa, Eyre & Spottiswoode, Comet Products, Gilmour & Dean, Johnsen & Jorgensen and PacPlas. Suddenly the company was a much wider organization. The new interests were based in London, Margate, Portsmouth and the US.

'We never, never buy a company aggressively,' says Watson. Perhaps the memory of the Norton-Opax and Maxwell bids is too painful. 'If we approach a company and they say no, then we walk back through the door.'

The company has a reputation as a high payer. A machine operator in the printing plant would be on £245 a week, and a packer £155. The company has a very good pension scheme, PPP for white-collar grades, a fair sick pay benefit plan, subsidized canteen facilities . . . and cost price Monopoly sets. More interestingly, the company introduced a share purchase scheme which allows staff to buy shares in the company.

Several people took part in the share option scheme when the share price was 17.5p. By the time the option was relinquished in 1987 the price had risen to 245p. Some people saving £50 a week made £40,000.

There are some very rich people at Waddington. The management is now having a hard time explaining to people that they will not always make as much money as this!

Not that people would have any compunction about speaking up. Waddington is the sort of company where people are not slow in coming forward. When the company was engaged in acquisition discussions, members of the work force spontaneously went to see the Monopolies Commission after there was some suggestion of a referral.

Peter Whitely, who works on the shop floor in the Leeds print factory, says: 'I did my training here. I have worked for seven or eight firms, but this is the one I always wanted to come back to. I have always found that they are an honest management. The money that we get is good.'

We found similar enthusiasm for the company at the sites we visited. There is a feeling of great warmth for the Waddington group, especially since the company has moved into a higher gear commercially. Its training policies are appreciated. Its pay and benefits are regarded as worthwhile, and while the company is not really a family concern, it certainly has that atmosphere.

WEETABIX

Weetabix is wholly owned by the George family of Northamptonshire. It employs 2300 people, of whom 1300 are at the factory in Burton Latimer, Northamptonshire. The company's 1987 turnover was £116 million, and pre-tax profits for the year were £12 million.

pay ☐		ambience ☐	
benefits ☐		environment ☐	
promotion ☐		equal opportunities ☐	
training ☐		communications ☐	

Weetabix, now in the hands of the third generation of the George family, is a family concern in every sense — and family values may well be at the core of the Weetabix success.

Weetabix was first produced in the early 1930s when miller Frank George came up with the simple idea for a nutritious wholewheat cereal. He hawked his wares to local shopkeepers and for a few years these were his only outlets. His original mill — a rabbit warren, say staff — is still preserved on the sprawling 55-acre site at Burton Latimer. It is unlikely that any Weetabix boss would have the nerve to demolish it. The ghost of Frank George, making his Weetabix by hand, would never permit it.

Demand for the product led to a massive expansion plan, and in 1967 the first fully-automated Weetabix production line was installed. Over the next five years the company's ten lines were all fully automated. George died in 1970, aged eighty-three, and his son Tony took over as chairman, overseeing a concern which goes from strength to strength.

New production lines were now churning out 52,000,000 biscuits a week. Even this could not meet world demand from 70 countries, and in 1975 a 100,000-square-foot extension, housing four new lines, was required. The £6,000,000 addition to plant not only increased production to 60,000,000 biscuits a week, but allowed the development of more new products.

Weetabix employs 2300 people worldwide. Of these, 1300, mainly shift-workers, are at Burton Latimer. At Corby, about ten miles away, a 9-acre site employs 150 people and a further factory will be opened by the end of 1988. Weetabix has its own packaging company – Vibixa – in Cheltenham, and wholly-owned subsidiaries are operating in Ontario and Boston. Just a few months ago Weetabix acquired Barbara's Bakery Inc. of California – a company which distributes a wide range of health-food products. Weetabix also owns a coupon redemption centre employing 50 people.

Weetabix and Kelloggs seem to have reached a gentleman's agreement that neither should rock the other's boat. Trevor Hart, marketing manager at Weetabix, says: 'We satisfy areas of the market that Kelloggs don't. We concentrate purely on cereals, heavily supporting high-quality branded products with dominant advertising, and we keep a high profile in a very competitive marketplace.' Hart is a former Kelloggs man: 'It is always a risk when you join a company. You know the pay and conditions but cannot know if you are going to fit in. Here there is a very informal atmosphere, but a very professional one too, which is a good balance. I found no barriers between myself and people who had been here for many years.'

Personnel manager Mike Winmill, a graduate mechanical engineer, was given the chance of a personnel job and never looked back. He says that the good old days of a family company are over as Weetabix strives to keep its hold in a fast-moving consumer goods industry. But even so he quotes a staff turnover of less than 5 per cent.

All the top jobs are advertised internally and recruitment from the relations of existing staff is actively encouraged. Every youngster that has come along on a Youth Opportunity Programme has finished up with a permanent job. Graduate entry is still something of a novelty, but of 30 graduates recruited over the last two years only four have left. Initial pay is low, but six-monthly reviews are held where performance is rewarded with pay increases.

Jack Williams is a full-time Usdaw convenor, and often acts as link man for the nine unions within Weetabix. 'We have a terrific relationship with management and get almost everything we ask for. There is no closed door and senior staff will see me any time I have a request. The days of banging on the table are long gone.

'We have never had a dubious sacking and only one walkout, nine years ago, over shift premiums. Even on picket duty the directors would chat and joke with us as they came in. It lasted a day.

'There is no closed shop but every new employee is given a union application form and I get to chat to them about the benefits of joining.'

Weetabix is fervently keen on safety and every shift has a meeting to discuss problems. There are regular inspections and no head-

355

shaking by management if the unions request a new and expensive piece of safety kit.

Weetabix has a sports and social club with a full-time secretary paid for by the company, and even boasts its own cricket pitch at Burton. There is a staff shop, regular outings, and parties and events for retired employees. The canteen is subsidized – roast beef and Yorkshire pudding costs just 54p – and a fleet of buses ferry staff to and from work for free.

As the third largest employer in Northamptonshire Weetabix is mindful of a duty to the community, recently donating £200,000 to a local college towards a management centre. It also sponsors a venture trust to help sixth-formers run small businesses, sponsors national sporting events and runs language courses for its many ethnic-minority workers.

Weetabix is a quintessentially family company. It produces brands which are highly regarded, and there is a vigorous and deep loyalty among the staff. The financial side of the business is impressive and there is no reason why it should not grow even further. As a dynamically-managed venture, Weetabix stands out in its region and its sector as a first-class employer.

WHITBREAD

Whitbread is a brewer and food and drinks retailer. Turnover in 1988 was £1.69 billion with pre-tax profits of £192.2 million. It employs 47,000 staff, mostly part-time. Head office is in London.

pay ☐	ambience ☐
benefits ☐	environment ☐
promotion ☐	equal opportunities ☐
training ☐	communications ☐

Whitbread is a company with some considerable history. It was founded in 1742 and it is still chaired by Sam Whitbread, a member of the originating family. The family still retains a controlling interest in the business and to a certain extent it shows. But in the last few years new life has been kicked into the company.

Whitbread has started up a chain of restaurants called TGI Friday, based on an American franchise. Its approach is to offer something slightly different in the way of eating. Two businessmen once ordered two prawn cocktails, two sirloin steaks and a bottle of house red at TGIF. The waitress told them that their order was too mundane and she would come back when they had picked something more exciting. This approach would probably cause heart failure among some of the old Whitbread hands.

Nevertheless, several managers in the company mentioned to us that this encapsulates the freshness and vitality which they want to spread throughout the whole company. It also emphasizes Whitbread's own perception of itself as being more of a food and drinks retailer than a brewer and wholesaler of beer. The company runs more than 6000 pubs and restaurants, including Beefeater and a share in Pizza Hut, but brewing and wholesaling through its 5000 tied houses represents half of the profits.

Assessing Whitbread as an employer can be a difficult task. It is not a run-of-the-mill company. The majority of its staff are part-time barmen or waitresses. Annual staff turnover can easily be as much as 100 per cent, but this reflects not so much on the company as on the industry. For these people, terms and conditions are established by wages councils. And the company rarely exceeds the statutory minimum. Similarly the quality of the working environment depends on the attitudes of the local manager.

The position of full-time staff – 22,000 – is rather different. The group has established a career structure and reward package which has given Whitbread one of the best reputations in the industry. And, to be fair, the company has tried to extend benefits beyond this section of the work force.

Whitbread's name rests on firm foundations – a long-established, tightly-knit company, and the considerable efforts made during the 1980s to meet the needs of individual employees. Some of the 'old school' Whitbread still shines through – a beer allowance for every full-time staff member once a month, and sherry and port at Christmas.

The new efforts stem directly from management reorganization in 1984 when Sam Whitbread became chairman. The company commissioned an attitude survey by MORI. While the findings were not universally bad, there was a definite feeling that people were not being informed about changes that were taking place. Another survey two years later reported a much higher level of morale, and a more positive attitude towards the company. Jackie Rimmer, a waitress in a Beefeater restaurant who has been with Whitbread for six years, comments, 'I would say that the company is going places. You'll never be out of work at Whitbread.'

Nessie Osment, who works in the accounts department of Beefeater, says, 'It is a company which likes to keep you happy.' Comments like these are commonplace in Whitbread. People generally believe that they are meant to get on with their jobs, unless there is a problem. Then there is someone there to help you. The persuasiveness of this view is reinforced by the accent on training – particularly for managers.

Managers of a steakhouse or pub are sent on leadership courses and are provided with personnel manuals to offer guidance when they have any problems which they cannot solve themselves. Staff turnover is acknowledged as a problem. Jim McGivern, human resources director in retail (restaurant chains), says that the necessary steps have been identified to create the sort of environment which will encourage people to stay. This includes training, pay and promotion.

McGivern says that the full-time staff are easier to deal with. Unit managers are provided with incentives, he says. Typically, a couple running a Beefeater could earn £25,000 jointly – 50 per cent of which is bonus. For part-timers McGivern is launching tactical incentives, such as a free trip or rewards in the pocket for meeting sales targets.

Promotion of existing staff has been unusual, but is now being actively encouraged. Richard Morris, personnel director of the inns division, says that most trainee managers are recruited from outside the company but that this is changing over a longer-term perspective.

An important part of the changes at Whitbread is the vast improvement in communications. The company always had a staff newspaper called *Whitbread News*. People acknowledged its high standards, but it was not widely read by the staff. In contrast, divisional newspapers – *Beefeater News*, for example – are much brighter and breezier. These enjoy much more support largely because they relate much more readily to people's jobs and activities.

There are regular briefing meetings for managers, at which unit managers will inform their people about company news. Employees identify quite strongly with their division, rather than with Whitbread as a whole.

Another communications innovation which was recently attempted at Beefeater head office was 'Intercom'. Management role play the problems facing the company, and answer anonymous questions which have been submitted.

A constant criticism of all brewers is their attitude to women, and sadly Whitbread is no exception. One Whitbread woman we spoke to stated quite boldly that 'Their attitude towards women is archaic.' Another said, 'Management here is for men – there are only a few women managers.'

Apart from this, Whitbread is making progress. As one of the largest players in the industry, it is dedicated to reforming attitudes and conditions, and is therefore beginning to offer its staff more diverse and exciting careers.

INDEX